Gender and Sexuality

Gender and Sexuality

Sociological Approaches

Momin Rahman and
Stevi Jackson

polity

First published in 2010 by Polity Press

Polity Press
65 Bridge Street
Cambridge CB2 1UR, UK

Polity Press
350 Main Street
Malden, MA 02148, USA

ISBN-13: 978-0-7456-3376-3
ISBN-13: 978-0-7456-3377-0(pb)

A catalogue record for this book is available from the British Library.

Typeset in 10.5 on 12 pt Plantin
by Servis Filmsetting Ltd, Stockport, Cheshire
Printed and bound in Great Britain by the MPG Books Group

For further information on Polity, visit our website: www.politybooks.com

Contents

Contents ix

Introduction

The aim of this brief introduction is to illustrate how the key sociological concepts of structure, culture, self and identity are important to understanding gender and sexuality and how they are dealt with in subsequent chapters. We also give guidance on the format of the chapters, which include exercises, learning outcomes and notes on further resources and reading. However, we begin with an example to demonstrate the importance of a sociological perspective in understanding gender and sexuality.

What Do You Think About Same-Sex Marriage?

In August 2010, a federal judge overruled California's Proposition 8, which had been passed in November 2008 during the American Presidential election. Proposition 8 overrode previous court rulings that had, since May 2008, permitted same-sex marriages, but it did not overturn the right to domestic partnerships, which California had enacted in 1999. It is worth reviewing some of the protests and the arguments both for and against same-sex marriage (available online at many news channels). You will see the strength of passion on both sides of this debate and we ask you to consider why it is that the right to marriage is such a trigger for social protest against lesbians and gays. In April 2005, one of your authors – Momin Rahman – attended a demonstration in support of the recent passage of a gay rights bill through the state legislature of Maine, USA. Fifty or so gay rights supporters gathered on the balcony of the capitol building, whilst, below, four or five times the number demonstrated their rejection of the proposed bill. Most of those opposed were religious, and we were told that many of these Christian groups had been bussed in from other states to bolster this show of 'traditional' moral values. The clothing of choice for the traditionalists was a t-shirt depicting a male and female figure holding hands, with the slogan that marriage was meant to be between a man and woman.

In fact, the proposed legislation was not concerned with same-sex marriage but with equalization of treatment for lesbians and gays [1]. However, given the controversies surrounding lesbian and gay civil union legislation in the USA, and the salience of this issue in the Presidential election of November 2004, it is perhaps not surprising that the possibility of marriage rights in Maine became the focus for the Christian Right. Furthermore, legislation to recognize same-sex civil unions and/or marriage is a truly global issue, with laws passed or under discussion in many countries worldwide, and always in the context of intense public debate [2].

How can we understand and explain the strength of emotion that the recognition of lesbian and gay marriage provokes? Of course, it could be argued that this particular civil right is the latest in a gradual extension of rights to lesbian and gay minorities, beginning for many in Western Europe and North America in the late 1960s and accelerating in the 1990s with the increasing cultural visibility of diverse sexualities. This trend could be seen as part of wider changes in western society that have also resulted in the advance of rights for women and ethnic minorities. We may then account for the controversy over same-sex marriage as the inevitable but temporary battle between traditionalism and democratic social progress. But is this an accurate picture? We suggest not.

A full understanding of such controversies is not possible without a thoroughly *sociological* analysis of the social organization of sexuality and gender and their social meaning. What such a perspective entails is discussed in the next section.

TASK: Set up a debate about legalizing same-sex marriage (or banning it if you live in a country that has already passed such laws).

Make sure that you have one person that is noting down the arguments made both for and against the motion.

Read the following section to see if the arguments made in the debate relate to the points made below.

Gender, Sexuality and Sociology

Our aim in this text is to demonstrate that gender and sexuality can be understood through the following key issues and concepts in sociology:

- social change;
- social conflict, social cohesion and social order;
- social hierarchies, divisions and inequalities;
- social identities;
- modernity/late modernity/postmodernity.

We discuss these key issues and concepts throughout the text, but we organize the discussion into parts that cover the central sociological concepts of structure, culture, self and identity. Let us stick with our introductory example to expand and explain. In the western world, the contemporary movements for women's rights and those of sexual minorities have developed from a period of significant **social change** since the post-war, mid-twentieth-century decades, affecting women's access to educational and financial resources, changes in cultural values, religious beliefs and decline in the deference to tradition. This period saw the rise of women's and gay liberation movements that demanded new political and social rights. These demands challenged tradition, resulting in **social conflict**. Social conflict thus often arises from social change. This is one way of explaining the common resistance across many cultures to the progress of lesbian and gay rights. If the social position of men and women is thought to be determined by nature – as religious and moral traditionalists believe – then lesbians and gays would inevitably be seen as a challenge to this 'natural' order.

Groups that are identified with traditional views on the role of women and on sexual morality often argue that social change has progressed too quickly, leaving a lack of **social cohesion** and **social order** in its wake. However, social conflict is not just the result of progress versus tradition. After all, in the case of marriage, we are talking about a relationship that has historically been seen as the foundation of family, kinship and, ultimately, society. In a period when there are widespread concerns about the decline of marriage and the stability it brings, why would traditionalists deny the extension of the right to marry to a small minority of the population? The answer lies in understanding the social significance of that minority, and its relationship to the majority. In this case of same-sex marriage, lesbians and gays represent a challenge to dominant ideas of masculinity and femininity (what we term gender) and the social, legal and cultural privilege given to traditional heterosexuality.

Underpinning the significance of gender and sexuality is the traditional 'naturalist' understanding of masculinity and femininity, usually based on ideas about biological reproduction and natural differences deemed to arise from it. Thus women are seen as 'naturally' suited to child-rearing and domesticity, historically justifying, for example, their lesser access to education and paid employment. In such naturalist explanations, lesbians, gays, transgendered people, bisexuals, are all seen to be going against the designs of nature – our genital reproductive function – and are thus subject to moral and social disapproval and often legal sanctions. If you believe that men and women are naturally designed to 'fit' together sexually, and that the ultimate purpose of sex is to reproduce, then lesbians and gays would inevitably be seen as perverted and/or immoral – as a result of their 'unnatural' desires. Such attitudes occur in western and many other cultures and are often expressed by religious groups and by political groups in favour of 'traditional values'.

In this traditional form of thinking – common to many cultures and religions – there is a **hierarchy of gender**, with men regarded as naturally superior to women, particularly in the sexual realm, and homosexuals at the bottom of the hierarchy since their existence is seen as a fundamental perversion of the gender order. Thus **divisions and inequalities between men and women, and heterosexuals and homosexuals**, are justified as natural and inevitable. The sociological literature describes such recourse to naturalism as **'essentialist'** or 'nativist' thinking, and one major achievement of sociological work on gender and sexuality has been to illuminate how essentialist thinking pervades many aspects of society, often through religion, but also in laws and policies and throughout institutions such as education, medicine and science and, most frequently, in popular culture and commonsense thinking.

The pervasiveness of essentialism often leads us to assume that social categories such as men and women, heterosexuals and homosexuals, are simply a literal reflection of natural 'types'. However, in opposition to essentialism, sociological work on gender and sexuality has shown the social origins of the categories into which individuals are placed, both through social classification over which they may have no direct control (your 'sex' has to be identified on most official forms, starting with birth certificates) and through their own identification ('I am a woman'; 'I am gay'). Sociological research and analysis has illuminated the development of these classification processes and their influence on the construction of our individual identities. In such academic work, biological 'sex' has been replaced with an emphasis on socially constructed gender and sexuality: how the categories of male and female become socially meaningful; how they are organized hierarchically; what consequences this has for life chances, sexual behaviour and identity; and which social groups are served by the social ordering of gender relations. Similarly, non-heterosexual identities are not seen simply as 'natural' types: homosexuality is meaningful or socially significant precisely because it forms the basis of an identity which is outside the conventional gender order and, as a result, is placed at the bottom of the gender/ sexual hierarchy. Any change in its status, as over the last thirty or so years, inevitably challenges traditional gender arrangements. Hence the current controversy over same-sex marriage can also be understood as a conflict over the social meaning and status of homo-sexuality *in relation to* heterosexuality. From a sociological perspective, then, **gender and sexuality are intimately intertwined:** the social construction and significance of one can rarely be understood without considering the other.

Gender and sexuality have relevance for all aspects of social life and thus sociological analysis: politics and power, cultural beliefs and values, social action, self and identity, and social structures. For example, the right of lesbians and gays to marry is seen not as a personal issue, or one simply of individual political rights, but rather as one for the scrutiny of the state. Claims for such rights are indicative of wider social changes that potentially threaten or undermine previously taken-for-granted essentialist beliefs and values and social structural arrangements associated with the traditional heterosexual gender order. Therefore, issues around sexuality and gender cannot be understood as merely personal and private since they raise key sociological questions about the connection between **structure, culture, the self and identity – and the operation of power** across all these aspects of social life.

Essentialism in Classical Sociological Thinking

Gender and sexuality received only scant attention within classical sociology and have only recently been established as 'proper' topics for sociological inquiry. Most introductory sociology courses and texts now cover gender and sexuality – but this is a relatively recent innovation, occurring over the last couple of decades of the twentieth century. It is useful to consider why it took so long for gender and sexuality to be included within what C. Wright Mills calls the 'sociological imagination' (Mills, 1959). Part of the reasons for this absence relates to the lack of 'presence' of both women and those of diverse sexualities in academia. A similar lack of ethnic and racial minority presence has often led to oversights on issues of racism, colonialism and post-colonialism. In both the UK and North America, these issues of race, gender and sexuality are more visible now in part because there is greater diversity in academia itself. It is important to note that much of the work around gender and sexuality has been driven by an attempt to understand personal experience in a sociological way. Indeed, both your authors have contributed to research on gender and sexuality largely because our personal identities and experiences have made us all too aware of various oppressions and how these have structured our lives in complex ways – Stevi as a heterosexual feminist from a working-class background and Momin as a gay, Asian man brought up in a Muslim family. For both of us and for many of those we discuss, work on gender and sexuality has presented a challenge to traditional assumptions of sociology as an objective, politically neutral science in terms of its topics, theories and methods of research.

Another important reason why gender and sexuality have been absent from much of sociology's history is that the key concepts and ideas developed by classical sociologists were not applied to these issues in any consistent way. One could suggest that this was again an issue of 'presence': sociology is often described as having founding 'fathers', and that is an accurate description of those who have come to represent the classical sociological canon – from which women thinkers such as Charlotte Perkins Gilman were excluded. The 'holy trinity' of classical theorists – Marx, Weber and Durkheim, with the inconsistent addition of Georg Simmel – were all male and all relatively privileged white Europeans. No doubt one can speculate as to their personal views on gender and sexuality, and there are many historical works that discuss their personal lives and experiences, and how these impacted on their theories and interests (see Pampel, 2000, for example). What is clear from the body of work produced by these theorists, however, is that they assumed that issues of differentiation and division between men and women (there is no reference to sexualities) were by and large derived from natural divisions based in biology. The founding fathers, on the whole, were essentialists [3].

The main achievement of sociological thought has been to challenge taken-for-granted ways of thinking about society, everyday social life, social change and social divisions and inequalities. The founding theorists were primarily interested in explaining the massive transformations brought about by the rise of modern capitalism: industrialization; urbanization; the advent of bureaucratic organization through the state; the reorganization of work and the new power of capital – in short, all that is 'modern' about our contemporary societies. The exclusion of gender and sexuality from this project, however, left us with only a partial understanding of modernity:

> If our view of modernity derived exclusively from the sociological classics, we would not know that a central part of the great transformation consisted of efforts to organize bodies, pleasures, and desires as they relate to personal and public life, and that this entailed constructing sexual (and gender) identities. In short, the making of sexual selves and codes has been interlaced with the making of the cultural and institutional life of Western Societies. (Seidman 1996: 2–3)

Gender and sexuality are proper topics for sociology because they are socially organized and socially meaningful and because the ways in which they are ordered and made meaningful interconnect with other aspects of modern social life. We have structured our chapters using the key concepts and theories developed by sociology to account for the social conditions that are characteristic of modernity. Sociological work on gender and sexuality has resulted in reinterpretations of these established concepts and theories and has also added new ones, thus enhancing our understanding of the social. For example, while the concept of 'patriarchy' appears in the work of Weber, feminist theorists have transformed the way it is used within sociology. Gender was adopted as a sociological concept only in the recent past, with the increasing influence of feminist and lesbian/gay theories, which also established sexuality as a legitimate field of sociological inquiry. Above all, the concept of essentialism – the fundamental starting point for the sociology of gender and sexuality – is a new concept and one that has now become established, enlarging the scope of the 'sociological imagination'.

The Structure of the Text

We begin, in Part I, with the development of essentialist ideas around gender and sexuality during the rise of modernity in the West. We then consider the challenges to essentialism associated with advances in sociological explanations of gender and sexuality. Taken with this Introduction, this first part provides a basic overview of sociological ideas around gender and sexuality, placing them in the historical contexts in which they developed. It will introduce some of the key concepts and central themes that will be dealt with in more detail in the subsequent chapters, but **Part I provides a self-contained and detailed introduction to the historical emergence of sociological thought on gender and sexuality.**

The **subsequent chapters offer more in-depth knowledge** and work towards fuller understanding through a more detailed examination of key concepts and ideas. Part II is concerned with structural accounts of gender and sexual inequalities – their social patterning – and how they are interrelated with other social divisions and inequalities (such as class and race). In Part III we discuss cultural values, beliefs and ideologies around gender and sexuality, linking these to the structural explanations in Part II, and to how we make sense of our own individual and collective identities, which is the main focus of Part IV. In the **Conclusion**, we discuss the continued contemporary relevance of the issues raised throughout the book, focusing on power, politics, contemporary social identities and social change.

Learning outcomes will be provided at the end of each part of the book. Your knowledge and understanding of key concepts and theories should develop through each self-contained chapter, but also with a cumulative effect as you progress through the book. To help along the way, each chapter is **cross-referenced** with other relevant sections throughout the text. **Notes** marked in the text direct you to **further readings and useful resources for further study**, to be found at the end of each part, just after the learning outcomes. The notes will help you to find further relevant materials and examples that will aid your understanding and preparation for any written assessments you may have. However, we have included examples of research in the text that illustrate concepts and theories, as well as **exercises for students** throughout the text that will develop skills of understanding and evaluation of the concepts and theories presented. These exercises come in two forms: first, **task-based exercises** which can be used in small groups or seminars; and, second, brief exercises which simply ask you as an individual reader to stop and think about a particular question in **Your World.** Finally, a full **bibliography of all the works cited** in the chapters and notes will be found at the end of the book.

Notes and Resources for Further Study

1 The law banned discrimination on the basis of sexual orientation in employment, housing, education and public accommodation and was passed in April 2005. It did not mention civil partnerships or marriage. Accounts from newspapers in Maine are available on *www.shgresources. com/me/newspapers*, and this particular demonstration and counter-protest took place on 28 April 2005.

2 Only a few countries give full marriage rights to lesbians and gays (Belgium, Canada, The Netherlands, South Africa, Spain). (The issue is unresolved in the USA, where the Supreme Court of Massachusetts has voted for full marriage rights, in conflict with most other states in the Union, provoking an on-going legal/constitutional battle.) However, a range of countries have legislation that recognizes some form of part-nership – either 'civil unions' or 'registered partnerships', or will at least recognize partnerships for the purposes of immigration. Most of these are in Western Europe but also include Australia and New Zealand, Israel, Argentina and Brazil. For country-specific information, you can check out Lesbian, Gay, Bisexual and Transgender rights organizations with information on current status of legislation and campaigns on a wide variety of issues, based in the USA and UK: *www.hrc.org*; *www. ilga.org*; *www.stonewall.org.uk*.These sites contain up-to-date campaign information on same-sex marriage, but for an excellent introduction to these issues in the USA, see the book by A. Sullivan, *Same-Sex Marriage, Pro and Con: A Reader* (2004).

3 In his comprehensive introduction to sociological theory, Swingewood points out that Marx's collaborator, Engels, did relate the subordina-tion of women within the family to the development of capitalism in *The Origin of the Family, Private Property and the State*, published in 1884, but that this approach used the usual concepts of sociology rather than thinking through gender as a distinct sociological concept (Swingewood, 2000: 237). It is interesting to note that in this third edition of the text, Swingewood still refers to feminist sociology and the sociology of sexual-ity as examples of new directions in sociological thought.

Part I

The Development of Sociological Thought on Gender and Sexuality

The aim of this first part of the book is to introduce sociological approaches to sexuality and gender and to place them in historical context. Sexuality and gender are commonly thought of as natural and eternal qualities of human individuals – what we call naturalist or essentialist thinking. In Chapter 1, we discuss the main features of 'essentialism' and we show how these ideas became the focus of sociological critique. In Chapter 2, we move on to discussing how feminists and lesbian and gay theorists have contested essentialist thinking and developed analyses of gender as a social division and of sexuality as central to this division. We conclude with a brief overview of some challenges to concepts and theories of gender and sexuality raised by issues of race and nation, masculinity and the question of how we think about bodies.

Introduction: The Unfortunate President

Lawrence H. Summers resigned yesterday as president of Harvard University after a relatively brief and turbulent tenure of five years, nudged by Harvard's governing corporation and facing a vote of no confidence from the influential Faculty of Arts and Sciences.

(*The New York Times*, 22 February 2006, Section A: 1)

In early 2005, President Summers delivered a conference speech in which he raised the question of whether inherent genetic or other biological traits were the reason that so few women made it to the top of the maths and science professions. The ensuing public arguments between Summers and his academic faculty made news across the world but particularly in the USA, where Harvard is the most verdant of the Ivy League universities, which make up the oldest and richest institutions in the American higher education system. It is instructive to consider this incident as a micro-example of the impact on contemporary societies of sociological thinking on gender and sexuality. That is not to say that the Harvard President eventually resigned only because of his stance on gender, since further reports during 2005 demonstrated that there were many aspects of his management style that were causing unrest amongst the staff. However, the remarks on gender did signal the beginning of making these issues public and, therefore, illustrate the importance of gender politics in contemporary culture. Summers made news precisely because he raised questions about the status of women and in particular their biological difference from men. In the early twenty-first century, such a position is newsworthy because it is controversial. Why is this the case?

In part the answer is because we live in societies in the West in which equality between the sexes is now a taken-for-granted aspect of how we should conduct our public life. We have social policies and laws that both protect individuals from discrimination and grant access to resources in terms of citizenship, rights and democracy. Women can now enter the same educational and employment sectors as men, and discrimination on the basis of sex – and increasingly on the basis of sexual identity – is regarded as unacceptable. We had a woman running for the Democratic Party's nomination for Presidency of the United States in 2008 and for most of the primary season Hillary Clinton was the frontrunner. We already have women in positions of political and public office around the world [1], as well as significant advances in lesbian and gay rights such as partnership, marriage, parenting and anti-discrimination rights. Popular culture has reflected a shift in understandings of women's status, and that of lesbians and gays, with successful television programmes such as *Sex and the City*, *Will and Grace*, *Queer Eye for the Straight Guy*, numerous films which attest to women's independence and, of course, successful women in both sport and entertainment (see Introduction to Part III). Indeed, if anything, the last few years has seen increasing concern about the problems of boys and men, often referred to as the crisis of masculinity in a post-feminist world [2].

Over the last thirty years or so, sociological analyses of gender have had a significant impact upon our political and popular culture, resulting in a shift in the understanding of the *reasons* for the differences and inequalities between men and women. Indeed, this point was made by many of the Harvard faculty who signed a letter of protest at their President's comments, drawing attention to the extensive academic research establishing that the status of women is social rather than biological or natural. We begin an introduction to these analyses in the following chapters, concentrating on the ways in which **essentialist** or **naturalist** explanations of gender inequalities and related issues of sexual behaviour and identity have been challenged. It is this particular issue of naturalism that the unfortunate Harvard President fell foul of (although his subsequent career did not suffer given that he went on to become a senior economic adviser to President Obama). While he actually discussed a range of reasons for women's limited progress within maths and science, including the lack of proper childcare facilities and the role of discrimination, he also invoked the notion of a biological basis to women's lack of ambition and success, provoking a substantial number of his faculty to criticize him on the grounds that he was ignorant of – or had wilfully ignored – decades of research on the social reasons for gender inequalities [3].

The chapters in Part I cover the main points of these sociological analyses, providing both a chronological introduction and a conceptual one. We thus demonstrate how gender and sexuality emerged as topics of sociological investigation and the historical importance of feminist/lesbian/gay movements in this development. We explain and illustrate the meaning of essentialism throughout and show how this naturalist explanation of differences has been subject to sociological critiques. Our focus is mainly on Anglo-American societies, and this is driven by the historical emergence of women's and sexual diversity movements, together with academic work, from within these societies. However, it is important to remember that gender and sexual inequalities are global phenomena, and are also structured by racial divisions both globally and within specific societies. We point out, however, that the significance of racial, ethnic and national differences for gender and sexuality has often been neglected and begin to explain how and why. Taken together with the overall Introduction to the book, Part I provides a basic-level introduction to the sociology of gender and sexuality.

1

The Trouble with 'Nature'

1.1 'One is Not Born But Becomes a Woman': Identifying 'Essentialism'

This is one of the most famous statements in feminist theory, made by the French philosopher Simone de Beauvoir in *The Second Sex* (1972 [1949]). Beauvoir was a writer and philosopher and her early ideas about the reasons for inequalities between women and men influenced what came to be known as the *second wave* feminist movement that developed in the 1970s. Beauvoir made the crucial argument that it was culture – in the form of western civilization – that delimited what women could become, and that this culture dictated the subordination of women to men through their exclusion from power, education, work and public life in general. Although Beauvoir was not a sociologist, her assertion that women are not 'born' resonates with sociological analyses of gender precisely because it summarizes the fundamental rejection of biological definitions. Moreover, this rejection of biological explanations by second wave feminist thinkers was based on the development of alternative, largely sociological, explanations for gender inequalities in western societies. Before we discuss those ideas in detail, it is worth reflecting on the radical implications of such a statement on women.

Cultural values and beliefs around men and women were still dominated by biological explanations not only when Beauvoir was writing in the 1940s, but also during the 1970s when the second wave of widespread feminist activism developed. Differences relating to genitalia, child-bearing, physical strength and mental and emotional capacities were all variously used to justify the social position of women as inferior to men in general, and subordinate to male counterparts in workplaces, education, politics and cultural life, and within the home as wives, mothers and daughters. Attitudes to and the regulation of homosexuality were even more oppressive, with homosexual acts illegal in Britain until 1967, and remaining so in many states of the USA, Canada (until 1969) and globally. Homosexuality was regarded as morally and psychologically deviant and above all as 'unnatural'. These values and beliefs were apparent in individual attitudes and were also reflected in laws, in social policies such as those on education, health and welfare, in politics and in everyday life. In short, the whole realm of the social, from social structures and culture to identities and everyday activities, was dominated by biological explanation of the differences and inequalities between men and women, homosexuals and heterosexuals. Indeed, the term 'gender' did not even exist as common cultural currency, with the biological term 'sex' used to contain and signify men and women (hence Beauvoir's characterization of women as the second 'sex').

This understanding of both the 'natural' division between men and women and the 'unnatural' deviance of homosexuals had become culturally dominant across the western world during the era of industrialization and urbanization, from around the late eighteenth century to the early twentieth century. For example, take this best-selling marriage manual advising men about sex with their wives:

> Woman is a harp who only yields her secrets of melody to the master who knows how to handle her . . . what both man and woman, driven by obscure primitive urges, wish to feel in the sexual act, is the essential force of maleness, which expresses itself in a sort of violent and absolute possession of the woman. And so both of them can and do exult in a certain degree male aggression and dominance – whether actual or apparent – which proclaims this essential force. (T.H. Van de Velde, *Ideal Marriage*, 1930, quoted in Jackson, 1989: 62)

It is clear that the woman is regarded as completely passive when it comes to sex, and that she is seen as 'naturally' unknowing until stimulated by 'the essential force of maleness', which enables her to re-connect to her own 'primitive' biological urges. Using this example, we can begin to define two key terms in sexuality and gender studies: those of essentialism and gender. These concepts will be developed later in the book but for now we offer working definitions. **Essentialism literally means any form of thinking**

**that characterizes or explains aspects of human behaviour
and identity as part of human 'essence': a biologically and/
or psychologically irreducible quality of the individual that is
immutable and *pre*-social,** as demonstrated above when sexual
urges are identified as 'essential' to 'maleness'. Woman's sexuality is
seen as naturally passive, but also buried deep in her essential biological being, awaiting arousal by a man. Biological explanations are
thus essentialist as they rely on reducing behaviour and identity to a
biological basis, whether genetic, hormonal or physiological. These
explanations are often referred to as 'naturalist' and/or 'nativist',
since biology is equated with 'nature'.

The idea of 'natural development' indicates that human conduct
and attributes follow evolutionary and/or genetically programmed
patterns, which are impermeable to social influence and are thus what
we are born with – the literal meaning of 'native'. Human 'nature' is
common cultural shorthand for the biological aspects of our character. In such naturalist explanations, it is perfectly reasonable to
state that women are 'naturally' maternal, and that homosexuality
is against 'nature' since it is not reproductive, that (heterosexual)
men are naturally sexually aggressive and, ultimately, that heterosexuality is the only 'natural' sexual behaviour. Essentialism can be
understood in terms of a determinist equation: biological sex *equals*
male or female *equals* sexual desire directed towards the opposite sex.
Anatomy is most definitely destiny in this equation, so child-bearing
is taken to define the natural role of women, and non-reproductive
sex does not fit within the equation's parameters.

Biology, however, is not the only basis of essentialism; spiritual
or psychological essentialism has also been a significant feature of
western thought. In this form of essentialism, gender and sexuality are often conceptualized in religious terms, as God-given (as in
discussions of abortion and child-care during the 1960s and 1970s
and homosexuality today), or in psychological terms, for example in
ideas of love, romance and sex as central to personal fulfilment and
emotional well-being. In both psychological and spiritual essentialism, social influences on gender and sexuality are either downplayed
or ignored. In such explanations, sexually active women have been
described as either spiritually 'fallen' or psychologically disturbed,
and, of course, homosexuals have been similarly characterized as
either sinful or perverted.

The simple statement that 'one is not born a woman' thus represents a considerable challenge to the essentialism that is deeply
entrenched in western culture.

TASK: Identifying essentialism.

In a small discussion group, ask your classmates to list the different ways in which they can safely say that they know that they are either a man or a woman, heterosexual or homosexual. It is best to do this as anonymously as you can.

Gather the written answers together and try to identify any essentialism in the explanations that people provide.

Think about the essentialist equation discussed above, and the combination of the biological/spiritual/psychological.

1.2 Identifying Gender: First Wave Feminism

As noted above, Simone de Beauvoir published *The Second Sex* in 1949, well before the second wave feminist movement developed in the West in the USA, UK and France. Nonetheless, her work became one the most influential texts across all these countries during the emergence of the women's movement and her statement that 'one is not born but becomes a woman' has come neatly to encapsulate feminists' rejection of essentialism in favour of sociological understandings. Crucial in the development of such understandings has been the introduction of a term that Beauvoir did not use: 'gender'. We have already used this term in the introduction and this first chapter, indicating that we can take for granted that, as students of sociology and as members of your specific culture, you will undoubtedly have a working understanding of what that term means, such has been the impact of feminist thinking on both sociology and everyday life. In non-academic contexts, however, 'gender' is now often used interchangeably with sex (most commonly on official forms which ask you to identify your 'sex' or 'gender' as male or female). Some clarification is therefore needed. **In short, gender refers to the social division between men and women; masculinity and femininity are thus understood as social attributes rather than natural ones.**

Historians of feminism in the West identify a first wave of feminist activism, located from around the 1840s to the 1920s, culminating in the achievement of women's right to vote in many democracies in the 1920s (Banks, 1990). The first wave of feminists campaigned against social inequalities between women and men and the disadvantaged position of women in society, but they did not develop a specific sociological concept – gender – as an analytical device. However, in their focus on education, employment, equal rights and, above all, the status of women in relation to men, first wave feminism began to identify what we now understand as gender – a *social* division between women and men. Evangelical, equal rights and socialist feminisms, which developed from the 1840s, all shared an assumption that some form of public intervention could be used to achieve better conditions for women through changes in politics, laws or cultural values [4]. Let us sketch some brief examples, beginning with the equal rights tradition, which has perhaps remained the most durable strand of feminist activism.

In her *Vindication of the Rights of Woman* (1792), a text that influenced both American and British first wave feminisms, Mary Wollstonecraft engaged with the emergent and urgent concern with rights brought about by the French and American revolutions. She deliberately echoes the classic statement of (male) human rights made by Thomas Paine in *The Rights of Man* (1792), arguing that women could equally fulfil the conditions of citizenship if given equal opportunity for education and employment. The implication of this is that access to employment and education affect the relative social positions of men and women and produce divisions between them, based not on biology, but on social exclusion and inequality. Such an analysis compels us to think of these groups as socially created rather than being defined solely or overwhelmingly by their biological or spiritual 'essence'.

Wollstonecraft acknowledged the different impacts on women of their economic positions, although her concern is really for 'idle' upper-class women, arguing that:

> With respect to virtue, to use the word in a comprehensive sense, I have seen the most in low life. Many poor women maintain their children by the sweat of their brow, and keep together families that the vices of the fathers would have scattered abroad; but gentlewomen are too indolent to be actively virtuous, and are softened rather than refined by civilisation. (1972 [1792]: 16)

Her critique challenged not only the economic dependence of 'gentlewomen', but also the emerging gender framework of the time for the middle classes, which separated men and women into the workplace and home, respectively, and which Catherine Hall (1992) subsequently named the 'domestic ideology'.

Although located within the equal rights or liberal feminist tradition, Wollstonecraft touches upon the impacts of class position, an issue which came to dominate the development of socialist feminism in the latter part of the nineteenth century, particularly in Britain when the influence of Marxist analyses of capitalism gradually displaced earlier forms of socialism (Banks, 1990: Ch. 4). Socialist feminism focused on oppression within the domestic realm, necessitated by capitalism's need for a social unit to reproduce and maintain a working-class labour force and for a system of marriage that protected the property and inheritance rights of the capitalist class [5]. Charlotte Perkins Gilman was also raising these issues of women's economic position in marriage in the American context, publishing 'Women and Economics' in 1898, in which she argued that marriage obliged women to perform domestic labour for free, subordinating them economically and thus socially. Again, the emphasis is clearly on how women *are made into* women by virtue of their social class, their economic situation, and through religious and cultural beliefs around femininity.

The beginnings of the idea of gender are evident in these first wave ideas – not as a specific concept but rather as a gradual movement towards explanations for women's position that do not rely on essentialist arguments. A caveat needs to be added here, however, not least because the issue re-emerges in second wave feminism (see Ch. 2.8): some aspects of equal rights/liberal, socialist and, above all, evangelical feminisms still either assumed or actively deployed the notion of an essential female difference from men, derived from biology and the maternal impulse, and/or an innate moral superiority, particularly in issues of sexuality. This is evident in the first wave feminist campaigns against prostitution in Britain and the USA.

Comprehensive regulation of prostitution began during the nineteenth century in Britain and the USA, provoked by increasing awareness of these activities in the newly urbanized towns created during industrialization. Crucially, regulation was the result of pressure from *both* religious and cultural moralists (including many women) *and* feminists who wanted to secure the protection of women, with these two groups often joining forces in political campaigns. The first of a series of Contagious Diseases Acts was introduced in 1864 in England to regulate sexually transmitted diseases among military personnel (who were all men in this era). However, both the framing and implementation of the law focused on women as the problem – allowing police to arrest any women suspected of being a prostitute and force them to undergo medical examination. Feminist campaigns against this law were led by Josephine Butler, who argued that women were being unfairly stigmatized by the 'double standard' of sexual morality, forcing them to bear the responsibility for, and consequences of, male sexual behaviours [6].

The 'double standard' referred to the common *biologically essentialist* understanding that men had compelling, natural sexual needs and could not be held responsible for trying to satisfy them by using prostitutes. Blame for transmitting disease, therefore, fell on the women who worked as prostitutes. They were seen as immoral for engaging in sex and thus going against the ideal of women as non-sexual and innocent of sexual desire (as illustrated in section 1.1 above). The consequence of enshrining such essentialist ideas into law is that the force of regulation becomes directed at women rather than men. While feminists argued vigorously against this injustice, many of the religious moralist *and* feminist campaigners also argued that women were naturally more moral and less sexual, only falling prey to such sin or immorality through financial circumstances or pressure put on them by men.

Victorian cultural ideals of asexual femininity arose in conjunction with the exclusion of women from many forms of paid employment and their relegation to unpaid domestic labour within marriage, all of which was a consequence of the reorganization of gender relations accompanying industrialization (Gilman, 2008 [1898]; Weeks, 1989; Hall, 1992). This new standard of femininity initially arose among the middle classes, since working-class women often had to work, either in domestic service or in industry. They were, nonetheless, subject to the same cultural ideology of femininity – working-class respectability in sexual morals and behaviour was based on the emerging middle-class ideology of femininity (Mort, 1987; Mason, 1994).

The movements that tried to challenge the 'double standard' of sexual conduct did, however, acknowledge that collective social regulation, in the form of laws, moral campaigns and providing alternative income through employment, could influence and change behaviours of both men and women. Thus, even in the essentialist aspects of first wave feminism, there are small inklings that masculinities and femininities are open to collective social influence through political reform campaigns and, more significantly, that cultural attitudes and men's and women's socio-economic locations also contributed to the formation of gendered conduct and identity.

Your World: Are there still 'double standards' when it comes to the sexual behaviours of men and women in your culture? Does this differ by age, ethnicity, class, sexual identity?

1.3 Consequences of Sex–Gender Beliefs: The 'Deviant' Homosexual

The Victorian reordering of gender relations was associated with a growing interest in documenting and categorizing sexual 'perversions': deviations from the expected norm of sexually passive women and heterosexually oriented men and women. This endeavour marked the beginning of the scientific study of sexuality – gathering statistical data on sexual behaviour and collecting legal, anthropological and proto-psychological case studies – which came to be known as sexology. Not all sexology was necessarily anti-homosexual. Karl Heinrich Ulrichs' work in the late nineteenth century focused on the natural basis for what he called Uranians – men who loved men in the manner of the god Uranus – and argued consistently for the decriminalization of homosexuality on this basis. The culture of the time, however, did not bode well for the reception of such ideas [7]. Partly this was due to the new prudery around sex during this time, driven by religion, the new middle-class ideology of asexual femininity and the more generalized concern of the middle classes with maintaining moral purity in the context of masses of people living crammed together in the newly urbanized industrial cities. In the minds of the middle classes, overcrowded housing raised concerns about the consequences of physical proximity for working-class sexual activity (Mort, 1987). The mass urban concentrations of population also led to the creation of many spaces where people could be anonymous to those around them and escape official scrutiny, creating the potential for lustful encounters and opportunities for men to use prostitutes (both male and female) in areas other than where they lived and worked. Such anonymity had not been possible in traditional, pre-industrial small towns or villages. The essentialist characterization of male sexual needs also raised a concern that men's potentially uncontrollable lust might lead to sexual perversion. As Weeks says in his comprehensive history of Victorian sexuality in Britain: 'In the debates before the 1885 Criminal Law Amendment Act was rushed through Parliament [which redefined and broadened the legal definition of homosexual acts as well as tightening the regulation of prostitution and raised the age of consent for girls to 16] male homosexual behaviour was quite clearly linked with the activities of those who corrupted young girls' (1989: 106).

Many of the major sexological studies published in the late 1800s and early 1900s were regarded as obscene, but this moral climate also meant that the 'science' of sexology was used to justify the contemporary social understandings of gender and sexuality. This, above all, meant the classification of a new type of person: the 'invert' or 'homosexual' as the antithesis of normal, moral, pure, natural masculinity. Many of the most influential works of the time focused on homosexual acts and, together with increased legal regulation, served to confirm homosexuality as a 'perversion' of the 'natural' order. The modern capitalist reordering of class and gender relations associated with the new middle-class morality also created a climate in which homosexuality was *increasingly* seen as a social problem and individual pathology, precisely as the 'inversion' of respectable heterosexuality. Moreover, this was focused on male homosexuality, with a lack of regulation of and public discussion on lesbianism (Weeks, 1989).

1.4 Defining Gender: The Second Wave

As Banks (1990) points out, it is difficult accurately to pinpoint the beginnings of second wave feminism because it emerged through a combination of grass-roots activism, nationally based political campaigns around key issues such as abortion, and the circulation of new ideas and research on women's status by academics and activists. Many feminists were also involved in and influenced by the battle for civil rights in the USA during the 1950s and 1960s, and later and elsewhere by the emergence of the New Left: a range of radical political movements, often associated with anti-war protests (particularly against the USA–Vietnam conflict), critiques of capitalism and student politics. Furthermore, many feminists have described how the impetus to develop independent political action for women was in part a response to the sexism encountered in these other movements [8]. In the following brief sketch we outline how the proto-sociological ideas of first wave feminism were transformed, as a result of second wave feminism and gay liberation, into specifically sociological concepts and theories. In doing so, we cover a time span that stretches across three decades, illustrating that the impact of feminist and lesbian and gay thought on academic sociology was a drawn-out process, with many key academic publications appearing some time after the activism and political writings that inspired them.

Most historians of feminist movements agree that Britain, France and the United States became the initial centres of second wave feminist activity. This is not to deny the emergence of such concerns across other western societies, or indeed around the world, but it is to identify these countries as significant contexts for the development of feminist theories. Second wave feminist activism is notable for the entirely new development of radical feminism – radical, in part, because of its sociological approach   but this period also saw the re-emergence of earlier first wave traditions, and so most histories of feminism categorize the movement from the 1960s as having three distinct but related strands: liberal or equal rights; socialist or Marxist; and radical.

TASK: The history of women's suffrage and feminist movements.

First, find out when women won the vote in your own country or locality and whether this was after men got the vote. How does the timing of this compare with other countries/localities?

Second, try to identify a relevant women's organization that was involved in suffrage campaigns. Was there an understanding of gender as social in their campaigns?

Some suggested starting points (and see note 8):

www.womenshistory.about.com;   *www.now.org*;   *www.unesco.org/women*

Equal rights feminism had developed during the first wave in the late nineteenth century, its main achievement being the right of women to vote in many nations in the early twentieth century. Its influence then declined in the mid-twentieth century, partly because of a loss of momentum once the vote was achieved, and partly as women entered professional and trade union organizations for the first time in significant numbers. Historians point to a resurgence of equal rights feminism in the 1960s in both Britain and the USA, with bodies such as the National Organization for Women emerging in the USA, and smaller such groups in Britain. Crucially, this resurgence was linked to wider changes in the social status of women, particularly in terms of their increasing participation in the labour market (Banks, 1990).

In Britain and Western Europe more often than the USA or Canada, feminist politics developed in the organized labour union movements in conjunction with, and sometimes in reaction to, the politics of class. Thus, a Marxist or socialist feminist tradition re-emerged during this period, as had the equal rights tradition, but both were markedly different from first wave feminism in their emphasis on the social basis of women's subordination, whether that was linked to employment and educational opportunities or the wider capitalist structure. Furthermore, both traditions were heavily influenced by what came to be termed radical feminism, which, for the first time, provided a range of analyses that conceptualized male domination as a social system. Feminists from all three traditions contributed to the development of a new concept: 'gender.'

A recent dictionary of sociology entry under 'gender' both shows its acceptance as a major sociological concept and defines its use:

> If the sex of a person is biologically determined, the gender of a person is culturally and socially constructed. There are thus two sexes (male and female) and two genders (masculine and feminine). The principal theoretical and political issue is whether gender as a socially constructed phenomenon is related to or determined by biology. (Abercrombie et al., 2006: 163)

This definition conveys the central point that the concept of gender contests biological essentialism but it does not expand on the ways in which the concept is used sociologically. For a little more insight, you can flick forward to the entry under 'sociology of gender', which outlines the 'ways in which the physical differences between men and women are mediated through culture and social structure' (Abercrombie et al., 2006: 371), thus reassuringly beginning to talk about key sociological concepts to which we can all relate. The entry goes on to mention briefly the issues of identity formation, public/private and divisions of labour, as well as ideologies of gender. This demonstrates that there is an understanding in mainstream sociology today that gender is a key sociological concept and social division.

Weber had talked about patriarchal authority, but his use of the term was limited to how legitimate power in traditional societies was vested in male heads of household, and he did not expand his gaze to discuss men and women as socially distinct groups. Engels had similarly focused on the family as a functional unit for capitalism in that monogamous marriage ensured control of women's reproductive sexuality so that bourgeois men could pass on their property to their 'rightful' heirs, but, like Weber, he saw women and men as 'natural' categories rather than social ones. Patriarchy is a term we will discuss in detail below, but first note that neither of these classical sociologists referred to gender in the way in which it is defined above. Early sociologists did recognize the differences between men and women's social position, but they did not develop a way of thinking about this as fully social.

In many, especially western, cultures, gender existed as a linguistic term denoting masculine and feminine, but as a social concept it was first used in the 1950s and 1960s by psychologists such as John Money and Robert Stoller to describe socially learned aspects of male and female behaviour as distinct from the biological categories male and female. This resonated with earlier anthropological work on the variability of sex roles, particularly that of Margaret Mead (1965 [1935]), which demonstrated that masculine and feminine behaviours and roles varied across cultures. Thus, the idea that masculinity and femininity might be acquired rather than innate was gradually taking root within some academic arenas, although its influence was not always progressive. John Money's work developed in his attempts to understand intersex infants, producing a concept of gender identity that serves to justify medical interventions to 'correct' anatomy (Hird, 2004: 133; see also Ch. 10.1). It was not until the 1970s that 'gender' became used in a critical sense, and this time lag is linked to the fact that it was only at this time that a significant number of feminist academics began focusing our attention on the social status of women as a social group, though it is important to note that there was some feminist sociological work on sex roles well before this time (see Ch. 3.4). There were two particularly influential contributions that established gender as a critical concept. The first of these was Ann Oakley's book *Sex, Gender and Society* (1972), in which she argued strongly for gender to be understood as a matter of culture – with historical and cultural variations – rather than as a simple matter of biology. Following this, Gayle Rubin's essay 'The Traffic in Women: Notes on the "Political Economy" of Sex' (1975) drew upon anthropological studies to describe how the social organization of marriage, kinship and reproduction gave rise to 'sex/gender systems', again making it plain that the social position of men and women, and their hierarchical relationship, could not be reduced to biological sex.

Other sociologists at that time began to produce research and theory on women's social situation, addressing such issues as housework, employment, sexual exploitation, as well as the overall structure of male-dominated or patriarchal society. Central to all such work was the development of the idea of gender as a sociological concept. Moreover, linked to this conceptualization of gender was an identification of sexuality as a key dimension of gender inequalities, and an increasing awareness that the essentialist sex–gender system privileges heterosexuality over homosexuality and other non-reproductive behaviours.

2
Sociological Challenges to Essentialism

2.1 *The Feminine Mystique* and Liberal Feminism

Although liberal or equal rights feminism had a long tradition of seeking legal reforms to promote equal opportunities for women, in this period it began to be more sociological in its framing. For example, in her 1963 book, *The Feminine Mystique*, Betty Friedan put forward a radical argument that middle-class women were ensnared in an *ideological* construction of femininity which had nothing to do with their biology or innate 'natures', and everything to do with subordinating women as domestic servants. So the post-Second World War advent of domestic labour-saving devices (like the vacuum cleaner and dishwasher) were not helping women to expand their role beyond domesticity, but rather enshrining this position by marketing the goods to women as routes to more *leisure* time for them, rather than opportunities for them to enter education and the labour market. Friedan's text became an early classic of second wave feminism, in large part because she provides a wide-ranging analysis of how the ideology of the 'feminine mystique' is sustained by social institutions such as the media, churches and the family (though she did not use the term 'gender'). Thus, even liberal feminists were acknowledging and contributing to a more sociological analysis of why and how women are subordinated by widening their gaze to include economic and educational resources and the beliefs that sustained particular definitions of masculinity and femininity. Friedan was a founding member of the National Organization for Women (NOW), America's most prominent liberal feminist political action group (see note 8). Their 'Bill of Rights', which was adopted at NOW's first national conference, in Washington, DC, in 1967, focused primarily on equal rights measures:

I.   Equal Rights Constitutional Amendment.
II.   Enforce Law Banning Sex Discrimination in Employment.
III.   Maternity Leave Rights in Employment and in Social Security Benefits.
IV.   Tax Deduction for Home and Child Care Expenses for Working Parents.
V.   Child Day Care Centers.
VI.   Equal and Unsegregated Education.
VII.   Equal Job Training Opportunities and Allowances for Women in Poverty.
VIII.   The Right of Women to Control Their Reproductive Lives.

(Morgan, 1970: 512)

First and foremost, this manifesto discusses how laws can provide equal rights to redress gender discrimination. But, crucially, discrimination is seen as *social*; as a general set of beliefs and ideas about women which have become institutionalized – through education, the tax system, medical systems and in family structures. Furthermore, this Bill of Rights also acknowledges the importance of other social bases of gender inequality, such as women's economic position, racial identities and child-care responsibilities. Indeed, this Bill of Rights makes it plain that *both* ideological beliefs in women's inferiority *and* other social bases of inequality, such as class, need to be challenged.

Your World: What are the contemporary expectations of femininity, masculinity and domesticity in your culture?

Friedan was reacting in part to the establishment of psychological essentialism, which, by the mid-twentieth century, was the dominant means of explaining masculine and feminine identities and attributes. Psychology had emerged as a discipline in the late nineteenth century and had influenced the contemporary discipline of sexology: the study of 'normal' and 'abnormal' sexual behaviour (see Ch. 1.3). Psychoanalysis, a branch of psychology developed by Sigmund Freud and his followers, became particularly influential in understandings of gender and sexuality, especially in the USA, where it was widely used in the clinical treatment of neuroses. Freud published a number of essays in the late nineteenth and early twentieth centuries, introducing the idea that gendered and sexual identity was established through the dynamics of family relationships rather than being inborn. Many have suggested, however, that as psychoanalysis

became more widely applied in clinical settings, it ultimately pathologized both women's sexuality and homosexuality. In large part this
was because Freud argued that psychologically 'healthy' adulthood
required appropriate heterosexual femininity and masculinity, suggesting that homosexuality was either a psychologically immature or
perverse identity and, furthermore, that adult heterosexual women
would be 'naturally' sexually passive. Freudian ideas therefore contributed to the variety of taken-for-granted essentialist ideas: that
male sex drives were dominant over female; that heterosexual sex was
the mature and normal form of sex; and that homosexuality was an
'inversion' of this natural order and limited to a minority of psychologically flawed individuals. Many liberal feminists in this era therefore rejected Freudian ideas, although their critique was focused on
gender subordination rather than the stigmatization of homosexuality
(see section 2.5 below).

2.2   Radical Feminism and the Concept of 'Patriarchy'

Going several steps further than liberal feminism, Kate Millett's
Sexual Politics (1971) detailed the multi-dimensional social aspects
of male domination, or what she termed 'patriarchy'. Millett's was a
theoretical argument developed from her analysis of literature, focusing on contemporary American male novelists' depictions of sex. She
took the broad position that literature reflected the wider cultural
meanings circulating in the society of its time, and her argument
was that these literary examples illustrated women's subordination
through the stories that the authors created and the language they
used. For example, she says of the 'four-letter' 'c' word that reduces
a woman to her vagina:

> Two ideas strike me – that the four-letter word derives from a puri-
> tanical tradition which is vigorously anti-sexual, seeing the act as dirty,
> etc. This in turn derives from a conviction that the female is sex and
> therefore both dirty and inferior to the intellectual and rational, and
> therefore masculine, 'higher nature' of humanity. The error is not a
> matter of language but of attitude . . . the study of meaning leads us to
> understand the motives language institutionalizes. (Millett, 1971: 325)

Although Millett starts from a literary analysis, she does make the
sociological point that cultural meanings – expressed in language –
reflect wider social power relationships. Along with other feminists

writing at that time, she used the term 'patriarchy' to describe these wider power relationships. Whilst patriarchy was not a new concept, having been used for some time by Weber and others to denote a power structure where senior men held authority over both junior men and women, the emphasis on patriarchy as a system in which men as a whole dominated women was new, as was the argument that this arrangement was social rather than biological. Millett's argument ranged over social structures (including the economy and the division of paid and unpaid labour between men and women), ideology (essentialist ideas in religion, culture, media) and identities and action (essentialist ideas providing the blueprint for socializing men and women into gendered behaviours).

Patriarchy has subsequently become a contested term within academia (see Ch. 4), but its use to describe the social structural form of gender, pioneered by radical feminists like Millett, forced a significant change in how we understand gender. It also inspired new thinking on the apparently natural realm of human sexual relations, locating sexuality within the power structures of gender, and therefore making connections between sexual identities and behaviours and patriarchal structures.

2.3   Radical Feminist Approaches to Sexuality

Sexuality plays a key role in analyses of women's oppression. Indeed, some theorists argue that it is *the* central technology through which structures of gender operate, whilst some suggest that it is important, but subordinate to other factors such as divisions of labour and class. As we saw in the previous chapter, first wave feminists attacked the 'double standard' of morality that stigmatized prostitutes but not their male clients, indicating that feminists have seen sexuality as central to women's subordination for generations. Specifically, in challenging the naturalist or essentialist construction of gender, feminists also questioned the biological rationalizations of sexual behaviour that underpinned ideas of gender difference. Second wave feminists took this further, contesting the idea that women's biological capacities for child-bearing determined their social position and developing critical analyses of sexual violence and exploitation and of the ideologies that justified them as inevitable consequences of men's 'natural' sexual desires and needs.

Kate Millett argued that sexuality was integral to the patriarchal order. She saw sexual violence and the sexual objectification of women as central to patriarchal domination, based on the ideological construction of dominant masculinities and passive, sexually subordinate femininities. Catherine MacKinnon argued that sexuality should form the principal focus of any analysis of gender:

> Sexuality . . . is a form of power. Gender, as socially constructed, embodies it, not the reverse. Women and men are divided by gender, made into the sexes as we know them, by the social requirements of heterosexuality, which institutionalizes male sexual dominance and female sexual submission. If this is true, sexuality is the linchpin of gender inequality. (MacKinnon, 1996: 185)

Other writers, such as Susan Brownmiller (1975), focused on the sexual violence committed by men towards women as a manifestation of male power, while Adrienne Rich (1980) provided a radical critique of heterosexuality as a social institution that trapped women into sexual and social subordination to men (see Ch. 4.5). The idea of 'men possessing women' is a key theme in many feminist analyses of sexuality and forms the basis of Andrea Dworkin's account of pornography (1981), which similarly focused on men's exploitation of women's sexuality, citing the widespread commercial businesses of pornography (in the days before the current expansion through the internet and video/DVD technologies) as evidence that the violent and exploitative treatment of women in pornography served to confirm and sustain the 'normality' of women's subordination.

In widening the scope of critiques of essentialist legitimizations of women's subordination to include sexuality, feminists effectively left no aspect of gendered relations to the realm of the 'natural' or inevitable. The radicalism of identifying sexuality as a technology of gender is that it puts the most intimate and apparently natural aspects of male/female relations under the sociological microscope, linking sexual practices and experiences to structural issues such as the existence of a patriarchal social system and to cultural issues such as ideological constructions of masculinities and femininities.

Moreover, as with gender, refusing to accept the naturalness of sexuality immediately raises the possibility that it can be subject to cultural, historical change, both through long-term social processes such as the increasing economic independence of women and lessening dependence on marriage and, crucially, through personal and political intervention. Indeed, the politicization of such an apparently intimate and natural part of our lives is all too evident in contemporary society, with public discussion of sexual expectations, prostitution and pornography as manifestations of male exploitation. We also live in a period in which rape within marriage is no longer legal in many societies, in which police services are in theory (if not always in practice) geared towards dealing sensitively with sexual violence, and in which expectations of younger generations have certainly moved on from the notion of a passive and subordinate female sexuality. These are achievements directly attributable to feminism. There are, however, counter-tendencies within the complexities of the contemporary globalized world, such as the expansion of commercial sex tourism (see Introduction to Part II) and the proliferation of diverse forms of pornography facilitated by new technologies, as well as the increasing sexualization of popular culture (see Ch. 8.2)

Perhaps the most important and durable consequence of these challenges to essentialism has been the widespread acceptance that sexual violence and exploitation are in part derived from wider, *social* inequalities of power between men and women. The achievement of the second wave has been that feminist arguments draw out the continuities between 'normal' heterosexuality and violence, focusing on the construction of masculine sexuality as aggressive and sexual violence as a form of patriarchal control. Two important sociological questions remain: first, whether 'normal' heterosexuality is fundamentally and irrevocably based on women's subordination; and, second, how the social structuring of gender and sexuality relates to, depends on or intersects with other social divisions, specifically class and race (see section 2.11 below and Parts II and III).

2.4   Sexuality and Social Structure: 'Compulsory Heterosexuality' and the Politics of Lesbianism

Feminist analysis of sexual inequalities initially focused on the cultural and physical oppression that women suffered at the hands of men, thus inevitably producing a focus on gender inequalities within heterosexual relations (Jackson and Scott, 1996a). The emergence of more explicit feminist critiques of heterosexuality was partly the logical consequence of characterizing heterosexuality as an oppressive institution, and partly driven by those who identified themselves as lesbians. In these debates, it is important to be aware of different strands of lesbian feminism. Political lesbians were those who saw lesbianism primarily as a form of resistance to patriarchy rather than simply a sexual preference. This tendency has retained a strong hold on contemporary cultural imaginations of feminism, with 'man-hating', 'masculine' looking and – above all – lesbian, stereotypes of feminists put forward as representing all feminisms. That such a negative caricature of feminism exists reflects the persistence of homophobia in that lesbianism is seen as deviant enough to use it to stigmatize feminists and regulate women's conduct. What this caricature also reflects is an interpretation of the ideas of political lesbianism which emerged during the second wave feminist movement, whereby the developing critiques of sexual inequalities led some to argue that any kind of interaction with men, particularly at the level of sexual and emotional relationships, constituted a betrayal of feminist positions and loyalties. In part, this was a reaction to the marginalization of lesbian concerns within the Women's Liberation Movement, but it was also an identification of lesbianism as a political stance. Groups such as the New York-based Radicalesbians argued that women should put their political and emotional energies into other women, not male-dominated political movements or intimate relationships with men. In the UK the Leeds Revolutionary Feminist Group (1981) maintained that heterosexual sex was a symbolic and material manifestation of male domination and that heterosexual feminists were colluding in their own oppression and engaging in 'counter-revolutionary activity'. Such sentiments are, of course, extremely radical and avowedly anti-male, but this was a minority tendency even among political lesbians, many of whom distanced themselves from condemnation of heterosexual women.

Political lesbianism ultimately made a lasting and significant contribution to radical feminism, and to second wave feminism as a whole, through more sociologically informed critiques of heterosexuality as an institution. Most influential among these was Adrienne Rich's essay 'Compulsory Heterosexuality and Lesbian Existence', published in 1980. Rich developed a social typology of male power to elaborate how a number of social practices effectively coerced women into a subordinated femininity as part of a 'compulsory' heterosexuality. She drew upon other feminist studies of the workplace, family structures, economic inequality and violence to produce a sophisticated theory of how heterosexuality and its gender divisions are imposed upon women, producing femininity in its current subordinated form while simultaneously stigmatizing lesbianism and rendering it invisible. Similarly, Monique Wittig writes: 'I describe heterosexuality not as an institution but as a political regime which rests on the submission and appropriation of women' (1992: xv), and, as a materialist lesbian theorist, she goes on to argue that 'the refusal to become (or remain) heterosexual always meant the refusal to become a man or a woman, consciously or not. For a lesbian, this goes further than the refusal of the role "woman". It is the refusal of the economic, ideological, and political power of a man' (1992: 13).

A later generation of feminists have continued to engage with these theorizations of heterosexuality. Significantly they have insisted that the critique of heterosexuality as an institution should not imply criticism of heterosexual women and that a more nuanced account of the complexity of heterosexual desires and practices is needed (see Jackson, 1999, 2006b). The analyses provided by lesbian feminists such as Rich and Wittig, however, have continued to inform explorations and critiques of heterosexuality as a social and political structure which privileges marriage and heterosexual families and influences laws, policies and ideologies affecting every aspect of social life (see Ch. 5.3)

2.5   Gay Liberation and the Beginnings of Sociology of Homosexuality: Challenging 'Deviance'

While lesbianism formed a central part of the development of second wave feminist politics and ideas, there was also an emerging sociology of homosexuality, which was influenced by feminist ideas, but developed in distinct ways because of its focus on sexuality *per se*, rather than gender. Moreover, as with their often uncertain position in women's groups, lesbians often found the developing gay liberation groups male-dominated and insensitive to gender difference and inequality. Thus, much of the early sociology of homosexuality reflects concerns about male homosexuality or gay identity, and, as demonstrated above, much of the academic energy of lesbian analysis remained within and transformed radical feminism.

In his excellent summary, Seidman (1996) describes the sociology of sexuality as a history of homosexuality and, often, male homosexuality. He argues that the impact of sexology and Freudian ideas at the end of the nineteenth century served to justify the status quo of heterosexuality as a 'natural' and inevitable state of affairs. Although some lesbian and gay organizations existed around the mid-twentieth century, these were relatively small and often argued for reform on the basis of sexological and psychological models that located homosexuality as innate conditions. This essentialism did not provide a basis for arguing that homosexuality was valid, it merely supported the view that those suffering from it had no conscious control over it, and therefore should be helped rather than criminalized. However, just as feminists had begun to react to sexological/psychological essentialism and the overwhelmingly oppressive gender ideology in the post-war period, so too do we begin to see the emergence of a more radical homosexual politics and movement, the beginning of which is often pinpointed as a riot at the Stonewall bar in New York City, in June 1969 [9].

As with feminist politics, the particular historical circumstances of late 1960s radical politics provided a training ground and context for gay liberation. One British activist recalls:

> GLF [the Gay Liberation Front] brought together politics which had been flowering in the social movements of the sixties and other political ideas which had lain dormant for many years. The immediate inspi-rations were the Civil Rights and Women's Liberation Movements, combined with the style of the counter culture. . . . For lesbians and gay men as individuals it meant coming out and taking pride in being gay, making the personal political, and trying to live out our ideals. It meant too, challenging the roles of the heterosexual nuclear family and the ideal of monogamy. (Birch, 1988: 51–2)

In academic terms, this explosion of a new positive claim for gay identity inspired an emergent sociology of homosexuality, with newly out and confident lesbian and gay researchers turning their gaze to their own identities, drawing on existing sociological concepts and theories. In a significant article published in 1968, the British sociologist Mary McIntosh argued that homosexuality should be understood as a social role which served to normalize mainstream behaviour: 'The creation of specialized, despised, and punished role of homosexual keeps the bulk of society pure in rather the same way that the similar treatment of some kinds of criminals helps keep the rest of society law-abiding' (1996 [1968]: 35). McIntosh is drawing on a sociological perspective known as labelling theory, which had developed as a way of exploring how certain behaviours came to be labelled as deviant and how stigmatized deviant identities were con-structed. In doing so, she demonstrated that the stigma attached to homosexuality arises from social control, rather than in response to some essential psychological, natural or moral deficiency.

Sociological studies of deviance, informed by a perspective known as symbolic interactionism, focused on the socially defined meanings of human actions negotiated through interaction with others. This emphasis was also apparent in John Gagnon and William Simon's pioneering book on the social sources of human sexuality, *Sexual Conduct*, published in the USA in 1973. Having worked at the

Kinsey Institute for Sex Research in the USA in the 1960s – which had already produced data that suggested human sexual orientation could be seen as a continuum – Gagnon and Simon produced a theory of 'sexual scripts', which turned attention to the ways in which sexual interactions were socially shaped, much as all other interaction, through a combination of learned behaviour and cultural codes (see Ch. 9.4) In doing so, they resolutely challenged the dominant psychological and biological essentialism of the time:

> We have allowed the organs, orifices, and the gender of the actors to personify or embody or exhaust nearly all the meanings that exist in the sexual situation. Rarely do we turn from a consideration of the organs themselves to the sources of the meanings that are attached to them, the ways in which the physical activities of sex are learned, and the ways in which these activities are integrated into larger social scripts and social arrangements, where meaning and sexual behaviour come together to create sexual conduct. (Gagnon and Simon, 1974: 5)

Ken Plummer, a British sociologist, took up this perspective in his empirical study of homosexuality, *Sexual Stigma* (1975). Plummer argued that using a symbolic interactionist perspective allowed us to understand homosexuality as an identity that is created by the social and interactional reaction to it, and that these provide the 'scripts' – or cultural codes – through which individual homosexual identity is created, inhabited and regulated. Plummer characterized different stages in homosexual identity: sensitization, signification and coming out, each of which depends on the meanings available to make sense of individual feelings. In the first stage an internal sense of homosexual experience develops, usually in relation to feeling different from prevailing heterosexual gender expectations, and then a negotiation of those feelings occurs within the immediate cultural and interpersonal context with a final resolution of coming out – an acceptance and creation of a new identity or role as homosexual.

The achievement of labelling and interactionist perspectives has been to reject essentialist ideas by challenging the notion that homosexuality is simply a psychological flaw, and to redefine purportedly 'natural' and 'normal' sexual behaviour as socially defined and learned. These theorists began the process of bringing homosexuality into the realm of the sociological, by insisting on the importance of the social meanings of sexuality and sexual identities, exploring how those meanings are socially constructed and investigating the social purposes they serve. They also made us aware that sexual interaction is not simply a natural response, but is as cultural and social as any other behaviour. One of the criticisms levelled at these theories, however, is their lack of attention to the structural aspects of society with which particular cultural meanings are associated and, in particular, to material social conditions and inequalities. It is here that analyses of the capitalist socio-economic order could be seen as illuminating the structural underpinnings of traditional scripts of marriage, monogamy and domesticity and the newly emergent commercial sub-culture of gay bars and clubs in which positive gay scripts were being constructed.

2.6   Marxist Feminism, Capitalism and Patriarchy

We have already mentioned Engels' characterization of gendered divisions within the family as serving the needs of capitalism (see note 5), but it was his more famous collaborator, Marx, who is credited as a significant founding 'father' of sociology, and he had little to say on the issue of gender. Marxist feminism is best understood as a consequence of the range of engagements with Marxist theory that arose from the second wave of feminist politics and activism. While some tried to use Marxist analytical concepts to explain gender, and some attempted to further the initial spirit of Engels' work and account for gender divisions as an effect of capitalism, others developed theories which positioned capitalism and the gender system – or patriarchy – as mutually reinforcing social systems (see Ch. 4)

Marxism and feminism (and subsequently gay and lesbian theories) have always had a problematic relationship, largely because of the difficulty of explaining gender and sexuality within a conceptual framework that was developed to account for the exploitation of industrialized, waged labour. Although some socialist feminists of the nineteenth and early twentieth centuries focused on the family as a social unit that reproduced and maintained male workers and argued for the need for women to engage in paid labour, in the vein of Engels' analysis (Banks, 1990), most did not extend this critique to the rejection of marriage and domestic labour; rather they posited that socialism could transform such arrangements. Second wave feminism challenged this through developing the idea that a gendered system of domination – patriarchy – existed alongside but distinct from capitalism. The logical implication was that neither gender divisions nor the social ordering of sexuality could be understood as simply the consequence of capitalism but both must be seen as social systems of domination in themselves.

The resurgence of New Left politics across Britain, France and the USA in the 1960s heralded a re-engagement with Marxist theory and class struggle as a reaction both to the fact that the increasingly wealthy capitalist societies retained significant populations in poverty despite social welfare programmes, and to the fact that the state socialism of the USSR and its satellite countries had become increasingly totalitarian rather than liberating. There was, moreover, a rethinking of revolutionary politics as involving more than simply class struggle, producing a focus on racism, imperialism and anti-war protests and, most radically, sexual freedom. However, the politics of what came to be known as sexual 'liberation' often rested on the essentialist premise that capitalist social relations were 'repressing' a 'natural' human sexual potential by organizing it into rigid bourgeois structures of family and reproduction, and some liberal feminists and early gay theorists endorsed this view of capitalism's consequences for gender and sexual relations.

One problem with traditional Marxist ideas of the material basis of social life is that they often led to a singular focus on the structures of the capitalist economy (who owns capital, who works for them, how this relationship is exploitative). This focus almost inevitably directed attention to the non-domestic realm, and largely thus to men. Marxist feminist ideas were therefore often developed in reaction to *and* in engagement with radical feminist ideas, particularly the concept of patriarchy. Heidi Hartmann (1981), in analysing the 'unhappy marriage of Marxism and feminism', develops a 'dual systems' approach, arguing that patriarchy has continued to coexist with capitalism, rather than having been superseded by it. Hartmann suggests that the main goal of Marxist feminism is to analyse the material basis for patriarchy in men's (and not just capitalism's) control over women's labour.

In the attempts to develop Marxist feminism, some of those who identified as Marxist could also be seen as radical, in the sense that they accepted the radical feminist conceptualization of patriarchy and, in some cases, the importance of sexuality as a material reality of gender divisions, whilst at the same time remaining committed to retaining the materialist groundings of Marxist theory. This tension has often led to a characterization of these ideas as materialist feminism, signifying a broader interpretation of Marxism. A key example is Christine Delphy's work on the exploitation of women's labour in the family (1984; Delphy and Leonard, 1992), in which she argues that Marxist concepts and methodology could be applied to analysing exploitation within the domestic realm as a patriarchal mode of production (see Ch. 4.3). Monique Wittig has extended this analysis by directly confronting the institution of heterosexuality, challenging the individualization of women as 'natural' beings within traditional Marxism and arguing that women's oppression had a material, and therefore social, basis:

> For women to answer the question of the individual subject in material-ist terms is first to show, as the lesbians and the feminists did, that sup-posedly 'subjective', 'individual', 'private' problems are in fact social problems, class problems; that sexuality is not for women an individual and subjective expression, but a social institution of violence. (Wittig, 1992: 19)

We will discuss the strengths and weaknesses of materialist and Marxist feminisms in chapters 4 and 5, but one of their most impor-tant contributions to second wave feminism has been an enduring concern with the broadly material (as economic) basis of gender divisions and inequality in capitalist societies. Furthermore, histori-cal analyses have highlighted capitalism's effects on the reordering of familial and gender relationships: for example, how property owner-ship was sustained through kinship and marriage (Kuhn, 1978), cre-ating a new dominant bourgeois class who promoted the 'domestic ideology' of femininity (Hall, 1979). These relationships have helped to delineate the material basis of male domination, even though the parties to the 'unhappy marriage' of Marxism and feminism never resolved their differences over the relative priority to be given to patriarchy and capitalism.

2.7   Gay Identity and Capitalism

Social historians such as Weeks (1989) and sociologists such as Adam (1985) and D'Emilio (1993) have demonstrated that the con-solidation of gender divisions through industrialization and urbani-zation had the simultaneous effect of increasing the regulation and stigmatization of homosexuality. This is demonstrated in the growth in legal regulation, such as the Criminal Law Amendment of 1885 in Britain (Weeks, 1989), and in the greater emphasis on controlling men's 'natural' lustfulness and channelling it towards monogamy and marriage. This concern was heightened by the opportunities for anonymous sexual encounters (paid or not) in the new urban spaces of work and leisure, which were now divided by gender, creating the potential for exclusive homosocial (same-gender) contacts. As homosocial environments at work and in leisure became the norm, the potential for homo*sexual* encounters increased, creating a need for greater ideological policing of this potential. Homosexuality was increasingly identified and stigmatized as the binary opposite of heterosexual masculinity. The *structural* changes wrought by industrialization and modern rational capitalism were the context for the increasing *cultural* influence of sexology in categorizing 'perversions' of sexual behaviour into types of people (see Ch. 1.3). Strictly Marxist ideas that explain culture (or ideology) as determined by social structure have been found wanting in explaining gender and sexuality because of this more complex link between structure and culture (or ideology), but many theorists drew upon, borrowed from and remain influenced by the *materialism* at the heart of Marxist sociology, particularly because the material social conditions produced by capitalism shape our social world. A materialist perspective also, and importantly, helps guard against the pull of naturalist and essentialist accounts of gender and sexuality.

One example is David Evans' work on homosexual identities in the late twentieth century, after gay liberation and decriminalization had occurred across most western capitalist countries. Evans (1993) uses a materialist framework to argue that post-Liberation gay identities have developed through the wider processes of commodification in advanced capitalism – gay male communities and identities came to be associated with consumption; through bars and clubs, sexual services and products, and wider lifestyle consumption made possible by male incomes that do not support a family. He argues that the advances in rights for homosexuals evident from the 1990s have been partly made possible by governments that are attempting to encourage new consumer markets for the benefit of capitalism – thus developing a traditionally Marxist theme that the democratic state ultimately works in the service of capital.

2.8   Women's 'Difference'

By introducing sociological analyses of 'sex', second wave feminism developed the concept of gender to challenge prevailing assumptions and politics about the naturalness of women's inferior social status. As in first wave feminism, however, there remained some distinct strands of feminist thought which focused on the fundamental difference that women's 'sex' entailed. Remember that many first wave feminist campaigners were part of religious movements that viewed women in traditional Christian terms, and that religion was the dominant framework for understanding human nature, social order and morality for many centuries, until its gradual decline in the industrialized era of the late nineteenth and twentieth centuries.

The campaigns for moral reform around prostitution exemplify this religious essentialist view of women, arguing as they did that women's naturally refined and weak natures need to be protected from the corrupting influence of male sexuality, and sexual pleasure itself (see Ch. 1). This essentialism was based on (admittedly contradictory) ideas of women's natural difference, whether that is characterized as their potential for moral superiority – being naturally more refined and less prey to sin – or their potential for susceptibility to moral weakness. These early ideas of women's 'difference' were not only contradictory, but also based on assumptions about both psychological and biological 'essences'. Given that these forms of essentialism are so problematic for women, it may be surprising to see them resurface during the period of second wave feminism, but in the sense that our culture remains focused on psychological and natural explanations of human nature, it is perhaps not wholly unexpected. Having said that, second wave feminists who proposed explanations of women's subordination based on biological or psychological differences also argued that these could be challenged through social action. Perhaps the best known example is Shulamith Firestone's *The Dialectic of Sex* (1972), in which she puts forward the view that women's role in biological reproduction has provided the basis for their social subordination and that this will remain the case until reproductive technology replaces child-bearing, and collective social responsibility replaces child-rearing in family units. However, she also pays considerable attention to the historical variability of family forms, and while she sees women's reproductive capacities as the root of their subordination she insists on 'the *relativity* of the oppression: though it has been a fundamental human condition, it has appeared in different degrees and different forms' (1972: 73, emphasis in original). Thus her essentialism is tempered by a degree of social constructionism.

Moving away from biologically based arguments, some feminists developed psychological arguments, particularly drawing on Freudian ideas, to suggest that children's early relationships within the family reproduce dominant masculinity and subordinate femininity at a psychological level. However, even in these cases, writers such as Juliet Mitchell (1975) acknowledge the potential for change, in her case calling for a 'cultural revolution' to transform femininity and masculinity. A more radical variant of psychoanalysis places the emphasis on women's essential difference. The most famous proponent of this 'difference theory' is the French philosopher and psychoanalyst Luce Irigaray (1985), who rejects what she sees as the masculinist form of knowledge underlying the main psychoanalytic traditions. She argues that women's specificity, based on their bodily difference, has been masked and denied by a patriarchal order that has defined them as lacking in relation to men. But again she envisages the possibility of change through recognizing and revaluing women's specificity and bringing into being a form of femininity that has heretofore not been allowed to exist.

2.9   Sexuality, Knowledge and Power: The Impact of Foucault

The French philosopher Michel Foucault has had a profound impact on feminism and the study of sexualities since the 1980s. Foucault published the first of a three-volume history of sexuality in France in 1976, and it was widely translated and began to influence academic work on sexuality in the English-speaking world. In the first volume, subtitled *The Will to Know*, Foucault argued that the history of sexuality in the West requires an understanding of how knowledge operates and how various different types of knowledge – sexology and psychology in particular – have come to dominate our ways of thinking about human gender and sexuality. By going beyond critiques of the essentialism in these disciplines, he created a new perspective on them.

Foucault argued that the regulation of sexuality was not only repressive but also productive, and that sexology, medicine and the law effectively *created* sexuality – both 'perverse' and 'normal' sexualities. These knowledges are a form of *discourse*. The French word *discourse* literally means 'speech', but Foucault used the term more broadly to denote ways of thinking about and constructing knowledge of the world. He argued that discourse creates its own objects: rather than 'things' being taken to exist outside of discourse (our ways of knowing and speaking about them), he focuses on what is produced through discourse. The knowledge constructed about sexuality in the Victorian era, then, was not knowledge about a pre-existing 'thing' called sexuality, but knowledge that brought it into being – including the modern usage of the word 'sexuality' and a whole lexicon of terms for classifying and categorizing sexualities. These are difficult ideas to understand and best illustrated by one of Foucault's well-known examples. What had once been merely a sinful act – sodomy – and a 'temporary aberration' was redefined as homosexuality, a proclivity of a particular category of person, or 'species' – the homosexual (1981: 43). It became possible, as Foucault said, to *be* a homosexual. Foucault therefore radically challenges the commonsense view that the Victorian age was one in which sexuality was repressed. Instead he argues that there was a 'discursive explosion' around sexuality in this era, from which emerged the modern ideas of sexuality as deeply rooted in our inner psychological being. Thus Foucault offers new insights into how biological and psychological forms of essentialism developed. His ideas have influenced historians of sexuality such as Jeffrey Weeks (1989), who draws on Foucault in his detailed historical account of the regulation of gender and sexuality in the Victorian era, showing how legal judgments increasingly relied on sexological and psychological explanations to make their case.

Foucault's theories are one of range that have been described as 'post-modern' because they radically question the possibility of any 'truth' existing outside discourse and therefore challenge modernist forms of scientific – and sociological – knowledge. These ideas are also associated with what has been called the 'cultural turn', which shifted the emphasis from structural forms of explanation to language and culture (see Parts II and III). Foucault's ideas have proved extremely influential in helping to challenge and historicize the culturally dominant forms of essentialist thinking that operate in society, but his characterization of identities as effectively *created* by discourse has been more controversial. Some feminists argue that he is largely insensitive to gender divisions, and others find his challenge to the authenticity of identities problematic for political action. Nonetheless, others have found it useful to think about identity from his rigorously anti-essentialist perspective, using it to challenge dominant or universal concepts of identities, showing, for example, how the category of 'gender' is produced by expert knowledges such as feminism which are, in fact, middle-class and white 'knowledges'. Similarly, those seeking to challenge white and male-dominated gay cultures have used Foucauldian ideas to show how identities are potentially multiple and unstable, but are disciplined into dominant versions (white, middle-class and male) by the production of discourses through gay politics and gay symbolic and economic culture, which create the 'norm' for being gay. Foucauldian theory has therefore been a useful starting point for those concerned with illuminating difference and so has impacted significantly upon feminism and lesbian and gay sociology, particularly in a contemporary version called queer theory, which has largely focused on the cultural operation of power/knowledge and how it is manifested through specific binary and hierarchical identity categories such as homo/hetero, male/female, black/white.

2.10   Significant Absences in Second Wave Feminism and Gay Liberation

The theories that have been discussed throughout these introductory chapters have had very little to say directly about how racialization structures the concepts of gender and sexuality and the inequalities that derive from their social organization. This exclusion is partly a matter of 'presence': that it often takes those who inhabit socially significant categories and experience the inequalities and injustice associated with them to speak up and make visible their oppression in order to put it on the academic and political agenda (see Introduction). Just as this was the case for issues of gender, so it has been the case for issues of racialized gender.

When other social differences, such as sexual identity, race, ethnicity and class, are factored in, it becomes evident that many of the founding texts of second wave feminism failed to provide a conceptualization of gender that was attentive to the differences *within* the category 'women'. Feminist characterizations of gender and sexuality, and some early sociology of homosexuality, often assumed a generalized sociological conceptualization of 'gender' and 'sexuality', creating 'universal' concepts which were not sensitive to the differences of race, ethnicity and class, either within specific groups such as women or homosexuals, or in allowing an understanding of how these social hierarchies work in intersecting and complex ways. Whilst there was some work looking at race, with discussions of the 'double jeopardy' of race and gender from the African-American perspective during the early second wave feminist movement (Beal, 1970), there has been little consistent integration of these perspectives into mainstream feminism. In particular, feminists from different ethnic or racialized groups have criticized feminist theories as too often based on a white and middle-class perspective. Patricia Hill Collins (2000) has produced a key black feminist critique, arguing for what she calls an 'intersectional' analysis which does not reduce black women's experience simply to gender or race, demonstrating in her work that many of the key targets of radical feminism, such as prostitution and pornography, are manifested in specifically racialized ways. Moreover, queer theory has challenged the notion of universal, unitary social categories, arguing that differences within such categories as 'women' or 'gays' undermine their legitimacy as the basis for all political action and theory (Seidman, 1996) (see Ch. 7.4).

Second wave feminism and theories of sexuality all position heterosexual masculinity at the apex of the hierarchies that oppress women and non-heterosexuals. However, more recent work has interrogated masculinity as a social construction and illuminated the complexities within this category – again, often of race and class but also in relation to sexual identity. Raewyn Connell (1987) developed the concept of 'hegemonic masculinity' both to describe the dominant ideal of masculinity in patriarchal structures, and to direct our attention to the many masculinities that do not conform to this dominant form.

As illustrated throughout this chapter, the overwhelming focus of sociological work has been to challenge the biological and psychological determinism that has dominated commonsense and 'scientific' thinking on gender and sexuality. This has inevitably meant a rejection of biological arguments based on how our bodies function and look: neither genital/reproductive organs nor other physical attributes such as breasts, body hair and musculature should determine our social positions. As a result, the role of the body as a site of femininity and masculinity has, on the whole, been characterized negatively, focusing on how bodily functions like child-bearing are represented ideologically, for example. However, we have seen a recent emphasis on how gender and sexuality are embodied. This takes two major forms: first, there has been a reconsideration of how we can theorize embodiment as social, effectively extending the sociological gaze on gender and sexuality to the processes of embodiment – how our bodies are understood by ourselves and what we do to them to fit in with gender/sexual categories (Witz, 2000; Jackson and Scott, 2007). Second, there has been a strand that questions whether we can reduce all embodiment to the cultural, or whether there is, in fact, a realm of bodily physicality that does constrain and structure our abilities, actions and identities (Grosz, 1994).

In conclusion to these introductory chapters we want to signpost these historical gaps in knowledge and highlight the fact that we discuss their more recent incorporation into sociological thought on gender and sexuality in the remainder of the book. The rest of the book builds on the introductory historical account presented in Part I, elaborating on current thinking and research, much of which addresses these significant absences.

Learning Outcomes

After reading the chapters in Part I you should:

- understand that the culturally dominant ways of explaining gender and sexuality are 'essentialist', locating gender and sexuality as 'innate' and pre-social;
- have an understanding of biological, psychological and religious variants of essentialism and how they have affected wider cultural beliefs and practices;
- be able to identify the hierarchical ordering of gender and sexuality and how this has been legitimated and reinforced by essentialist ideas;
- have knowledge of the ways in which first wave feminism contributed to the sociological understanding of men and women as social groups, paving the way for the second wave conceptualizations of gender;
- understand how and why feminist, lesbian and gay scholars have challenged essentialism;
- be aware of the variety of perspectives existing within second wave feminism and how they have influenced each other;
- understand how the stigmatization of homosexuality is interdependent with the development and maintenance of binary gender divisions;
- be aware of the neglect of race/ethnicity within second wave feminism and lesbian and gay theories.

Notes and Resources for Further Study

1 For statistics on women in politics look at the United Nations Educational, Scientific and Cultural Organization's site, *www.unesco.org/women/sta/*, and check links to other information. The global average of women political representatives is 17 per cent, with the Nordic countries at around 40 per cent and Europe overall and North America around the average.

2 See Connell's *The Men and the Boys* (2000). As one of the world's leading sociologists of masculinity, Connell's work is an excellent introduction and guide to the research on masculinities: from concerns around work, the impact of feminism, male violence, and the consequential remaking and remarking of identities. Her concept of 'hegemonic masculinity' has proven to be a key analytic for the exploration of the complexities of masculine experience and dominant symbolic expectations of men.

3 The text of the speech can be found at *www.president.harvard.edu/speeches/summers_2005/nber.php*, whilst some of the responses from the faculty are at *www.boston.com/news/education/higher/articles/2005/01/19/harvard_womens_group_rips_summers*. If these sites are unavailable, a search through *www.cnn.com* or *www.bbc.co.uk/news* should bring up details. In 2007, Harvard faculty elected a woman to replace Summers

– historian Drew Gilpin Faust is the first woman President at the oldest, richest and most famous university in the USA.

4 Banks' *Faces of Feminism* (1990) is an excellent historical account of first wave feminisms, its complexities and interrelationships, alliances and connections to second wave feminism.

5 See Introduction note 3 on Engels here.

6 For the historical accounts from this period of first wave feminism, see Weeks (1989), Banks (1990), McBride-Stetson (2004), and the essays on prostitution in section two of Nye (1999). Walkowitz's *Prostitution and Victorian Society: Women, Class and the State* (1980) is also an excellent study. Eventually in the USA, the essentialist moralists, or social purity reformers, joined with these first wave feminist reformers to control regulation in every state in the USA, and forcing a Congressional Federal law in 1910 which prohibited the 'traffic' of women across state lines for prostitution and any other 'immoral' act. This remains on the statute books but has been amended to be gender-neutral, protect minors and remove any reference to immoral acts, focusing instead on any act which is illegal in the destination state. Only Nevada now has legalized prostitution (McBride-Stetson, 2004: 312–13).

7 We will discuss sexology in greater detail in Part III on culture, but some major studies were Karl Heinrich Ulrichs' work, published from 1864 to 1879, in which he put forward the first classifications of sexual types, arguing for a natural basis to these sexualities and thus regarded as a liberationist. Richard von Krafft-Ebing, an Austrian psychiatrist, published *Psychopathia Sexualis* in 1886, which is often credited with beginning the specific scientific study of sexuality, although, as the title indicates, his collection of case histories focused on non-reproductive, 'deviant' acts and their source in mental disorders. For an excellent review, see Ch. 1 in Bristow's *Sexuality* (1997) and Ch. 8 in Weeks' *Sex, Politics and Society* (1989).

8 For example, for a range of essays detailing second wave feminism in Europe and the USA, check Dahlerup (ed.) *The New Women's Movement: Feminism and Political Power in Europe and the USA* (1990). Banks (1990) is excellent on first wave feminism and draws some links to the second wave, although she tends to underplay the development of radical feminism in the UK compared to the USA. The history of the American National Organization for Women can be found at *www. now.org/history*. The second wave of feminist politics is often associated with the term Women's Liberation, or the Women's Movement, but you should be aware that this description does not denote a unified or coherent organization or set of politics. See also Jackson and Scott (eds) *Feminism and Sexuality* for both their introductory essay mapping second wave feminism (1996a) and key classic readings throughout the book (1996b).

9 The Mattachine Society, for gay men, was formed in 1954, with the Daughters of Bilitis society, for lesbians, formed in 1955, both arguing for the public acceptance of homosexuality on a psychologically essentialist basis. The Stonewall riots, following a police raid of 28 June 1969 on the Stonewall Inn, a gay bar in New York's Greenwich Village, are credited with bringing together a range of people who became activists for a more radical acceptance of homosexuality, spawning similar groups across the USA, Canada and Britain, which all came to identify as gay liberation movements. In England, homosexual acts between men were decriminalized in 1967 for those over 21, and subsequent gay rights groups emerged, such as the Campaign for Homosexual Equality in 1971 and the Gay Liberation Front, beginning in London in 1970.

Part II

Inequalities and Social Structure

Part II is concerned with the ways in which gender and sexuality are socially patterned and ordered. We will therefore focus on social structural perspectives, which emphasize the 'systems' and institutions that generate social divisions and inequalities – including gender and sexual inequalities. In Chapter 3 we will consider early sociological accounts of gender and sexual inequality and how they laid the foundations for later, more radical approaches. We will move on, in Chapter 4, to second wave feminist theories of patriarchy and capitalism and explore how sexuality, once largely neglected by sociologists, came to be seen as a further source of inequality, closely related to gender through the institutionalization of heterosexuality. In Chapter 5 we will discuss more recent developments, particularly the increasing appreciation of the ways in which gender and sexuality intersect with other social divisions and inequalities such as class and race. Here we will also address the impact of social change in our late modern, globalized social world.

Introduction: Local and Global Structuring of Gender and Sexual Inequalities

A British man, a sex tourist, travels to a resort in Thailand. He arranges his trip through a western company, flies on a western airline and stays in a hotel belonging to a large international chain. While in Thailand he can have his pick of young Thai women sex workers and can hire one for the night for less than the cost of a brief encounter with a British street prostitute. It is estimated that at least 60 per cent of what he spends goes to international conglomerates, based in rich nations, and that the many women with whom he has sex during his stay share about 10 per cent of his expenditure among them (see O'Connell Davidson, 1995).

Julia O'Connell Davidson's study of British sex tourists in Thailand was conducted in the 1990s, but the situation she describes persists to this day. The phenomenon of sex tourism is indicative of patterned or structural inequalities surrounding gender and sexuality and the ways in which these are interwoven with other inequalities: those between rich and poor countries and those of class and race. It is primarily men who purchase sex (whether from women or men), and the vast majority of the world's sex workers are women and girls. This reflects a long history of male dominance in which men have historically enjoyed sexual rights to women. That a British man travels to a distant land to buy sex, however, is a consequence of the relations between rich and poor nations and of the existence of a global marketplace. These global relations enable a man from a wealthy western country to take advantage of opportunities for travel and recreation in a country where the cost of living – and the cost of sex – is far cheaper than at home. Local economic conditions, such as rural poverty and the lack of alternative means of making a decent living, lead many young, uneducated women to enter the sex trade. Thus both the demand for prostitution and the supply of sex workers are a consequence of complex and intersecting local and global inequalities. This situation also raises questions of culture, of the meaning of sex and gender and beliefs about them in different cultures, and of the western racialized image of Thailand in general, and Thai women in particular, as exotically other. There are also questions of agency and identity: our male sex tourist makes a choice to go to Thailand, and his choices reflect his masculine identity; the women who service him have fewer choices, but are not necessarily lacking in agency and may be acting in terms of their own identities, for example as filial daughters sending money back to their rural families. These issues will be addressed in Parts III and IV. For now it is worth noting that in any social situation, structural, cultural and subjective aspects of sociality are all in play.

In Part II, however, we are concerned with social structure and systematic gendered and sexual inequalities. These include not just those evident in our example, but the inequalities within our own modern western societies, which are so much part of our social landscape that they are frequently taken for granted as 'just the ways things are'. We will also be considering the social institutions that shape and regulate gender and sexual relations, from the global commodity market that features in our example to institutionalized heterosexuality. We will therefore be dealing with sociological perspectives that seek to analyse the structure of societies, explain how particular structural arrangements arise, persist and change, and how they have shaped gender and sexuality.

3
Gender, Sexuality and Structural Inequality

3.1 Approaches to Social Structure

Structural approaches take a 'view from above' and see society as having an ordered existence independent of its individual inhabitants, which shapes and constrains their lives. Society has sometimes been explicitly characterized as a system, with its component institutions, such as the family, performing functions that ensure its continuity. Thus society is thought of rather like a living body, the working of whose organs (institutions) ensure its survival – what is known as the 'organic analogy'. Individuals are integrated in the social system by playing designated roles and subscribing to shared norms, beliefs and conventions that govern how things are done. Here social hierarchies, such as those of class or gender, are seen as necessary or *functional*, for example by ensuring that social roles are performed by those best qualified for them, as with the idea that women are best suited to domestic and caring roles. Alternatively, a social system or structure can also be seen as founded on fundamental inequalities and divisions, which produce conflicts of interest between the privileged and less privileged. Individuals are then seen as occupying locations within hierarchical structures, which are legitimated through a dominant belief system or *ideology* that serves the interests of the powerful and privileged. It is this latter approach to social structure, best exemplified by the Marxist tradition, which has proved more influential in studies of gender and sexuality.

From a structural perspective, gender can be defined as a hierarchical social division between women and men. Sexuality as a sphere of life is not itself a structural phenomenon, but it is *structured through* social regulation, notably through the institutionalization of heterosexuality, which gives rise to hierarchies of normative and non-normative sexualities. Second wave feminist and early gay liberation-ist approaches to gender and sexual inequality were initially largely structural ones, influenced particularly by Marxism, but also formu-lated in critical engagement with other structural sociologies. These perspectives, moreover, sought to analyse the position of women, gay men and lesbians within a particular form of society – western industrial capitalism – and were shaped by the history of that social formation and the ways in which sociologists had theorized its rise, development and characteristics.

The origins of structural sociology lie in nineteenth-century think-ers' attempts to make sense of the momentous social changes accom-panying the rise of industrial capitalism and the growth of urban society. Transformations of gender and sexual relations are now seen as integral to these changes, though they were not initially central to the emergent discipline of sociology. That it was 'founding *fathers*' who shaped the early contours of the discipline reflects the male-dominated society in which they worked; and their ideas were also influenced by taken-for-granted assumptions about gender deriving from the historical epoch in which they lived – the nineteenth and early twentieth centuries.

3.2   The Gendered and Sexual Landscape of Late Nineteenth- and Early Twentieth-Century Western Societies

Industrialization and urbanization produced major shifts in family life, in relations between men and women, in conceptualizations of masculinity and femininity and in the regulation of sexuality (Seidman, 1997). Many aspects of gender and sexual relations that we now see as 'traditional' were established at this time: the rel-egation of women to the domestic sphere; the notion that men are sexually active and women sexually passive; and the definition of homosexuality as a 'perversion'. It is important to note, however, that homosexual *acts* (defined as sodomy or buggery) had long been illegal under Church and secular law and that women were already con-sidered to lack legal personhood. Only a few unmarried or widowed women who had property or the means of economic self-sufficiency had some autonomy. Under English common law (which also shaped legal systems in North America, Australia and other erstwhile British colonies), a married woman had no independent existence and no right to her own earnings, property or children. Husband and wife were considered to be one person in law, and personhood was vested in the husband. With industrialization, however, the distinction between women and men initially became even more marked, with an increasing divide between the private realm of home and family and the public realm of work and commerce.

Until the industrial phase of capitalism, most production, whether agricultural, craft or domestic industry, was centred on households; everyone – men, women and children – contributed his or her labour under the authority of the (usually male) head of household. Not all households, however, were productive units: some had too few resources to be self-sufficient, while more prosperous craft and agricultural households might contain a number of living-in paid employees, usually young people between their early teens and late twenties. Industrialization gradually removed production from households, creating a split between home and work. While some forms of work had always been carried on outside households (Davidoff et al., 1999), industrialization made it the normal means of earning a living. For working people this separation of home and work was a matter of necessity, but for the rising bourgeoisie it signalled the adoption of a new lifestyle. Among this class a new 'domestic ideology' emerged, enshrining the notion that women and men were suited to separate spheres – and women's sphere was the home (Davidoff and Hall, 1987; Hall, 1992). This ideology subsequently spread to other classes; a 'family wage' sufficient to enable men to keep a wife at home became an aspiration of organized labour (Walby, 1986), though it was rarely attained by poorer sections of the working class. Middle-class women, who had once played key roles in family enterprises, were largely excluded from business and commerce during the first few decades of the nineteenth century. Meanwhile working-class women were increasingly restricted to low-paid unskilled jobs, making them dependent on higher-earning husbands for survival (Hartmann, 1979).

The restructuring of gender relations was accompanied by a reconceptualization of sexuality and changes in its regulation. Even by the eighteenth century the state's jurisdiction over moral and marital matters had displaced the older authority of the Church. In the nineteenth century the professionalization of medicine created a new institutional base and a scientific rationale for the definition and control of sexuality. Sexuality, once thought of in terms of bodily, and potentially sinful, appetites, increasingly came to be redefined as an attribute of individuals (Foucault, 1981). With women now positioned as radically 'other' than men, rather than merely inferior to them, the old medieval idea that women were as prone to lust as men, if not more so, was overturned. Women were now viewed as '*the* sex', lacking autonomous sexual desire yet governed by their sexual and reproductive organs. As an early twentieth-century physician put it: 'Man possesses sexual organs; her sexual organs possess woman' (Otto Weinenger, 1906, quoted in Kent, 1990: 24). Sodomy, once defined as a sin to which all men were susceptible, was recast as homosexuality – a property of particular, perverse individuals (Foucault, 1981; see Ch. 2.9).

Gender and sexuality were, from the late nineteenth century, policed in the interests of 'healthy' monogamous marriage and the social stability assumed to follow from a solid family life. With homosexuality defined as both an illness and a crime, it was not until the late twentieth century that it became possible to contest the institutionalization of heterosexuality. In the nineteenth century, however, women began to challenge their subordinate status and to gain greater rights within and outwith the family: middle-class women resisted their exclusion from public life and fought for access to education and the professions; working-class women campaigned for better wages and conditions; both began to demand the vote. As a result there was much debate in the nineteenth century and early twentieth century about 'the woman question', and both male and female writers, such as J.S. Mill, Cicely Hamilton and Charlotte Perkins Gilman, challenged the confinement of women to the domestic sphere. Mainstream sociology, however, largely reflected the status quo of the time: just as women were institutionally excluded from the public realm, social theorists excluded them from their specifically masculine conceptualization of the social (Witz and Marshall, 2004).

3.3 Structural Sociology and the Neglect of Women

The founding fathers of sociology produced theory shaped by their social location as white, western men, and this theory continued to inform assumptions about gender well into the twentieth century [1]. Some of them did provide conceptual tools useful to later, more radical, perspectives – especially Karl Marx and his collaborator, Friedrich Engels. Marx, however, had little to say about women; he was concerned primarily with class, with the exploitation of the proletariat (working class) by the bourgeoisie (capitalist class), and implicitly treated both workers and capitalists as men. While his analysis of inequality and exploitation was later to provide inspiration for second wave feminist theorists, it was Engels who initially provided a Marxist account of women's subordination, linking its origins to the beginnings of private property and the state (see Ch. 4.4).

Other influential early sociologists, such as Max Weber and Émile Durkheim, seemed not to find it necessary to explain gender inequality. Weber identified patriarchal authority as the oldest form of socially legitimated power, in which male heads of households had authority over all their dependants, not only over wives and children but also over younger men, servants and slaves. Here, however, he was not primarily concerned with gender inequality but with the ways in which patriarchal control of households was incorporated into the wider exercise of authority within traditional societies through each household head's allegiance to an overlord in a hierarchical chain of social relations, with the monarch at the top. He did not question the basic division between men and women and saw the mother/child unit as natural and therefore not sociologically significant – it was only through men that women were linked into the wider society (Sydie, 1994 [1987]: 63).

Durkheim also treated differences between the sexes as natural. He argued that the division of labour among men became more elaborated and specialized as societies progressed, but that women were reduced to a single, simple specialization, shared by them all, in the private sphere of the home. Durkheim saw this sexual difference as fundamental to marriage, making men and women dependent on each other in a complementary relationship in which 'one of the sexes takes care of the affective functions and the other of intellectual functions' (1964 [1893]: 60). These ideas influenced sociology well into the twentieth century, particularly functionalist sociology, which dominated the discipline in the USA from the interwar years until the early 1960s. More generally, sociology continued to be concerned with the public sphere, deemed to be masculine, and thus rarely considered women as part of society at all except when the private sphere came under scrutiny. Even then, the more conservative implications of social thought largely held sway.

One example is Kingsley Davis's functionalist account of prostitution. Davis sees the demand for prostitution as 'the result of a simple biological appetite' (1937: 753), by which he clearly means men's appetite. He argues that prostitution provides 'relief' for those who cannot find it elsewhere and for the gratification of 'perverse' desires which might be denied in marriage. While he does acknowledge the possibility of women seeking sexual gratification, it is male sexual needs, taken as given, which determine the functional necessity of prostitution, which in turn enables a small number of women to cater for the needs of large numbers of men and thus ultimately safeguards the stability of marriage and society in general. This account is, of course, thoroughly essentialist: it takes both gender divisions and heterosexuality for granted and assumes, as an early feminist critic pointed out, that no institutional arrangements are necessary to satisfy women's sexual needs (see McIntosh, 1978).

A better-known example of functionalist analysis is that of Talcott Parsons. Parsons was writing in the 1940s and 1950s, by which time women in most western societies had won basic citizenship rights, including the vote. Despite women's contribution to the work-force in the two world wars, they were still predominantly destined to be housewives; indeed reasserting the naturalness of the conventional division of labour between women and men was central to the ethos of the period following the Second World War – to what Betty Friedan (1963) called 'the feminine mystique (see Ch. 2.1). Parsons, like the social theorists of old, treated this state of affairs as normal. He argued that the nuclear family, divested of wider kin ties, was 'functional' for modern industrial societies since it rendered (male) workers socially and geographically mobile: their wives and children would follow them wherever they moved. This functionality was enhanced by specialization within the family. Echoing Durkheim's analysis, Parsons argued that husbands and wives played complementary roles, with men specializing in instrumental (goal-oriented) functions and domestically oriented women specializing in affective (emotional) functions (Parsons and Bales, 1956). This reduced any potential strain between the instrumentally oriented world of work and the emotional ambience of family life.

Parsons' view of society was of a system in equilibrium, a functionalist assumption that did not go unchallenged. Another key thinker of the mid-twentieth century, Norbert Elias, argued, *contra* Parsons, that change rather than equilibrium was the normal condition of society. Unusually among sociologists of the time, he focused considerable attention on sexuality as a key element in the 'civilizing process', analysing changes in the sexual relations between women and men from medieval to modern times. More influential at the time, in terms of emerging ideas about gender and sexuality, were those who began to take up the concept of 'sex roles' for more radical ends. A few, mostly women, theorists were beginning to question the 'naturalness' of the gendered social order. Within academic anthropology and sociology, the foundations for a more critical approach to gender and sexuality were being laid.

3.4 Early Critical Approaches

In their encyclopaedic survey of anthropological work on sexuality, *Patterns of Sexual Behaviour*, Ford and Beach demonstrated not only that active masculine sexuality and passive feminine sexuality were far from universal, but also suggested that the number of societies that accepted homosexuality as normal indicated that heterosexuality might be a result of 'cultural conditioning' (1951: 14). It was not until the 1970s, however, that the implications of this insight began to filter into sociological work; initially it was easier, though still radical, to question the differences between men and women than to challenge the naturalness of heterosexuality. Among the pioneers of anthropological research on gender was Margaret Mead, who used evidence from other societies to demonstrate that what counted as masculinity and femininity varied across cultures and therefore could not be ordained by nature (Mead, 1965 [1935]). Mead was more concerned with culture than structure and said little about the relative power or status of women and men, but did suggest that, despite cultural diversity, what is deemed masculine also tends to be seen as superior:

> Men may cook or weave or dress dolls or hunt humming-birds, but if such activities are the appropriate occupation of men, then the whole society, men and women alike, votes them as important. When the same occupations are performed by women, they are regarded as less important. In a great number of human societies men's sureness of their sex role is tied up with their right, or ability, to practise some activity that women are not allowed to practise. (Mead, 1962 [1950]: 157–8)

At the same time that Mead was writing, sociologists such as Viola Klein in Britain and Mirra Komarovsky in the USA, also began to question the social ordering of 'sex roles' and to critique the inequities they produced. Viola Klein's groundbreaking work, *The Feminine Character* (1946), exposed the masculine bias underlying supposedly 'objective' social science and argued that 'femininity' was social rather than biological in origin. For Klein, women's social being was shaped by their domestic responsibilities, which absorb 'a preponderating part of women's energy' (1946: 181). Klein, in association with Alva Myrdal, conducted one of the first studies of women's strategies in combining paid work with domestic work: *Women's Two Roles* (Myrdal and Klein, 1956). At a time when mainstream sociologists assumed that women were primarily 'housewives', Myrdal and Klein were alert to the increasing participation of women in the post-war labour force and the double burden this imposed upon them.

They also, however, saw the integration of women into the labour force as potentially emancipating. Challenging the Parsonian view of contented full-time housewives, they suggested that women at home experienced social isolation and boredom exacerbated by financial dependence and the low status of the housewife role.

Mirra Komarovsky, like Klein, was aware of the ways in which social change was impinging on women, often subjecting them to contradictory expectations. In a study of women college students, she explored the tensions between the pursuit of educational success and the demands of sexually desirable femininity. College women, she found, admitted to 'playing dumb' in male company, allowing their boyfriends to explain things they already understood in order to flatter men's egos and preserve their own 'femininity' (Komarovsky, 1946). Her later study of *Blue-Collar Marriage* (1962) revealed the divergences between working-class men's and women's expectations and experiences of married life. While the women generally accepted an inequitable division of domestic labour, many expressed dissatisfaction with the lack of emotional intimacy and companionship in their marriages.

These early studies of sex roles began to mark out new terrain for sociology and establish some of the preconditions for the later conceptualization of sexual divisions as social divisions and gender as a social category. Outside mainstream social science, too, feminist pioneers such as Ruth Hersberger (1948) in the USA and Simone de Beauvoir (1972 [1949]) in France, like Cicely Hamilton and Charlotte Perkins Gilman before them, challenged assumptions of women's inferiority, their sexualization and their confinement to domesticity. Taken together, such foundational studies made three main contributions:

• They questioned the naturalness of sex differences.
• They cast doubt on the idea of an unproblematic complementarity between men's and women's 'roles'.
• They began to establish that 'sex roles' were not merely markers of differences between women and men, but represented a form of social inequality.

3.5   From 'Sex Roles' to 'Sexual Divisions'

The idea that 'sex roles' were hierarchically ordered paved the way for the more radical analyses developed by feminist sociologists in the 1970s. The term 'sexual divisions' made its entry onto the British sociological stage through the landmark 1974 British Sociological Association conference in Aberdeen, the theme of which was 'Sexual Divisions in Society' (Barker and Allen, 1976; Allen and Leonard, 1996). The conference organizers, Sheila Allen and Diana Leonard Barker, rejected the term 'sex roles' because of its association with a static, consensual and functionalist model of society. While the term 'gender' had just entered the academic vocabulary (Oakley, 1972), it was more often used to denote masculinity and femininity as social attributes rather than to conceptualize the hierarchical relation *between* women and men. Only later did structural analyses of gender itself emerge (see Ch. 5). The concept of 'sexual divisions', on the other hand, drew on Marxist political economy, emphasizing the oppositional relationship between women and men as two mutually constituted, class-like groups and linked this relationship with the idea of divisions of labour. In employing this concept the feminist conference organizers sought to establish 'a paradigm in which questions of power and control, oppression and exploitation between men and women (and within these categories), would be addressed' (Allen and Leonard, 1996: 22).

The conference was the first occasion on which issues of gender took centre stage in sociology anywhere in the world and was a major victory for feminists, few of whom were then established members of the profession. The papers given were indicative of the structural orientation of analysis at the time, focusing on such issues as inequality in the workplace and in families. There were only four papers on sexuality presented at the conference since working on sexuality in the 1970s remained a risky enterprise and was marginal to what were seen as the main structural features of inequality between men and women. The pioneering work on sexuality being undertaken in the early 1970s tended to be influenced by forms of social constructionism that emphasized everyday interaction and the meanings of sexual conduct (see Part IV). In one of the few papers to deal with this subject, Mike Brake linked sexuality to the structuring of gender 'by the heterosexual division of labour' (1976: 175), thus presaging later critiques of institutionalized heterosexuality (see Ch. 4.5).

Establishing sexual divisions as a major, structural inequality constituted a considerable challenge to mainstream sociology. British sociologists had long been critical of American functionalist orthodoxy and, as part of this, had given a great deal of attention to conflict and inequality. While this made them potentially receptive to the inclusion of gender, the stumbling block was that most saw social class as the fundamental form of 'social stratification' (or structural hierarchy), which rendered other forms of inequality secondary. Some sought to defend this position against feminism. Notable among these was Frank Parkin, who argued that 'sex' could not be regarded as an 'important dimension of stratification', since the 'disabilities attaching to female status' did not override those of class (1972: 15). Parkin, like other British sociologists, insisted that the family, rather than the individual, was the appropriate unit of stratification. Although sociologists were aware that there was a division of labour between women and men within families, they assumed that wives occupied exactly the same social location as their husbands. According to Parkin, feminists were in error because women's social location was basically the same as that of their male kin and, therefore, 'inequalities between different members of the family . . . cannot really be said to provide the basis of a distinct form of social stratification' (1972: 15).

The idea of sexual divisions unsettled these assumptions in two ways. First, inequality *within* families and households was reconceptualized as a social division and, second, the labour market was analysed as a source of sexual (gender) inequality as well as class inequality. Thus the patterned, structural basis of relations between women and men began to be established. The recognition that male domination was both systematic and pervasive led on to attempts to analyse it as a system in itself; just as capitalism was conceived by Marxists as a system of class domination and exploitation, so the term 'patriarchy' came to be used to denote the system of male domination. In the 1970s and into the early 1980s, as we shall see in the next chapter, the concept of patriarchy was much debated among feminists as they strove to develop a theoretically grounded explanation for the persistence of male dominance and women's subordination.

TASK: Oral history exercise on gendered divisions of labour.

Conduct a short interview with an older person who was an adult in the 1960s and/or early 1970s, asking them about their memories of men's and women's work in the home and the labour market during this period. Discuss your findings in class.

4

The Idea of Patriarchy

4.1 Women's Subordination and Sexual Exclusion in the Early 1970s

Second wave feminist debates on patriarchy should be understood in historical context – in terms of the gender and sexual relations prevalent in the early 1970s. While there were differences among western countries in the legal framework under which women and gay people lived their lives, there were many similarities. The British case will serve as an example. In Britain male homosexuality *in private* had been decriminalized only in 1967. While decriminalization made it possible for a gay liberation movement to organize openly, many homosexuals remained closeted because of persistent stigma and because of the lack of any protection from discrimination. Gay men were far from equal to straight men at this time: for example, the age of consent for homosexual acts remained at 21 (as compared to 16 for heterosexual women) and public displays of same-sex intimacy could still result in prosecution under indecency laws. Lesbianism had never formally been against the law but it was heavily stigmatized: for example, lesbians often lost custody of children conceived within heterosexual relationships since their deviance from 'normal' femininity was held to make them unfit mothers.

In 1970 the majority of British women married, did so by the time they reached the age of 21 and gave birth to their first child soon after marriage. While women had been drawn into the labour market in increasing numbers in the previous two decades, many still gave up paid work on marriage and most did so once their first child was on the way. To be married, then, was to be a housewife and mother – and perhaps a part-time worker once children were older. Most women who were employed worked in a very few, low-paid occupations; equal pay legislation was introduced in the UK in 1970, seven years later than in the USA, but did not come into effect until 1975, when the first sex-discrimination legislation was also enacted. Married women in Britain had limited rights to pension and social security benefits, since they were regarded as their husbands' dependants; single women found it difficult to get credit or mortgages without a male guarantor. Women were beginning to have the potential to control their own fertility with the introduction of oral contraception, which became more widely available in the 1970s, and somewhat easier access to abortion, through a 1967 Act which permitted it on health grounds (though not in Northern Ireland). Men, however, still had the legal right to rape their wives and there was no legal protection for women whose husbands assaulted them – and there were no refuges (the first of these came into being in the 1970s). Thus married women were economically dependent on their husbands with little ability to challenge their power – which two male British sociologists of the time characterized as the power of the purse supplemented with the power of the fist (Bell and Newby, 1976). It is not surprising, then, that feminist analyses during this period focused on women as housewives, mothers, underpaid workers and victims of physical and sexual violence. Radical gay theorists and gay liberation activists at this time joined feminists in critiquing the patriarchal family, which was regarded as central to the oppression of lesbians and gay men as well as women. The hierarchical divisions between women and men and between heterosexual and homosexuals thus came to be seen as interconnected.

4.2 The Influence of Marxism: Capitalism, Patriarchy and Sexual Politics

During the 1970s, most feminist thought was concerned with understanding fundamental inequalities between women and men. Its basic premise was that male dominance derived from specific social, economic and political arrangements. Since this entailed radical critique of the entire structure of society, liberal feminists were not involved in developing these analyses; they sought only to improve women's situation *within* the existing social order and continued to pursue a reformist agenda. Marxist and radical feminists, on the other hand, though often supporting reforms that would bring immediate benefits to women, were interested in a more revolutionary transformation of society in order to end inequality and oppression. The gay liberation movement also endorsed the ideal of radical social change, which marked it apart from more liberal organizations pursuing homosexual rights.

Marxism resonated with these revolutionary aspirations since its central rationale was the explanation of inequality as social in origin and as built into the structure of society. Marxism was also a theory of social change, one which held out the promise of a more egalitarian future. Many feminists and gay activists, particularly in Britain and Europe, were drawn from the ranks of left-wing groups and campaigns, which were very active during this period, and were already familiar with Marxism. Yet Marxism posed problems since it had developed as a theory of class oppression rather than gender or sexual oppression. Traditional Marxists were often reluctant to take women's issues seriously and had even less time for the politics of gay liberation; they either ignored issues of sexuality or saw them as 'personal problems' that should not be brought into the political arena. Gay theorists themselves often found it difficult to make Marxism fit with their concerns. It was common for gay theorists in the 1970s to argue that the oppression of lesbians and gay men was related to the containment of sexuality within heterosexual marriage and the patriarchal family (see, for example, Brake, 1976) and some linked this to capitalist regulation of sexuality through the family, but they found that much about sexuality and its regulation remained unexplained (see Ch. 2). Many who defined themselves as part of the 'gay left' began to look beyond conventional Marxism and were among the first to pursue more cultural explanations of the social ordering of sexuality (see Gay Left Collective, 1980; see also section 4.6 below)

Feminists, on the other hand, initially found the engagement with Marxism more productive. Its appeal was not limited to those who identified as Marxist or socialist feminists; many who defined themselves as radical feminists also took up Marxist ideas and concepts and sought to apply them to an analysis of the social origins of women's subordination. The difficulties of extending Marxism to cover the latter led to heated debates around interpretations of Marxist thought and its potential utility for feminism. Central to these debates was the status of the concept of patriarchy, used to denote a social system based on male domination, and its relationship to capitalism. The key participants in this debate were ranged along the spectrum from Marxists to radical feminists. Many textbooks give the impression that these two variants of feminism occupied polarized political camps, and we ourselves, in Chapter 2, identified them as two distinct tendencies. Now, however, it is necessary to paint a more complex picture in order to capture the diversity of positions within this debate. Rather than there being a sharp divide between two opposing feminisms, there was actually more of a continuum between those who saw contemporary society as primarily capitalist and those who insisted it was primarily patriarchal, with many arguing that it was a product of the interrelationship between these two systems of inequality [2].

Within these debates, patriarchy was a highly contentious concept. Hardened Marxists insisted that women's oppression was part and parcel of capitalist social relations and saw the concept of patriarchy as an irrelevant product of 'bourgeois feminism' – a position some on the left maintained well into the 1980s (see, for example, Petty et al., 1987). Marxist feminists generally saw male domination as a systematic feature of modern society, but some of them were reluctant to accept that patriarchy was a separate social system existing alongside capitalism. Many worried that the concept of patriarchy was ahistorical. Some felt that it aptly described past societies based literally on the rule of fathers, but was not applicable to our own (Rubin, 1975; Barrett, 1980) or shared Sheila Rowbotham's (1981) concern that positing the existence of patriarchy as a system which long pre-dated capitalism might lead feminists into a fruitless search for its pre-historic origins. Defenders of the concept of patriarchy, whether Marxist or not, countered these critiques by resisting its trans-historical usage (Delphy, 1984) or by seeking to historicize it (Walby, 1986).

Among those who used the term 'patriarchy', whether from a Marxist perspective or not, there was no consensus on how to define or theorize it (see Beechey, 1979; Barrett, 1980; Walby 1986). These disagreements were related to another set of differences, cutting across the capitalism–patriarchy continuum, about where the causes of women's subordination should be located. Many Marxist feminists argued that rather than being rooted, like class, in relations of production, women's subordination was either a consequence of specific relations of reproduction or was primarily ideological. Some theorists at the radical feminist end of the spectrum did focus on productive relations while others developed analyses of reproduction and sexuality – and many of these were also influenced by Marxist ideas or concepts. This rather complicated picture is simplified in Table 4.1, which represents, on one axis, the continuum between analyses of patriarchy and capitalism and, on the other, distinctions between explanations founded on productive, reproductive, sexual and ideological relations.

In the table, the first column is populated only by orthodox

Table 4.1. Varieties of feminism in the 1970s

THEORIES EMPHASIZING	Capitalism	Capitalism + male dominance	Patriarchy or male dominance
Production	Orthodox Marxism	Some Marxist and materialist dual-systems theorists (**Hartmann**, USA; **Walby**, UK)	Materialist radical feminists (**Delphy**, France)
Reproduction		Relations of reproduction (e.g. **McDonough & Harrison**, UK) Male alienation from reproduction (**O'Brien**, Canada)	Male control of reproduction as the basis of sex-class (**Firestone**, USA)
Sexuality		Sexuality reinforced by culture/ideology – psychoanalytic Marxist feminism (e.g. **Mitchell**, UK)	Male appropriation of women's sexuality (**MacKinnon** (USA; **Jeffreys**, UK/Australia) The heterosexual contract (**Wittig**, France) Compulsory heterosexuality (**Rich**, USA)
Culture/ideology		Some Marxist feminists (e.g. **Barrett**, UK)	

Source: Adapted from Jackson, 1998: 15.

Marxists, the second by both Marxist and radical feminists and those who would identify with neither camp, and the third primarily by radical feminists. A few words of caution are needed in relation to this table. It has been constructed in order to help map the field so that you can more easily understand where particular theorists stand in the debates, but there were, in fact, many positions that cut across those lines on the table. In what follows we will elaborate more on these positions, starting with theorists who focused on economic, productive relations, moving on to reproduction, sexuality and, finally, culture and ideology.

4.3 Relations of Production: Theorizing Women's Paid and Unpaid Work

Marxist analysis takes its point of departure from the way a given society organizes production, specifically the 'relations of production' between those who own or control the means of production and those who do not. These relations of production give rise to class relations: in capitalism between the capitalists, or bourgeoisie, and the workers, or proletariat, whose labour is appropriated by the bourgeoisie. This was also the starting point for many feminists. Those who sought explanations for male domination in terms of the exploitation of women's labour ranged from orthodox Marxists, who saw women's subordination as a consequence of capitalism, to radical feminists, arguing that the productive processes of modern society entail both capitalist and patriarchal relations. This form of analysis was founded on two aspects of women's economic situation. First, women are disadvantaged in the labour market: they tend to be lower paid, concentrated into fewer occupations and employed less continuously than men and/or part-time. Second, in addition to any paid employment women undertake, they are typically also engaged in unpaid domestic work in the home.

One line of inquiry was to focus on women's labour in the capitalist economy. The conditions of women's employment, particularly its intermittent character, led to women being dubbed a 'reserve army of labour'. This term refers to workers who can be called upon at times of economic boom or labour shortage and discarded when no longer needed, such as short-term migrant workers. Women, it could be argued, similarly provide capitalism with a pool of cheap, flexible and disposable labour. However, a number of objections to this model have been raised, suggesting that it may be applicable to some situations but not as a general explanation of gender inequality (see Breugel, 1979; Walby, 1986). For example, women very clearly were used as a reserve army of labour during the two world wars, when they took over men's jobs, only to be returned to the home or to low-paid 'women's work' once peace returned. In other circumstances, however, the model has less validity. If women are employed because their labour is cheaper than that of men, why are they not always given jobs in preference to men? Women may be a flexible labour force, but that flexibility is not utilized in such a way that they are potential replacements for male workers. Indeed women rarely do the same jobs as men and are employed instead in a different range of occupations. Moreover, this approach does not explain why it should be *women* who constitute the reserve army – it is simply taken for granted that women's primary role is a domestic one and that this renders them marginal to the wage economy.

Your World: Think about which occupations are dominated by women and which by men in your country and what this tells us about gender divisions in the labour market. Is it possible to relate these differences to divisions of labour in the home?

Women's domestic work itself clearly needed analysis – and it was subjected to a great deal of theoretical scrutiny. Marxists theorized housework in terms of the contribution it made to capitalism, within what became known as 'the domestic labour debate', which dominated theoretical discussions on housework in many western countries, particularly in Britain and Canada, throughout the 1970s. The debate was premised on capital's need for a constant supply of labour, which must be 'reproduced'. Reproduction, according to Marx, works in two ways: first the worker must be kept fit enough to work each day and thus must be fed and clothed; second, the next generation of workers must be conceived, born and raised. In the former sense the working class is reproduced through the conversion of workers' wages into 'fresh labour power' via the consumption of food, clothing, and so on. What Marx ignores is that this 'conversion' also requires labour – that of the male proletarian's wife who cooks his meals and launders his shirts. Marxist feminists sought to make this work visible, to establish that housework involves servicing the existing labour force and rearing future workers and is therefore necessary to capitalism (see, for example, Benston, 1969). What began from feminists' attempts to challenge the orthodox view that this work was marginal to capitalism subsequently became a highly technical discussion about Marxist economics and whether domestic labour contributed to profit and was therefore productive in the Marxist sense (for summaries, see Kaluzynska, 1980; Walby, 1986).

The debate raised more problems than it solved, and by the end of the 1970s it had become clear that this was not a fruitful line of feminist inquiry. Participants in the domestic labour debate took divisions of labour between men and women for granted; they never paused to consider why it was women who performed domestic labour or why men apparently 'needed' to have it done for them. The competing claims made about the value of domestic labour were entirely contingent upon the position of the housewife's *husband* within the capitalist economy. It was in terms of his labour that her work was conceptualized. Yet relations between husbands and wives, particularly inequalities between them, were largely ignored. Marxism, a theory designed to analyse wage labour, could not easily explain domestic labour, which is performed under very different social conditions.

From the early 1970s a rather different approach, deriving from a more radical adaptation of Marxism, was being developed by French materialist feminists, particularly Christine Delphy. According to Delphy, the peculiarities of housework arise from the social relations within which it is performed. She argues that these relations are patriarchal and that within families men systematically exploit and benefit from women's labour within a domestic mode of production (Delphy, 1976, 1977, 1984). Women's domestic work is undertaken as a personal service to a male head of household. He effectively appropriates her whole person and the labour she embodies, so that the work she does is potentially limitless and depends on his requirements. Hence housework has no fixed job description, does not directly involve the exchange of a set number of hours or an agreed amount of work for a given return. The maintenance a wife receives is not related to the work she does, but is determined by her husband's income and his generosity (so an inefficient housewife married to a rich, generous man receives more than an efficient housewife married to a poor or mean man). The direct appropriation and non-exchange of women's labour is particularly clear when a wife is also in employment, earning enough to meet her own maintenance costs, but is still expected to do the housework. In this situation she is clearly working for nothing (Delphy and Leonard, 1992).

TASK: How much is domestic labour worth?

See if you can calculate how much a wife would receive for her work if she were paid the going rate for the job in your country. Think of all the tasks housework usually involves – shopping, cleaning, cooking, laundry, child-care, and so on – and remember it's not just about getting the chores done, but supervising and coordinating the doing of them to ensure that the needs of the household are met.

Delphy's analysis received some very hostile responses from Marxist feminists (see Jackson, 2001). Some raised technical difficulties, such as whether two modes of production can coexist within one society (Kaluzynska, 1980; Molyneux, 1979), and, while recognizing that housework is subject to relations of production distinct from those of capitalism, denied that these relations were patriarchal. These objections, though, were not only technical, but sprang from a refusal to accept that men (especially proletarian men) benefit directly from the work their wives do and therefore directly exploit them (see, for example, Barrett, 1980: 216–17). This view has been contested. Men do not, as Barrett would have it, simply 'evade' their share of housework; they have their share done for them, and there was much empirical evidence by the 1980s that it was also done to suit men's routines and tastes (see, for example, Finch 1983; Charles and Kerr, 1988). Moreover, as Walby (1986) pointed out, a wife is not merely a 'dependant' whom her husband is obliged to support from his wage; she contributes to his ability to earn that wage.

The materialist feminist approach can also be used to account for women's disadvantaged position in the labour market and to explain why women and men are not exploited equally in the capitalist economy. The most thorough analysis of the interconnections between capitalism and patriarchy in the structuring of labour markets was developed by the American Marxist feminist Heidi Hartmann (1976, 1981), and subsequently extended by Walby (1986). Hartmann, though a Marxist feminist, shares common ground with Delphy in seeing patriarchy as a distinct system of inequality founded upon male control of women's labour, but devotes more attention to women's paid work outside the home. Hartmann sought to establish interconnections between patriarchy and capitalism, arguing that the development of capitalism within societies which were already patriarchal had consequences for gender divisions in both the home and the workplace. During the nineteenth century, organized working-class men used their social advantage to exclude women from well-paid skilled occupations: for example, in the printing trade (Hartmann, 1976). A vicious circle was established, such that women's disadvantage in the labour market constrained them into dependence on marriage for survival. Within marriage they exchange domestic services for maintenance, and housework and child-care become their primary responsibilities. Because of the burden of domestic work, they cannot compete in the labour market on equal terms with men, thereby compounding their original disadvantage. Walby (1986) adds to this analysis, drawing on Delphy's work to argue that the benefits men receive from this arrangement are mediated through the exchange of labour power. She argues that a man realizes the value of the domestic labour he has appropriated when he exchanges his labour power – which his wife's work has produced – for a wage that he controls. This, for Walby, is the main mechanism of exploitation within the patriarchal mode of production.

4.4 Relations of Reproduction: Marxism, Feminism and Motherhood

Marxist feminists, although reluctant to view domestic work as productive or exploitative, continued to see housework as *reproducing* labour power. Many therefore suggested that women's subordination was located in social relations of reproduction, rather than production. One problem with this approach is its essentialism: when women's work is said to 'reproduce' the proletariat or capitalist social relations, the implication is that they do this work because they have babies. Sometimes this connection was made explicit: 'An analysis of childcare and women's position with regard to the reproduction of the species would lead to an analysis of the role of women in reproducing labour power, and the forces and relations of production more generally' (Barrett and McIntosh, 1979: 102). It might seem strange for feminists to succumb to such blatant biological determinism, to reduce women's oppression to their reproductive capacities, but this was a common means of theorizing the relationship between capitalism and women's oppression among Marxist feminists. This idea derives from Marx's collaborator, Engels, and the argument he presents in *The Origins of the Family, Private Property and the State* (1942 [1884]). Engels starts from the proposition that at some time in pre-history women and men were equal – but different. He assumed (wrongly) that the division of labour between male breadwinners and domesticated women had always existed. He thought, however, that the contributions of women and men had, in pre-historic times, been equally valued. He also maintained that the original human societies had traced descent through the female line (what he called 'mother-right), and that fathers, therefore, had no rights in their offspring (another presupposition now recognized as flawed). He argued that 'the world historic defeat of the female sex' came about with the development of private property, which led men to seek control over women's sexual and reproductive capacities in order to pass their worldly goods onto their own offspring. This led to the overthrow of 'mother-right' in favour of 'father-right', to monogamous marriage and the subordination of women within the family.

Although Engels' work was known to be based on flawed nineteenth-century anthropology, the essentialist assumption of a 'natural' sexual division of labour and the equally essentialist presupposition that men possess an innate desire to transmit property to their biological offspring, it was drawn upon by some Marxist feminists. Engels supplied the Marxist authority to ground the search for the roots of women's subordination in reproduction. For example, Rosin McDonough and Rachel Harrison (1978) locate patriarchy in men's control of women's sexual and procreative functions. They suggest that this trans-historical subordination of women is mediated through given modes of production and class relations. The emergence of social classes, they argue, divided women into two groups: 'those who procreated heirs (future owners of the means of production) and those who procreated future . . . labourers'. Thus women perform 'two economic functions necessary to perpetuate the social relations of capitalist production' (McDonough and Harrison, 1978: 34).

The attraction of the idea of relations of reproduction was that it kept Marxist analysis of productive, class relations intact while simultaneously providing a means for arguing that patriarchy exists to service capitalism. Other Marxist feminists, however, were wary of leaving Marxist analyses of productive labour relations untouched by feminism, and were therefore sceptical of arguments based only on reproduction (see, for example, Beechey, 1979). It was not only Marxists, however, who had an interest in establishing reproduction as central to women's subordination. This was also a strategy adopted by some who sought to displace class relations from the privileged place they occupy in Marxism, and concentrate on the significance of gender relations in the progress of human history.

One of the best known examples of this tendency is Shulamith Firestone (1972). Often taken as an exemplar of radical feminism, Firestone's analysis is in fact highly idiosyncratic. She attributes women's subordination directly to their reproductive functions. 'Unlike economic class, sex-class sprang directly from biological reality: men and women were created different, and not equal' (Firestone, 1972: 16). Firestone employs Marxist rhetoric in order to rebut the Marxist conception of history as class struggle, replacing it with a view of history as founded upon 'the division of society into two distinct biological classes for procreative reproduction, and the struggles of these classes with one another' (1972: 20). She claims that the organization of the biological family is the crucible of all forms of domination and inequality, and that this is the motor of history, but there is nothing in her model to explain how historical change comes about.

A far more sophisticated account of the historical development of relations of reproduction is offered by Mary O'Brien (1981). She argues that feminists need a theory of reproduction and male domination analogous to Marx's analysis of production and class domination. O'Brien's conceptualization of reproduction includes the biological processes of conception and gestation and the social relations involved in nurturing a child. She argues that reproduction is a legitimate object of materialist analysis, that paying attention to reproduction is no more biologistic than Marxist accounts of production. Both production and reproduction, she points out, start from basic human needs: to survive as individuals and as a species. However, in satisfying these basic human needs we enter into *social* relationships, and it is these which shape the conditions under which we produce and reproduce and have historically produced structural inequalities of class and gender. O'Brien sees reproductive relations as subject to change and posits two major historical transformations: the discovery of biological paternity and the recent development of technologies of fertility control. The outcome of the latter is still uncertain and is a site of feminist struggle. The discovery of paternity, however, presaged the beginnings of patriarchy. This knowledge simultaneously included men within reproduction and excluded them from it. Men became aware of their alienation from their own contribution to reproduction and lack of an experiential sense of generational continuity. To establish their place in the succession of generations they appropriated the fruits of women's reproductive labour as their own, cooperating with other men to maintaining their individual rights. O'Brien thus supplies what is missing in analyses deriving from Engels: an explanation of why men should seek to pass on property to their biological offspring. But whether she does, in fact, avoid biological essentialism is a moot point.

4.5 Sexuality, Sexual Exploitation and Institutionalized Heterosexuality

In the above accounts, heterosexual acts figure only in relation to reproduction. Other feminists focused on sexuality itself, and in so doing began to question what others had taken for granted: the heterosexual norm. Two strands of feminist activism fed into this analysis: campaigns against sexual violence and exploitation and lesbian feminist claims that lesbianism constituted an act of resistance to patriarchy. While these ideas had been current in grass-roots feminism throughout the 1970s, it was at the end of the decade and at the beginning of the 1980s that they resulted in influential theoretical propositions.

One of the most significant of these was Adrienne Rich's essay 'Compulsory Heterosexuality and Lesbian Existence' (1980). It is also unusual in being less influenced by Marxism than most other analyses of the time. Rich argued that heterosexuality, far from being natural, was a coercive imposition, and that a great deal of social control, including violence, was needed to enforce it and to silence and suppress the alternative: lesbianism. Compulsion was involved both in keeping women inside the bounds of heterosexuality and in rendering them subordinate within heterosexual relations. Women's oppression was thus linked directly to the institution of heterosexuality. While Rich assumed that heterosexuality was not natural, there is an implication that lesbianism might be, in that she sees all women as united on a 'lesbian continuum': from lesbianism itself through to friendship and other forms of female solidarity. There is, thus, an element of essentialism in her argument.

Another influential variant of the argument that women's oppression is founded on sexuality is that offered by Catherine MacKinnon, who does directly engage with Marxism. She begins by establishing parallels between the object of Marxist analysis, labour, and the object of feminist analysis – which, for her, is sexuality: 'Sexuality is to feminism what work is to Marxism: that which is most one's own, yet most taken away' (MacKinnon, 1982: 515). She does not use the term 'class' to denote gender relations, but nonetheless sees gender as analogous to class and as constituted through men's appropriation of women's sexuality. The division of gender is founded on 'the social requirements of heterosexuality, which institutionalizes male sexual dominance and female sexual submission' (1982: 533). MacKinnon thus provides a theory of the social foundations of gender itself, linking it, as did Rich, with heterosexuality.

Monique Wittig, who began developing her analysis in the late 1970s [3], also linked women's subordination, and gender itself, to heterosexuality. Unlike MacKinnon, however, she does not see this only in terms of sexuality. Wittig was a French materialist feminist who drew on Delphy's (1984) work on the exploitation of women's labour within marriage and Colette Guillaumin's (1995 [1978]) conceptualization of the public and private appropriation of women's bodies and labour. In articles originally published between 1976 and 1981 she analyses the heterosexual contract as founded upon both sexual and labour relations, which produce women and men as classes since 'there are no slaves without masters' (Wittig, 1992: 15). Because it is the heterosexual contract that defines women, she likens lesbians to runaway slaves, as 'escapees from our class' (1992: 20). Since the category 'woman' has meaning only in terms of heterosexual relations, she says: 'Lesbians are not women' (1992: 32).

Wittig was not alone in seeing lesbianism as the vanguard of feminism: this stance was adopted by some other lesbian activists in western countries. In Britain, for example, the Leeds Revolutionary Feminist Group (1980) argued that heterosexual feminism was a contradiction in terms and that heterosexual woman colluded in their own oppression. As in Wittig's analysis, revolutionary feminists saw women as a class, but they did not define this in Marxist terms and focused exclusively on men's sexual appropriation of women. Prominent among this group was Sheila Jeffreys, who argued that heterosexuality was eroticized inequality whereas lesbianism eroticized equality. She has continued to treat sexual domination as fundamental to and symptomatic of patriarchal power (Jeffreys, 1990, 1993, 1997).

Your World: Can you see signs of eroticized male dominance in your own culture, for example in advertising in magazines or in films?

While aspects of these accounts of sexual domination have been contentious and fiercely opposed by other feminists, some of them have had a lasting impact. The work of Wittig and Rich, in particular, opened up the possibility of analysing heterosexuality as a social institution rather than merely a sexual preference or practice, which also resonated with the ideas circulating in gay movements at the time. Marxist analyses of reproduction, on the other hand, have proved to be less durable. Among Marxist feminists, the most significant developments took place in the sphere of ideology and culture.

4.6   Ideology, Discourse and Culture

By the end of the 1970s, many Marxist feminists were aware of the inadequacies of analysing the subordination of women in terms of the capitalist economy alone. This strategy could not explain why it should be *women* who occupied particular niches within capitalism as, for example, 'reproducers of labour power' – except by falling back on essentialist assumptions about women's 'natural' role in biological reproduction. Moreover, as the prominent Marxist feminist Michèle Barrett argued, it was becoming clear that women's oppression under capitalism could not be explained 'in terms of the supposed needs of capitalism itself' (1980: 248). Marxism also offered little help with issues that were important to feminists – and gay men – such as subjectivity and sexuality. For those, like Barrett, who rejected the idea of patriarchy, an alternative approach was needed, and many turned their attention to theories of ideology. While Barrett (at least, at that time) counselled against taking ideology in isolation from material social relations and practices, the turn to ideology and ultimately to culture presaged a gradual move away from a materialist, structural analysis.

The shift was evident in the increasing influence of Louis Althusser's structural Marxism and, in particular, his essay 'Ideology and the Ideological State Apparatuses' (in Althusser, 1971). Althusser reformulated the traditional Marxist model in which the economic base of society determined all else, arguing instead that each level or instance of the social (economic, political and ideological) was relatively autonomous and that each had material effects. This was potentially attractive to feminists: if ideology no longer had to be seen as a mere superstructural reflection of the economic base of society, this created a space to theorize women's subordination without having to relate it to the capitalist mode of production. Moreover, Althusser argued that ideology constituted us as subjects, which was read as promising a way of theorizing gendered subjectivity.

In a pioneering application of this perspective, Juliet Mitchell (1975) drew on Althusser in combination with psychoanalysis to argue that ideology is reproduced in our psyches in such a way as to perpetuate male domination. She claims that women's subordination once had a material base, rooted in the social ordering of kinship, but that the rise of capitalism has made kin ties much less important to the socio-economic order. Women's subordination is therefore now guaranteed only by the workings of ideology on our unconscious minds and is a cultural rather than a structural, material problem.

Other Marxists and Marxist feminists were also becoming interested in French structuralist theory, experimenting with combinations of Althusserian theory and structural linguistics, particularly the idea that ideology is effective through the capacity of language to shape our thoughts and desires (see, for example, Coward and Ellis, 1977).

Ideology is usually seen by Marxists as a distortion or concealment of real or 'true' conditions of existence, which works in the interests of the ruling class. This began to be challenged by the adoption of the theories of Michel Foucault. For Foucault, the concept of ideology is untenable since 'truth' is an effect of discourse, the linguistically constituted frameworks through which we 'know' the world (see especially Foucault, 1980; see also Ch. 7.2). Because Foucault (1981) saw homosexuality as a discursively constituted category rather than an essential property of individuals (see Ch. 2.9), his work was particularly attractive to gay theorists, including some who positioned themselves as Marxist or socialist. Many of those who contributed to a British collection edited by the Gay Left Collective (1980) were critical of what they saw as the crude assumption that capitalism 'repressed' sexuality (Mort, 1980; Watney, 1980; Weeks, 1980), an idea that had previously informed much theorizing from the gay left, and drew on Foucault both to develop this critique and to propose alternative analyses. Simon Watney, for example, criticized the politics of the Gay Liberation Front as rooted in the idea that sex represents the 'truth' of our being and of therefore perpetuating an essentialist conceptualization of sexuality as some kind of instinct that could be 'liberated'(1980: 72–3). Jeffrey Weeks (1980) pointed out that the assumption that capitalism repressed sexuality was untenable since capitalism seemed actively to promote sexuality in certain respects, for example through advertising, while new forms of sexuality were emerging within and were produced by capitalist society. Weeks drew on Foucault to argue that the object of critique and political struggle should be 'the very ideology of "sexuality", that artificial socially constructed unification of the variety of pleasures of the body' (1980: 19).

What is notable in Weeks' analysis, and others from the Gay Left Collective, is that this argument was still framed in terms that treated ideology and discourse as synonymous and still couched in terms of a critique of capitalism. Soon, however, Foucault's concept of discourse as distinct from ideology became more widely accepted. In the 1980s many erstwhile gay Marxists and Marxist feminists, dissatisfied with Marxism's limited applicability to issues such as sexuality and subjectivity, turned their backs on materialist analysis in favour of a focus on culture. Postmodern scepticism about truth claims and metanarratives (grand theories such as Marxism that aim to explain the totality of social relations) further discredited the analysis of systematic economic and social oppression. These developments severed the analytical link between the symbolic and the material world. Gradually these new forms of feminist and gay theory evolved into poststructuralist and postmodern feminisms and queer theory, associated with 'the cultural turn' in social theory (see Ch. 7.3).

Michèle Barrett (1992) characterized the 'cultural turn' in feminist analysis as a shift in emphasis from 'things' (such as women's work and male violence) to 'words', to issues of language, representation and subjectivity (see also Ch. 7.3). This development was associated with a change of direction away from sociologically grounded materialist analyses towards approaches derived from literary criticism, philosophy and cultural studies. Macro-level models of social structure, along with the concepts of patriarchy and capitalism, disappeared from many feminist analyses. Previous feminist theory came to be branded as mistakenly totalizing, foundationalist and essentialist. Women's subordination could no longer be assumed to be universal, and even the category 'women' was called into question (see, for example, Adams et al., 1978; Riley, 1988; Butler, 1990a). This approach effectively denied that gender could be thought of as a structural social division and diverted attention away from investigating material inequalities between women and men.

The new postmodernist cultural theorists were interested in countering the idea of 'women' as a fixed, natural category, and approached this through studies of language, discourse and subjectivity – in other words focusing on women as a cultural and linguistic category rather than a social category. There was, however, another important reason for questioning the category 'women', in that it often served to conceal differences and inequalities *among* women.

4.7 Challenging White Feminism

The analyses of women's oppression which shaped feminist debate in the 1970s were framed almost entirely from a white western perspective. By the end of that decade, white feminists found themselves confronted by black women, Third World women and women of colour [4], angrily denouncing those who had excluded them or unthinkingly subsumed them under the banner of 'sisterhood' without allowing them to speak for themselves and without recognizing the specific, racist oppressions they faced. Hazel Carby summed this up when she asked of white feminists, 'what exactly do you mean when you say WE?' (1982: 233) As the clamour of critique grew in the 1980s and 1990s, it became abundantly clear that the category 'women' was not, and could not be, unitary, and that any theory attempting to distil women's subordination into a single explanation was doomed to exclude the experiences of the majority of the world's female population (Flax, 1990). Moreover, attention was increasingly being drawn to the complexities of women's lives in a post-colonial era with its global economy, its history of colonial diasporas and its current labour migrations and displacements of refugees.

All of this was taken by some feminists as a further mandate for postmodern theorizing, seen as a means of avoiding the exclusions of an assumed universal womanhood and the simplifications of causal models of oppression (see, for example, Riley, 1988; Flax, 1990). Whether postmodernism was the only means of coping with the complexities of gender in a post-colonial world, or whether materialist, structural analyses still had something to offer, however, was and remains a matter of debate. Tania Modleski (1991) accused postmodernists of failing to confront the realities of racism, while Jacqui Alexander and Chandra Mohanty questioned postmodernists' destabilization of the categories of race, class, gender and sexuality:

> This strategy often forecloses any valid recuperation of these categories or the social relations through which they are constituted. If we dissolve the category of race, for instance, it becomes difficult to claim the experience of racism. . . . [T]he relations of domination and subordination that are named and articulated through processes of racism and racialization still exist, and they still require analytic and political specification and engagement. Global realignments and fluidity of capital have simply led to further consolidation and exacerbation of capitalist relations of domination and exploitation. (Alexander and Mohanty, 1997a: xvii)

While there are feminist post-colonial theorists, influenced by postmodernism, who speak from the position of the previously marginalized 'other' (Spivak, 1988; Trinh, 1989), many of the challenges to white western feminism remained concerned with material inequalities. It was not white feminists' focus on 'things' (rather than 'words') that was the problem, but *what things* they concentrated on and how they defined them, in particular the neglect of the material effects of racism. For example, white feminist preoccupation with 'the family' as a source of oppression was subject to a great deal of criticism on these grounds. bell hooks (1982) demonstrated how the heritage of slavery had impacted on black American families and made much of white feminist analysis inapplicable. In the British context white feminists were criticized for neglecting the differing family forms of those of Asian and African Caribbean descent, for failing to take account of the ways in which bonds of solidarity within families could be a source of resistance to racism, and for not acknowledging impact of racist immigration laws and social policies on families (Carby, 1982; Amos and Parmar, 1984; Bhavnani and Coulson, 1986).

Black feminists and women of colour were also confronting political realities and the difficulties of struggling simultaneously against racism and gender oppression. How that politics was manifested varied from one national and local context to another and depended on the specific histories of racism in different countries, but it always involved fighting on several fronts. For example, in the UK, Southall Black Sisters, a predominantly Asian group, have been active since 1979 in anti-racist, anti-fascist and anti-imperialist campaigns, as well as combating violence against women within black and Asian communities – which has, at times, brought them into conflict with elements of those communities (see Gupta, 2003). Black feminists in the USA often faced similar problems (see Collins, 2000). Writing as a black American lesbian feminist, Cheryl Clarke (1981) drew attention to the intersections of gender, sexual and racist oppression and the difficulty of resisting institutionalized heterosexuality and racism while combating the sexism and homophobia of black men. These experiences and the analyses they engendered led to what would later be called intersectional approaches to the consequences of racist, gender and class divisions – which will be elaborated in the next chapter.

5

Rethinking Gendered and Sexual Inequalities

5.1 The Persistence of Material Inequalities into the Twenty-First Century

Not all feminists were convinced by the turn to culture. Many continued to conduct empirical and theoretical work on such issues as inequality in the workplace and the home and violence against women. Indeed it may be that the impact of the 'cultural turn' has been overstated, for, while it certainly affected what was considered theoretically fashionable and the stories told about the 'progress' of feminist theory (see Hemmings, 2005), much of the work feminist sociologists were undertaking in the 1990s and beyond continued to be informed by ideas about material inequality (Torr, 2007). Many feminists remain wary of ignoring the material conditions of women's lives and giving up on the quest to explain them.

We live today within a global context characterized by extremely stark and worsening inequalities – and it is often women who are most disadvantaged by the intersections between global and local exploitation (see, for example, Alexander and Mohanty, 1997a; Mohanty, 1997). 'Differences' among women are not merely cultural'; the most significant of them are founded upon real, material inequalities deriving from institutionalized racism, the heritage of centuries of slavery, colonialism and imperialism and local and global divisions of labour. If we neglect the structural, material dimensions of social life, we may risk valorizing cultural differences that are products of oppression and inequality. For example, in the Indian context, Meera Nanda (1997) questions the conceptualization of cultural difference (such as Indian women's supposed affinity with the natural environment) as a site of resistance. She argues that this stance can lead to neglecting local patriarchal relations and to glorifying women's status as underdogs. Within the wealthy nations, too, gender, class and racial inequalities are still with us. The 'things' that feminists identified as oppressive in the 1970s – male violence, the exploitation of women's domestic labour and low-paid waged labour – have not disappeared. Violence remains an intractable problem, despite legal changes improving facilities for and the treatment of women who experience it. Rape, in particular, largely goes unpunished in many western countries as a result of under-reporting, lack of prosecutions and the difficulty of obtaining convictions (see, for example, Kelly et al., 2005).

Despite equality legislation and the advances women have made in education in western countries, gender segregation in labour markets persists, with women, especially those from ethnic minorities, still over-represented in low-paid service occupations. As a result, the gender pay gap, though narrowing to some extent, remains: in most western countries women earn, hour for hour, around 20 per cent less than men even in full-time jobs, with a wider gap when part-time jobs are taken into account (Irving, 2008). In households based on heterosexual couples the old male breadwinner and female housewife model is in decline: from the 1980s two earners became the norm in both Britain and the USA (Irwin, 1999; Castells, 2004). But because of the gender pay gap and because women with young children are likely to work part-time, the typical pattern is not a move from a single male breadwinner to dual breadwinners, but, as Jane Lewis (2001) suggests, to a one and a half breadwinner model of family life. These patterns are also affected by ethnicity and by racism: in the UK, for example, white and African Caribbean women are far more likely to take paid work than women of Pakistani or Bangladeshi descent, and when the latter are economically active they are over-represented in the lowest paid, least secure jobs and are more vulnerable to unemployment (Dex, 1999; Irving, 2008).

It is still largely women, as wives or partners and mothers, who take primary responsibility for caring for home and children and who give up paid work or take part-time employment after the birth of children (Lewis, 2001). 'Fathers appear to be fitting family commitments around their working lives . . . for mothers it is their labour market activity that usually has to be fitted around their family' (Dex, 1999: 37). Men are now more willing to be involved in child-care, but have barely increased their participation in routine household chores, even when wives are working (Dex, 1999). Both men and women have been reported as noticing that this is 'unfair', but this recognition seems not to have produced a change in the actual distribution of domestic labour (Lewis, 2001).

Well-paid women in wealthier nations increasingly ease their double burden by buying the services of other, poorer, women in an increasingly international market (Romero, 1992, 1999; Cheng, 2003; Lan, 2003, 2006). Wealthy American women often employ Chicana women (Romero, 1992), while their counterparts in Taiwan and Hong Kong employ maids from the Philippines or South East Asia (Cheng, 2003; Lan, 2003, 2006). In poorer countries such as India, labour comes so cheap that it is routine for middle-class families to employ at least one servant. As Pei-chia Lan (2003) argues, there are important continuities between paid and unpaid domestic labour. This holds for both employers and employees. Women who do other women's housework are often also responsible for domestic labour in their own homes; if they are migrant workers, they often have to make arrangements for others to care for their children and send money home for this purpose (Romero, 1999; Lan, 2003, 2006). Women who employ such workers often exert a high degree of control over them, but in 'managing' their foreign maids they reconfirm their responsibility for running the home (Cheng, 2003: 183).

Your World: Who is responsible for the housework in your home and/or your parents' home. What inequalities can you observe in how domestic labour is organized?

It has been more privileged women who have benefited most from the changes that have occurred, who are able to find well-paid jobs that allow them to lead independent lives or to buy the services of other women to do the housework. The extension of citizenship rights to lesbians and gay men in many countries also has uneven effects. A high-earning gay male couple, for example, benefit from partnership rights that safeguard their standard of living and right to inherit from each other. For poor lesbians, on the other hand, its effects might not be so positive: in the UK, for example, if one of a lesbian couple is unemployed, she may lose her right to benefits and be forced into economic dependence on her partner (Browne, forthcoming).

5.2   New Materialisms

Since the 1990s there have been signs of a revival in structural, materialist theorizing, with the recognition of the continued need for a 'critique of social totalities like patriarchy and capitalism' (Hennessy, 1993: xii). Some of this recent work reaffirms basic Marxist principles (Hennessy and Ingraham, 1997; Hennessy, 2000). Others have moved away from 'grand theory' towards empirically grounded work on specific issues and contexts, in keeping with Mary Maynard's (1995) suggestion that feminists should develop what sociologists have called 'middle-order' theories, which offer grounded generalizations rather than totalizing models of entire societies. This approach is more easily integrated with empirical research, fostering analyses of everyday gender relations and the meanings women give to their lives without losing sight of structural patterns of dominance and subordination.

This kind of work facilitates the making of connections between aspects of the social once thought of as discrete spheres of inquiry, such as sexuality and work. Lisa Adkins (1995) has drawn our attention to the sexualization of women's labour in the service sector. Analyses of gendered labour markets have largely ignored sexuality, or, where it has been considered, have often treated it as an aspect of workplace culture unrelated to the gendered structuring of jobs. Adkins' empirical investigations of a hotel and a leisure park, however, enabled her to see that the persistent sexualization of women's labour – their use as display, the particularities of dress codes, the expectation that coping with sexual harassment from customers was 'part of the job' – was far from incidental. This 'heterosexualization' was coded into the gendered division of labour: it was a covert aspect of the 'person specification' for particular jobs and the everyday practices of recruitment and work discipline. More recently Liu Jieyu (2008) has applied Adkins' analysis to the sexualization of women's white-collar work in China, showing how women's sexuality is used as an organizational resource in securing sales, contracts and business connections – linking sexuality to the changing economic relations accompanying China's integration into the global market economy. Such analyses suggest that sexuality may play a much larger part in the structuring of gendered labour markets than is usually assumed.

Your World: Do you have experience of work in the service sector, for example in cafés or bars? Is women's work sexualized in these occupations, and if so how?

The relationship between sexuality and the capitalist economy has been explored from a more explicitly Marxist standpoint by

Rosemary Hennessy (1995, 2000). Hennessy focuses on the material bases of queer lifestyles – in the sense of those who organize their lives around a self-identification as 'queer'. She argues that consumer capitalism has accommodated queer practices as lifestyle choice, but that these are not equally available to all. The celebration of queer lifestyles by the materially privileged rests upon the exploited labour of the underprivileged who produce the commodities on which that lifestyle depends (Hennessy, 2000). Opportunities for pursuing sexual lifestyle choices are not equally distributed, however: working-class lesbians and gay men often both lack the economic means to take advantage of fashionable queer spaces and do not feel comfortable in them (see, for example, Taylor, 2007). Heterosexuality can also be seen as increasingly commodified. One example is the increasing commercialization and cost of weddings, which Chrys Ingraham (1999) characterizes as 'the wedding industrial complex'. Gay couples are now buying into this in countries where some form of formal partnership is recognized, creating a niche market for gay and lesbian weddings. Here, too, economic divides are evident: one reason why poor cohabiting heterosexual couples do not marry is that they say they cannot afford to – meaning that they cannot afford a 'proper wedding' (Lewis, 2001).

The emergence of new materialist arguments has led some of those most associated with postmodern theorizing to acknowledge material inequalities. For example, Judith Butler (1997), seen by many of her critics as epitomizing an exclusively cultural focus, has argued that sexuality is not 'merely cultural'. She suggests that queer studies might be a means of returning to critiques of the family 'based on a mobilizing insight *into a socially contingent and socially transformable account of kinship*' (1997: 276, emphasis in the original). But what the current structuring of gender and sexuality is contingent on, according to Butler, is the functionality of the heterosexual family for capitalism. Ironically, Butler thus returns to early forms of Marxist feminism, which were found wanting precisely because of their failure adequately to account for gendered and sexual inequalities (see Ch. 4). Butler also reduces the material to the economic (Fraser, 1997) and the economic to capitalism and class relations, which conceals the operation of non-capitalist economic processes, in particular men's appropriation of the labour of wives and dependants (Delphy, 1984; Delphy and Leonard, 1992). Hence Butler fails to make a connection between the oppression of lesbians and gays and the inequality *within* heterosexual relations – despite her earlier reliance on the work of Monique Wittig (Butler, 1990a). As we saw in the last chapter, Wittig (1992) conceptualizes the heterosexual contract as a labour relationship, as well as sexual one, and one that constitutes women and men as hierarchical social categories. Wittig's argument suggests that gender and heterosexuality might be considered as structural phenomena *in themselves* rather than merely being shaped by structural factors external to them.

5.3   The Structural Dimensions of Gender and Sexuality

The idea that gender might be structural goes back to the early years of its theorization – in particular to Gayle Rubin's conceptualization of a sex/gender *system* (see Ch. 1.4). According to Rubin, each society 'has a sex/gender system – a set of arrangements by which the biological raw material of human sex and procreation is shaped by human, social intervention' (1975: 165). These arrangements vary from one society and culture to another and serve as conventional means of organizing human sexual relations, especially through the structuring of kinship and marriage. Gender, for Rubin, is 'a socially imposed division of the sexes' and 'a product of the social relations of sexuality' (1975: 179). While Rubin thus emphasizes the structural basis of gender division, she nonetheless leaves 'sex' as a residual biological category so that, ultimately, gender rests on a biological basis. This residual essentialism has been challenged by an alternative theorization of gender deriving from French materialist feminists such as Delphy and Wittig (see especially Delphy, 1984) [5].

The materialist feminist approach also answers the concerns of those who argued from a cultural perspective for the need to denaturalize gender categories themselves (see Ch. 4.6). Rather than seeing 'women' and 'men' as discursive constructs, however, materialist feminists argue that they are *social* categories, products of a hierarchical social order. This idea was developed from the 1970s but took longer to reach the English-speaking world. In the first issue of the journal *Questions Féministes*, originally published in 1977, its collective argued that men and women are social, not natural, categories. In a non-patriarchal society, they claimed, there would be no social distinctions between men and women. This does not mean women becoming like men, since 'men' as we know them would no longer exist: 'for at the same time as we destroy the idea of the generic "Woman", we also destroy the idea of "Man"' (1981: 215). This position on gender follows from a conceptualization of men and women as existing in a class-like relationship. Rather than seeing male domination as based upon pre-existing sex differences, the collective argued that gender only exists as a social division because of patriarchal domination. As Delphy and Leonard later put it: 'For us "men" and "women" are not two naturally given groups who at some time fell into a hierarchical relationship. Rather the reason the two groups are distinguished socially is because one dominates the other' (Delphy and Leonard, 1992: 258). This argument is in keeping with a Marxist method of analysis. For Marxists, classes only exist in relation to one another: conceptually and empirically there can be no bourgeoisie without the proletariat, and vice versa. Similarly 'men' and 'women' exist as socially significant categories because of the exploitative relationship which both binds them together and sets them apart from each other. Conceptually and empirically there could be no 'women' without the opposing category 'men', and vice versa. To repeat the quote from Monique Wittig, '[T]here are no slaves without masters' (1992: 15).

The materialist feminist perspective thus treats 'sex' – in the sense of biological 'sex differences' – as itself the product of society and culture. This is clearest in the work of Christine Delphy, who is unusual among the French materialist feminists in using the term 'gender'. Delphy reversed the usual logic of the sex–gender distinction, suggesting that rather than gender being built upon the foundation of biological sex difference, 'sex has become a pertinent fact, hence a perceived category, because of the existence of gender' (1984: 144). Gender creates anatomical sex 'in the sense that the hierarchical division of humanity into two transforms an anatomical difference (which is itself devoid of social implications) into a relevant distinction for social practice' (1984: 144). These ideas were further elaborated in Delphy's later work (Delphy, 1993), where she continues to question the idea of 'sex' as a natural distinction, arguing that sex is as social as gender, a product of the way 'society represents biology to itself' (1993: 5). She further points out that men and women as we know them are a product of the hierarchical relationship between them. She therefore counters the argument that under conditions of equality women would become like men: 'If women were the equals of men, men would no longer equal themselves. Why then should women resemble what men had ceased to be?' (1993: 8). This argument also has implications for how heterosexuality is conceptualized – as integral to the way gender is constructed and ordered and therefore structural and institutional. This was the basis of Monique Wittig's argument that the heterosexual contract creates us as men and women (see Ch. 4.5) [6].

Since the 1990s there has been a renewed focus on heterosexuality as an institution (Richardson, 1996; Jackson, 1999; Seidman, 2002). Attention has been drawn to heterosexuality's normative status, its institutionalization through law and the state, and the privileges heterosexuals have without often being aware of them. Feminists have also, and importantly, focused on heterosexuality as a gendered institution – and in so doing made it clear that it is not simply a sexual institution. While founded on a sexual union between a man and a woman, the heterosexual contract, as Wittig calls it, has always involved more than sex. It also entails a domestic division of labour which has, historically, also been reflected in the labour market, where men's higher wages and more secure jobs have been related to their role as family breadwinners.

Following the logic of this argument, Chrys Ingraham (1996) advances the thesis that heterosexuality should displace gender as the central category of feminist analysis. Inspired by the work of Monique Wittig, Ingraham exposes the 'heterosexual imaginary' to scrutiny. The heterosexual imaginary, she maintains, masks the ways in which gender has consistently been defined from a hetero-normative perspective. She argues that sociologists (including feminists) have failed to see the heterosexual ends to which this gender divide is directed. As Ingraham points out, the definitions of gender employed by feminist sociologists indicate that it is a binary 'organizing relations *between* the sexes' (1996: 186, her emphasis). She goes on to suggest that heterosexuality 'serves as the organizing institution and ideology . . . for gender' (1996:187). She proposes the term 'heterogender' to capture the ways in which the heterosexual ordering of gender is implicated in the operation of all social institutions at all levels of society, from family to workplace to the state.

While it is evident that heterosexuality is *an* organizing principle of many aspects of social structure and social life, and an important one, there are still some doubts about whether it should be accorded primacy in analyses of gender (see Jackson, 2005, 2006a, 2006b). Defining heterosexuality so broadly that it encompasses all aspects of gendered relations, and then collapsing heterosexuality and gender into one term – heterogender – might make it more difficult to analyse their interrelationship. Hence it would be wise to maintain an analytical distinction between gender, as the hierarchical relation between women and men, and heterosexuality, as a specific institutionalized form of that relation. We also need to think about how the social ordering of gender and heterosexuality intersects with other social divisions and inequalities.

An alternative concept is 'heteropatriarchy'. This term has been used by some radical lesbian feminists to emphasize the link between heterosexuality and women's subordination (see, for example, Kitzinger and Wilkinson, 1993). From a rather different perspective M. Jacqui Alexander adopts this concept in analysing how hetero-sexualization and patriarchy combine in the state regulation of female sexuality in the Bahamas, a Caribbean nation that was a British colony until 1973. Unlike Kitzinger and Wilkinson, Alexander sees heteropatriarchy not as a stable, monolithic entity, but as unstable, constantly requiring shoring up, and as operating at discursive and material levels. Through a close reading of legislative changes out-lawing lesbianism and homosexuality and regulating family life, she argues that the state reinforces patriarchal privilege within families, creates 'a subordinate class of lesbians, gay men, prostitutes and people with HIV' and a class of 'loyal heterosexual citizens' co-opted into the tourist trade, where they are sexualized as commodities for the benefit of predominantly US tourists and international capital (Alexander, 1997: 69). In so doing she highlights the intersections between gender, sexuality and race within the neo-colonialist state.

5.4   The Idea of Intersectionality

The concept of intersectionality is attributed to Kimberlé Crenshaw (1989, 1991) in arguing that white feminist analyses marginalized the concerns of Black women. The idea, however, had its origins earlier, in the critiques of white feminists mounted by Black feminists and women of colour in the 1970s and 1980s (see Ch. 4.7) [7]. Indeed, the idea could be said to go back even further. In an oft-quoted speech made at a women's rights convention in Akron, Ohio, in 1852, a black ex-slave, Sojourner Truth, directly countered asser-tions of women's innate weakness:

That man over there says women need to be helped into carriages, and lifted over ditches, and to have the best place everywhere. Nobody ever helps me into carriages and lifted over ditches, or over mud puddles or gives me any best place! And ain't I a woman? Look at me! Look at my arm! I have ploughed, and planted, and gathered into barns, and no man could head me! And ain't I a woman? I could work as much and eat as much as any man – when I could get it – and bear the lash as well! And ain't I a woman? I have borne children and seen most of them sold into slavery and when I cried out with a mother's grief, none but Jesus heard me. And ain't I a woman? (As quoted in Carby, 1982: 214–15; see also hooks, 1982: 160).

This speech has a number of contemporary resonances, First, and most obviously, Sojourner Truth challenges essentialist ideas of womanhood and femininity: she contradicts a white man's depiction of women and demonstrates, forcefully, that women are not (or not all) innately weak and delicate creatures. Her repeated rhetorical question (ain't I a woman?) is provoked, however, by a very specific construction of womanhood: one that is white and middle class. Simultaneously she asserts her inclusion in the category of women, both through her reiterated question and through her mention of motherhood, while demonstrating her visible difference from frail white femininity ('Look at me! Look at my arm!') and emphasizing her capacity for hard physical labour. But her embodied difference is more than just difference. It is the result of extreme oppression – 'bearing the lash' and seeing her children sold into slavery – and a mark of her exclusion from the normative conduct and privileges of white women. This speech has been read as demonstrating the instability of the category 'women' (Riley, 1988). Our reading, however, is that while it reveals that women is not a unitary category, that lack of unity is better understood in terms of its intersections with other categories, other structural inequalities that position Sojourner Truth simultaneously within gender and racial hierarchies. She is not just a woman; she is a black woman and ex-slave. While the inequality and oppression to which she draws attention are particularly stark and brutal, it should remind us that we all occupy multiple social locations, and that our position within any one hierarchy is always related to and intersected by our location within others.

Intersectionality has become a 'buzzword', a term without a precise agreed definition that has multiple applications (Davis, 2008). Often it is used in relation to identities: the idea that we each embody simultaneously several identities, classed, racial, gendered, sexual and other, which can lead to a potentially limitless list of categories (see Butler, 1990a: 143) and a very fragmented view of social divisions (Yuval-Davis, 2006). This is a problem if we think of identity in isolation from social structure, and can be avoided if we focus instead on the ways in which we are each positioned in relation to intersecting social divisions and inequalities and on 'the ways different social divisions are constructed by, and intermeshed with, each other in specific historical conditions' (Yuval-Davis, 2006: 202). Nira Yuval-Davis argues that under given historical conditions it is possible to specify which social divisions are most important in relation to axes of power and inequality. Some social divisions, including class, gender and ethnicity, 'tend to shape most people's lives in most social locations', while others – for example caste – affect particular people in particular locations. Also, Yuval-Davis suggests, some categories come to be constructed and defined as culturally and politically significant (2006: 203). On the other hand, some differences are just differences and therefore do not structure inequalities.

Intersectional analysis derived from feminist theorizations of the social location of black and ethnic minority women, but it does far more than simply arguing for the recognition of multiple oppressions of race, class and gender. While some black feminists did, in the 1970s and 1980s, argue in terms of 'triple oppression' (race + class + gender), there have long been feminists who are critical of an 'additive' approach, pointing out that race, class and gender are inextricably intertwined in shaping the lives of black women and men – and indeed of all of us (see Brah and Phoenix, 2004; Yuval-Davis, 2006). The privileged and powerful (such as rich, white, heterosexual men) are positioned by intersecting locations within hierarchies as much as the underprivileged or powerless. Intersectional analysis requires us to interrogate inequalities among women and among men – and indeed within sub-categories of women and men. Avtar Brah (1991) has illustrated this in relation to her own location as a British Asian woman. As such, she is subjected to racism, but 'as a member of a dominant caste' in her community she also occupies 'a position of power in relation to lower caste women' and is thus 'differently positioned within these social hierarchies' (1991: 172).

Such multiple positionings reveal another problem with the additive approach and another reason why intersectional analysis is necessary: positions within different hierarchies are not always congruent. For example, while people from ethnic minorities are over-represented in the working class, not all are working class; while women are more likely than men to be poor, not all women are poor. Thus women may be positioned in some hierarchies above some men as well as other women: the wife of a white slave-owner may have been dominated by her husband but had material power over male slaves; today a woman in a managerial position has material power over subordinate male workers within her organization. Men generally retain patriarchal privileges relative to women in their own social group, but under conditions of total abjection may be denied even this: historically male slaves in the USA and colonized men elsewhere were often denied the patriarchal privileges white men enjoyed – for example exclusive control of 'their' women.

A further complication is that the hierarchies through which we are socially located differ from each other: they do not all have the same ontological basis – they are not all founded on the same social relations (Anthias and Yuval-Davis, 1992; Anthias, 2001; Yuval-Davis, 2006). Gender, class and race and ethnicity are generally identified as the three main lines of social cleavage within contemporary western societies. Whereas most theorists think of class as having a material basis, racial and gender divisions are often seen as matters of cultural or symbolic difference. Floya Anthias (2001) contests this distinction, arguing that all three are elements of stratification, entailing struggles for resources, both material and symbolic; and, of course, all interconnect with the others. They have differing 'social ontologies' and 'parameters of location': class is based in economic life; gender (and by extension sexuality) in the social ordering of sexual difference and reproduction; and ethnicity in collective bonds related to geographical origins or cultural differences. This might seem to echo the old Marxist feminist distinction between the spheres of production and reproduction, but Anthias's argument is more complex, since each impacts on the other, so that class, gender and ethnicity in any concrete situation intertwine and overlap in the production and reproduction of specific social conditions.

The idea of intersectionality, then, attunes us to the complex relationships between intersecting hierarchies and the need to be specific about how they intersect in any given situation. We have discussed these issues primarily in relation to western societies, but the conditions that produce these social divisions are products of global socio-economic relations and not merely local ones.

5.5   Global Modernity, Global Inequality and the Ordering of Gender and Sexuality

As we have seen in earlier chapters, the rise of modernity has in many ways reshaped gender and sexual relations. We are now said to be living in an age of postmodernity or late modernity, and a number of theorists have associated this with further shifts in the gendered and sexual landscape. Unlike postmodernity theorists, theorists of late modernity see recent social transformations as an intensification of processes already evident *within* modernity, rather than a break *from* modernity (see Heaphy, 2007). Late modernity is, for them, characterized by 'detraditionalization' and individualization (Beck and Beck-Gernsheim, 2002), the weakening of normative constraints and a disembedding of the individual from solidaristic bonds accompanied by a reordering of gender and intimate relations. Thus we are said to be living in an era of 'the normal chaos of love' (Beck and Beck-Gernsheim, 1995) or witnessing a 'transformation of intimacy' (Giddens, 1992). Anthony Giddens locates women and gay men at the forefront of social change and the pursuit of more democratic relationships. He posits a shift from romantic love (based on the premise of an ideal partner for life) to 'confluent' love and the 'pure relationship', which is contingent on mutual satisfaction rather than life-long commitment. Ulrich Beck and Elisabeth Beck-Gernsheim (2002) are more cautious, and cast women as less individuated than men, caught between living for others and forging lives of their own. Feminists have been critical of such propositions, arguing that they underestimate the continuing importance of intimate social bonds, the degree to which choices we make about social life are shaped by our socio-economic location, and, in the case of Giddens, the persistence of gender inequality (Jamieson, 1999; Smart and Shipman, 2004; Irwin, 2005). Others, however, are more optimistic about recent social change, especially in relation to sexual freedoms (see, for example, Weeks, 2007).

A further problem is that these theories are highly ethnocentric, focused entirely on western societies and ignoring societies elsewhere that might be considered equally modern – such as those in East Asia. Western modernity theorists have been challenged by Asian sociologists, who point out that not only is Asian modernity built on different traditions, but it is also on a different relation between tradition and modernity – precisely because of the historic dominance of the West (Tanabe and Tokita-Tanabe, 2003; see also Jackson et al., 2008). Some western theorists have begun to discuss the idea of multiple modernities, but even this, as Gurminder Bhambra (2007) points out, can still imply a modernity originating in the West and then modified elsewhere. Bhambra suggests that modernity is better conceptualized in terms of global, connected histories, but with uneven consequences [8].

Global interconnections have existed since antiquity through ancient trade routes and the concomitant movement of people and commodities. The era of western exploration and colonial expansion strengthened global ties further (often in highly oppressive ways). Indeed, far from being a western phenomenon, modernization has always been global, facilitated through colonial exploitation and

its post-colonial aftermath. From this point of view, poorer societies more usually thought of as pre-modern cannot be thought of
as 'outside' modernity but must be seen as located within it and
shaped by the heritage of colonialism and the inequalities that global
modernity has produced. Conversely, this history has also shaped
the imperialist nations themselves. Not only was the rise of western
industrial capitalism fuelled by the exploitation of the resources
and labour of subjugated nations (the latter including slavery and
indenture), but it also resulted in the invention of the concept of
'race', which affected social relations within the imperial nations. As
Anne McClintock argues, the idea of race was central 'not only to
the self-definition of the middle class but also to the policing of the
"dangerous classes": the working class, the Irish, Jews, prostitutes,
feminists, gays and lesbians' and others (1995: 5). The 'pure' white
middle-class woman was defined not only in contrast to disreputable
working-class women, but also against colonized women; in colonial
situations her purity was seen as needing protection from the potential threat of indigenous men, while white men expected to have easy
access to the bodies of local women. These asymmetrical economic
and social, gendered and sexual, interrelationships persist. Think,
for example, of Rosemary Hennessy's point that fashionable queer
lifestyles depend on the exploitation of workers elsewhere (see above,
section 5.2), or more generally how western women's (and men's)
access to cheap fashionable clothes depends on the sweated labour of
women and children in poor countries.

> **TASK: Global inequality and the clothing industry.**
>
> Look at the labels in your own clothes and shoes to find out where
> they are made. Find out what you can about the conditions of
> labour in these countries and the gender and age of those working
> in clothing factories. What else can you find out about gender
> inequalities and sexual rights in these countries?

Since the turn of the millennium, some of those who have characterized the late modern sexual climate as one of increasing freedom,
flexibility and diversity have begun to acknowledge that their analysis
is applicable only to privileged corners of the globe (Plummer, 2005;
Weeks, 2007). Plummer, reflecting on his previous neglect of global
inequalities, produced a table highlighting the contrast between
the rich, modern world of choice and the poor, traditional world

characterized by lack of choice. We reproduce our own version of this in Table 5.1, but with modifications, in part to avoid a rather problematic opposition between 'traditional' and 'modern' and to avoid some of the more stereotypical representations of the poor world. Even with our amendments, however, the contrasts outlined here need to be carefully qualified.

There is no doubt that poverty constrains sexual lives and has gendered impacts. So why is it necessary to qualify the table? First, we must be careful to avoid the forms of homogenization and stereotyping of the 'third world' that Chandra T. Mohanty (1991b) has warned against. Secondly, while our table does map, in broad terms, some crucial inequalities, the global picture is rather more complicated. To begin with, rich and poor nations are not homogeneous: there are inequalities within them and thus the categories 'poor' and 'rich' do not map directly onto particular countries or regions of the world; the rich in poor countries can avail themselves of many of the sexual and reproductive freedoms available to the rich elsewhere. Cultural differences also change the picture: for example, some wealthy East Asian countries such as Japan and South Korea, despite changes in patterns of intimate relationships, have kinship systems that differ from, and are stronger than, those of the West (Jackson et al., 2008). More restrictive sexual laws and morals are not necessarily the product of poverty. For example, South Africa, a country in which there is a great deal of very obvious poverty, has (in contrast to other African countries) one of the most liberal sexual

Table 5.1.   Contrasting sexual lives: the distribution of choice and constraint

High-income world	Low-income world
Travel for business and pleasure	Travel to seek work or escape poverty, war, oppression
Buyers of sex and importers of wives and sex workers	Sellers of sex and exporters of wives and sex workers
Body projects and bodily aesthetics	Malnourishment and vulnerability to disease
Weak kinship, 'families of choice'; diversity of sexual identities and lifestyles	Strong kinship; less individualized sexual and relationship choices
Assisted conception; new reproductive technologies	High infant mortality; high risk of death in childbirth

Source: Adapted from Plummer, 2005.

regimes in the world, where protection against discrimination on grounds of sexuality is enshrined in the constitution – though here again ability to access this protection and the freedoms it guarantees is far from universal (see Reddy et al., 2009). In many cases laws against homosexuality derive not from indigenous 'tradition' but from the colonial legacy: most of the countries that were once part of the British Empire have had such laws, initially imposed by the British. Paradoxically these laws are now often defended in the name of local tradition: for example, those who opposed the Indian Supreme Court's overruling of the old colonial anti-homosexuality laws in 2009 did so on the grounds of defending 'Indian culture'. In some cases, though, new laws against lesbians and homosexuals have been introduced in ex-colonies (see, for example, Alexander, 1997), including, as we write, in Uganda.

Notwithstanding these reservations, global inequalities do impact on gender and sexual relations, and nowhere is this clearer than in the global sex trade, illustrated by the example with which we started Part II, which makes it clear that commercialized sexual exchanges are influenced by global economic inequalities. In recent years a great deal of attention has been paid to the issue of trafficking in women, which once more reveals the gap between rich and poor countries, with women from the latter destined for the sex industries in the former. As with prostitution as a whole, it is important to recognize that not all 'trafficked' women are subject to the same conditions. Some are coerced or duped into prostitution; others are sex workers who choose to migrate in search of better pay, conditions or lifestyles – some writers emphasize the former (for example, Monzini, 2005), others the latter (for example, Agustín, 2007). Some sex workers therefore are effectively economic migrants, as are many women who participate in the global marriage market. Here, too, a similar pattern occurs, with a pattern that could be called 'global hypergamy' (Constable, 2005), whereby women from poorer countries seek to improve their position by marrying men from richer nations. Often this does not result in actual hypergamy, since the men concerned are usually those disadvantaged in their local marriage markets. European and American men seek wives from Eastern Europe and Asia; men from Japan and Taiwan find brides in poorer, more 'traditional' countries in South East Asia (Constable, 2003, 2005; Suzuki, 2005). Other patterns of migration are also gendered, and also follow similar patterns, as in the case of the domestic workers discussed in Chapter 4 (Ch. 4.1). Women from poorer countries use whatever strategies are available to improve their lives, and may employ different ones at different times (Lan, 2008a), reminding us that we should not ignore individual agency (see Part IV).

In investigating the persistence of local and global inequalities and the intersections between various axes of inequality, a social structural analysis is essential but not sufficient. We need also to take account of the cultural contexts in which sexual and gendered inequalities are made sense of, justified and sometimes challenged, and the ways in which these inequalities are experienced subjectively, negotiated by individual social actors and influence the construction of identity. These issues are addressed in Parts III and IV.

Learning Outcomes

After reading the chapters in Part II you should:

- understand the concept of social structure and the structural bases of inequality;
- be able to demonstrate awareness of the ways in which social change has affected both gender and sexual inequalities and sociologists' understandings of them;
- have knowledge of theories of patriarchy and capitalism and, in the process, have a revised understanding of varieties of feminism;
- understand why a structural analysis of gender and sexuality remains relevant and essential to sociological analysis;
- be aware of the structural intersections between gender and heterosexuality;
- have an understanding of the ways in which gender and sexuality intersect with other social divisions, especially those of class and race, and an appreciation of the complexity of these intersections;
- be sensitive to the global dimensions of gendered and sexual inequalities.

Notes and Resources for Further Study

1 For further reading on the gendered assumptions of the founding fathers, see Barbara Marshall's *Engendering Modernity* (1994), R.A. Sydie's *Natural Women, Cultured Men* (1994 [1987]) and Barbara Marshall and Anne Witz (eds) *Engendering the Social* (2004).

2 Overviews of these debates are inevitably marked by the position taken by the author. Two of the fullest are referenced in what follows, but can be recommended with the caveat that you remain aware that these are not disinterested accounts; these are Michèle Barrett's *Women's Oppression Today* (1990 [1980]) and Sylvia Walby's *Patriarchy at Work* (1986), Chapters 1–4.

3 Note that the works cited in this paragraph were published in French from the early 1970s up to 1981 and did not become available in good English translation until much later.

4 These various terms were adopted in different national contexts. In Britain the term 'black' was adopted in the 1970s and 1980s as a political identity uniting ethnic minorities, especially those of African Caribbean and South Asian descent, and continues to be used by some of the latter, for example by Southall Black Sisters, who are predominantly Asian: see Rahila Gupta (ed.) *From Homebreakers to Jailbreakers: Southall Black Sisters* (2003). A selection of writings from black British feminists, from a variety of ethnic groups, can be found in Heidi Mirza (ed.) *Black British Feminism: A Reader* (1997). In the USA the term 'black' was more often used exclusively for African Americans, as in key texts such as bell hooks' *Ain't I a Woman* (1982) and Patricia Hill Collins' *Black Feminist Thought* (2000). American women from other ethnic minorities more often called

themselves 'women of colour': see, for example, Cherrie Moraga and Gloria Anzaldua (eds) *This Bridge Called My Back*. Other terms were also adopted. 'Third world women' usually refers to women from poorer countries. In her introduction to *Third World Women and the Politics of Feminism*, Chandra Mohanty (1991a) uses the term as one that unites all women struggling against the effects of racism, colonialism and imperialism as an 'imagined community', while at the same time being critical of homogenizing accounts of 'third world women' produced 'under western eyes' (1991b); see also M. Jacqui Alexander and Chandra T. Mohanty (eds) *Feminist Genealogies, Colonial Legacies and Democratic Futures* (1997b). The term 'third world', though, is a contested one. All the sources mentioned here are useful reading for getting a flavour of challenges to white feminism as well as debates among black and third world feminists and women of colour.

5 Rubin's essentialism has also been challenged from other, non-structural perspectives: see especially Suzanne Kessler and Wendy McKenna's *Gender: An Ethnomethodological Approach* (1978), which we discuss in Ch. 4.2.

6 For further reading on materialist feminist analyses of sex and gender, see Stevi Jackson's *Christine Delphy* (1996) and Diana Leonard and Lisa Adkins (eds) *Sex in Question* (1996).

7 For a discussion of the development of intersectional analysis from earlier black feminism, see Avtar Brah and Ann Phoenix's 'Ain't I a Woman: Revisiting Intersectionality', *Journal of International Women's Studies* (2004); an introductory overview of the debates can be found in Kate Reed's 'Racing the Feminist Agenda: Exploring the Intersections between Race, Ethnicity and Gender', in D. Richardson and V. Robinson (eds) *Introducing Gender and Women's Studies* (2008); for some recent theoretical elaborations on the utility and definition of the concept, see the special issue of the *European Journal of Women's Studies* on intersectionality, Vol. 13, No. 3, 2006.

8 Gurminder Bhambra's book *Rethinking Modernity: Postcolonialism and the Sociological Imagination* (2007) provides an excellent and thought-provoking critique of the ethnocentrism of both classical and contemporary sociological theories of modernity. Unfortunately, however, it says little about gender or sexuality.

Part III

Culture, Ideology and Discourse

In Part III we discuss cultural beliefs and values around gender and sexuality and detail their historical emergence during the period of modernity. We show how science, psychology and ideas of an inner spiritual nature have contributed to developing and enshrining essentialist understandings of gender and sexuality and aligning them to patriarchal gender relations. We then move on to sociological critiques of this dominant ideological formation. We conclude with a discussion of the complexities of contemporary values and beliefs around the sexual with specific reference to sociological debates about whether we live in a postmodern era where a diversity of identities and lifestyle choices have rendered traditional values and ideologies obsolete – or at least less relevant.

Introduction: The End of a 'Queer' Era?

Sad news arrived in August 2006: *Queer Eye for the Straight Guy* was cancelled after three seasons of top-rated television viewing in over ninety countries. *Queer Eye* is a makeover show, originally aired by Bravo TV in the USA in 2003. In it, five gay men take a nominated heterosexual man under their collective wing in order to improve his appearance, grooming habits, lifestyle knowledge and general presentability, often with the explicit goal of achieving, saving or furthering a romantic relationship [1]. The most significant thing about *Queer Eye* is that it ever existed; a programme about five gay men 'making over the world, one straight man at a time', would have been impossible to commission just a few years ago, and would have been unimaginable before the days of second wave feminism and gay liberation in the 1970s. *Queer Eye*'s arrival on our screens in the early twenty-first century was a clear sign of the times, and, more precisely, a sign of progress in the visibility and acceptability of lesbian and gay lifestyles (Streitmatter, 2009). At first sight, we must credit the political movements of gay and lesbian liberation and second wave feminism with achieving this progress. As argued throughout this book, the political impact of these ideas has been enormous, resulting in the gradual acceptance of laws and social policies that attempt to equalize the treatment of women and men, and homosexuals and heterosexuals. However, a full sociological understanding of the progress of equality cannot look only at politics but must also consider the shifts in values and beliefs around sexuality and gender that have helped to promote political change. In short, we must understand changes in culture.

Given that television is a major global media technology, the production and popularity of *Queer Eye for the Straight Guy* can be seen as a consequence of widespread cultural changes that created audiences for it. Audiences are consumers, and only in sufficient numbers do they make media products profitable, through sales of the show and associated advertising. Thus, we can infer that in the last few years production executives have been secure enough about male homosexuality to promote it intentionally as socially acceptable and, moreover, as something from which heterosexual masculinity can learn a thing or two. Sociologically, this means that beliefs and values have changed, now permitting the positive portrayal of gay men, and permitting people to admit their enjoyment of such a show.

Given that gender and sexual inequality are interrelated, *Queer Eye* must also be understood in the context of cultural changes around gender as well as sexuality. Perhaps *Queer Eye* could not have been possible without the preceding hit show about financially, professionally *and* sexually independent heterosexual women, *Sex and the City*, which aired in western countries during the late 1990s and early 2000s. Indeed, the straight male subjects of *Queer Eye* have often been nominated by their female partners, who want them to shape up, or by their family members or friends, who are concerned that they will never secure a relationship unless they shape up. The meaning system of *Queer Eye* – or, in Foucauldian terms, its *discourse* – is *both* that gay men are better at grooming themselves than straight men (and so can give good advice) *and* that straight women are now in a position to be independent of men, and can make demands on them to conform to their expectations and standards. At the beginning of the twenty-first century, consider how different this cultural meaning of femininity is from the oppressive ideology of the *Feminine Mystique* (see Ch. 2.1).

This change in cultural values and beliefs is not limited to the realm of media entertainment, since the use of gay identity as a source of profit would not be possible unless wider cultural changes had made gay identity publicly legitimate. These began in the 1970s with Gay Pride marches and the demands of gay liberation movements for political rights, subsequent increasing public visibility and recent gains such as civil partnerships and gay marriage in some countries. Similarly, we have discussed the advances in women's rights, which have changed cultural values to the extent that the Harvard President's brief flirtation with biological essentialism helped to ruin his credibility (see the Introduction to Part I). Shifts in cultural beliefs are thus widespread throughout society, evident in education, governing institutions, legal systems and the media.

Feminist, lesbian and gay analyses of how dominant beliefs and ideas are sustained in these social settings by specific cultural practices – the doing of actions, if you will – indicate key sites of ideological reproduction such as education, the family, law, medicine, science and popular culture (see Chs 7 and 8). Moreover, cultural practices are sustained at the most personal level, both in interpersonal relationships with family, friends and colleagues, and within our own subjective beliefs. Sociologically speaking, we cannot think of culture as merely related to structural phenomena, but must see it as linking structural aspects of society to our most individual sense of self, identity and action – issues dealt with in Part IV.

Sociological theories of postmodernity have suggested that the foundational concepts and theories of sociology are no longer adequate for understanding the contemporary globalized, mediatized and de-traditionalized world. That argument is made precisely because classical sociology developed out of an attempt to understand the advent of industrial capitalism – what is often referred to as *modernity*. Moreover, a significant component of arguments for postmodernity is that the realm of culture is now displacing social structure in shaping social relations, identities, action and experience. In a postmodern world the sphere of consumption has, it is said, become a more important determinant of lifestyle and identity than the sphere of production and the class divides characteristic of modern capitalism, so that class and community are less salient to our lives and our sense of who we are. It is argued that identities are now based on what we consume rather than our place in capitalist divisions of labour, giving rise to greater diversity and choice in lives that are no longer constrained by old community norms. It is not difficult to see how the contemporary emphasis on diverse sexualities, and the associated 'liberation' of women, may point to, or be implicated in, these arguments about the shift to a postmodern society. Our example of *Queer Eye* testifies to an era in which the emphasis on the self – on pleasure, identity, self-improvement and lifestyle – is meaningful to audiences. Indeed, the proliferation of reality makeover shows seems only to confirm the notion of the individualized society in which traditional social structures of class, gender, ethnicity, are no longer barriers to social mobility and self-reinvention. After all, in the *Queer Eye* world, we watch traditional patriarchal men being taught how to become new and better 'selves' with the help of those arbiters of self-invention, gay men.

There are, then, a number of critical issues to explore when thinking sociologically about the formation of gender and sexuality in our culture. We begin with a detailed introduction to the cultural development of knowledge around sexuality and gender in Chapter 6, demonstrating the institutionalization of essentialism during the period of modernity in the West. In Chapter 7 we move on to critiques of this institutionalized knowledge from second wave feminism and lesbian and gay theorists and the challenges raised by postmodernism, which views knowledge as socially constructed rather than a literal 'truth'. However, it is important to recognize the distinction between postmodern*ism* as a *theory* and the idea of postmodern *society* – or the condition of postmodern*ity*. We move to discuss the latter in Chapter 8, where we focus on popular culture and what it tells us about gendered and sexual relations within contemporary globalized capitalism. We consider the implications that current sexual values and beliefs have for the question of whether we live in a postmodern culture, or whether traditional relationships between structure, culture and identity still persist. This question is important for the political projects of feminism and sexual diversity, since core sociological concepts from second wave feminism and gay liberation have been central to analysing oppression and inequalities in the realm of the sexual. However, these were developed through an engagement with classical sociology and its emphasis on social structures and systems, and if these have become less relevant, the implication is that we need new concepts and theories to understand gender and sexuality in the new, postmodern era.

6

Gender and Sexuality as Cultural Constructs

6.1 Identifying Patriarchal Culture

Sociological approaches to culture began from analyses of normative or dominant value systems, how 'norms' or social expectations of correct behaviour derived from these and how they shaped the meanings available to us as individuals through language, symbols and ideologies. Culture was then seen as mediating between social structures and individual conduct and identity. For example, we have already referred to Betty Friedan's 1963 classic feminist text, *The Feminine Mystique* (see Ch. 2.1), which focused on ideological constructions of domesticated femininity. This 'feminine mystique' was also the focus of critique from a first wave feminist, Mary Wollstonecraft, writing in 1792 (see Ch. 1.2). Wollstonecraft argues that 'gentlewomen are too indolent to be actively virtuous, and are softened rather than refined by civilization' (1972 [1792]: 16). She is focused here on privileged women who have no need to work, instead running their husbands' households and adopting appropriate feminine behaviours and pastimes, a situation that had changed little by the time of Friedan's critique. This understanding of women as naturally more suited to the domestic realm developed largely during the Victorian era in the West and, we can argue, is still with us today, with most domestic labour being performed by women and most cultural representations – through either television, films or advertisements – still emphasizing the role of women as the primary domestic carers, whether for children, partners or the house itself. For example, in Britain in 2007, a major grocery chain Asda (a subsidiary of Wal-Mart) ran an advertisement for a new range of healthy and quick-to-prepare meals from pre-packaged fresh ingredients. The advertisement depicted a mother using the product, whilst her young daughter mimicked her by her side, on her own toy stove, thus relying on well-understood and widespread cultural beliefs. Not only does the time span demonstrate the durability of cultural beliefs around masculinity and femininity, but it also shows how culture defines women as domestic servants.

Second wave feminists developed analyses that connected 'civilized' values and beliefs with a social system of male domination – patriarchy – which promoted a culture that confined women's agency and their sense of self-identity within narrowly defined limits. Our culture can be seen as patriarchal in that it is characterized by essentialist or naturalist beliefs around men and women, which have often served to legitimate their relative social positions. Essentialist beliefs are pervasive features of our culture, linked to social structures such as the economy and labour markets, through institutions that reproduce and sustain cultural values, such as religion, media, popular culture, education, thus providing the major ways in which we can make sense of gender and sexuality at the individual and interactional level. Essentialism impacts on our actions and identities precisely because it is first and foremost a system of meanings on which we draw in thinking about how to 'be' a man or woman. Whilst we have covered the basics of essentialism in Chapter 1, we detail below some more specific historical processes in its emergence.

6.2   Religion, Culture and the Sexual

Religion makes an important contribution to contemporary cultural debates around issues of gender and sexuality, particularly in the USA, where religious 'values' feature prominently in opposition to gay rights and abortion (Rayside and Wilcox, 2010), and increasingly in other Western countries, where established Christian churches are often now joined by the minority religions of immigrant communities in discussions or campaigns around sexuality and gender. Given that Christianity often shares a conservative viewpoint on gender and sexuality with other world religions, it is not surprising that social conflict arises when the rights of women and homosexuals are promoted by the state. Notably, there has been a major emphasis in the 'War on Terror' on the rights of women as a justification for challenging Islamic civilizations, and even invading specific countries (Razack, 2008), but *all* major world religions have at times had an oppressive influence on women and homosexuals.

The function of religion has been a substantive focus of sociology since its inception as an academic discipline, particularly in relation to the transformation from industrial to modern societies with the advent of capitalism, urbanization, industrialization and science. Durkheim emphasized the social cohesion provided by religion, whereas Marx argued that religion served a bourgeois ideology that legitimized class inequalities as part of 'God's plan' and Weber saw the value system of ascetic Protestantism as contributing to the successful rise of the capitalist class. What these views have in common is that they suggest that organized religion provides a system of values that served to legitimize certain social structures and relations by providing an authoritative framework of meaning that guides individual conduct. Given that all the major global religions – Christianity, Islam, Judaism, Hinduism, Sikhism, Buddhism – have plenty to say about the proper roles of men, women and sexuality, it is important to question the ideological purpose of religious pronouncements on and beliefs about sexuality and gender.

In pre-Victorian western Christianity, women were often characterized as sinful. Drawing upon biblical accounts of original sin, women were cast as lustful and dangerous temptresses (Karras, 1996). This thinking is captured in a statement from two fifteenth-century Dominican friars who actively engaged in the persecution of those, mostly women, deemed to be witches: 'All witchcraft comes from carnal lust, which is in women insatiable' (Sprenger and Kramer, 1486, in O'Faolain and Martines, 1974: 221). Lust, of course was one of the seven deadly sins and thus antithetical to a pious life – hence the emphasis on celibacy among Catholic clergy. There had, however, been a gradual movement towards sanctifying reproductive sex within marriage over the course of the Middle Ages and Renaissance (around the 900s to the 1700s), which was seen as controlling or channelling the human potential for lust (Nye, 1999). This cultural understanding shifted during the period of industrialization when the ideal of chaste, spiritual feminine purity gradually came to the fore, but continued to be defined against the 'fallen' woman, epitomized by the prostitute, creating the dialectic of Mary/ Eve, or Madonna/whore. As we have seen, first wave feminists did not usually challenge the contemporary religious conception of femininity as passive, spiritual and asexual, but rather turned it to their own ends, as in campaigns around prostitution (Banks, 1990 and see Ch. 1.2). Second wave feminists were much more critical, arguing that religious beliefs converged with patriarchal ideology and thus were a significant source of women's oppression (Daly, 1970). At the time, most religions around the world, and certainly most western forms of Christianity, defined women as subordinate to men in their doctrines, and this was reflected in both their institutionalization of marriage and their internal organization and hierarchies, with many excluding women from positions of authority.

Furthermore, social historians have shown how Christian injunctions against homosexuality have varied in enforcement over time, again suggesting that religious doctrines are historically and culturally specific. For example, in his study on Christianity and homosexuality, John Boswell (1980, 1992) describes how ancient civilizations and early Christianity viewed sexuality as a natural human quality expressed through the impulse to physical lust. He argues that many ancient societies were untroubled by any form of sexual behaviour as long as it did not undermine personal responsibilities to family or state or threaten normal social arrangements. However, a reformed Christian attitude began to emerge around 400 CE, wherein sex could be tolerated only within marriage, for procreative purposes, accompanied by an increasing concern with non-reproductive sex, particularly 'sodomy' – or homosexuality, as we would understand it today. The emphasis was now on the subjugation of lust by the individual as necessary for a pure spiritual soul. This dualist conception of the body and soul developed over subsequent centuries and came to dominate intellectual frameworks, characterizing human action as a constant battle between the physical impulses of the body – such as lust – and the will imposed by the rational and spiritual mind or soul. This framework combines an essentialist, pre-social and primarily God-given view of the mind or soul with a naturalist view of the sexual drive, but, of course, it leaves the two in potentially perpetual conflict. It does, however, link the choice of moral behaviour with the mind – which paves the way for the subsequent scientific focus on 'immoral' or 'abnormal' behaviour as located within the psychology of the individual.

During the twentieth century, the influence of religious ideas gradually lessened through secularization: the decline of faith-based or mystical foundations for the organization of society and human conduct. The advent of scientific explanations of human nature, bodies and behaviours, which developed from the nineteenth century onwards, certainly had an impact in loosening religion's ideological hold. At the same time, fewer and fewer people in western societies attended church regularly, thus weakening the link between religious teachings and gendered and sexual behaviour. Nonetheless, because religious doctrines had provided the basis for sexual and moral codes for centuries, even with the declining power of religious institutions this inheritance continues to influence many aspects of culture, including legal rationales for regulation, the values underpinning sex education in schools, commonsense ideas about gendered and sexual conduct and, perhaps most enduringly, our understanding of an inner spiritual and moral self. While we may not believe in religious doctrines as much as in previous times, much of the current social ordering of gender and sexuality derives from religion. The prospect of gay marriage, for example, is controversial precisely because marriage was originally a religious rite, sanctioning a union between a man and woman, and this was the basis of secular legislation that superseded religious laws. Although religious groups have tried to move with the times and re-examine their attitudes to sexual morality, divorce, abortion, and so on – in part to stem declining memberships – conservative views on these matters persist within most strands of Christianity, Judaism and Islam.

Your World: Do you see any continuing influence of religion on sexuality in your culture? Think about issues such as sex education, abortion rights and the rights of sexual minorities.

6.3   The Advent of Scientific Essentialism

Biological rationalizations of human sexual activity are widespread throughout our culture and they form a significant, perhaps dominant, component of essentialist ideas around gender and sexuality. Biological explanations are regarded as self-evident and underpin most legal, cultural, medical and commonsense understandings of sexuality and gender differences. Indeed, sociologists such as Raewyn Connell and Gary Dowsett (1992) argue that science gradually came to challenge and displace religion as the dominant framework of explanation from the late nineteenth century. However, both sets of explanations are essentialist or nativist. As with religion, then, we should consider the role that scientific explanations serve in society, whether they are biological or psychological.

Sexology is the name given to the scientific study of sexuality and gender that developed as a discipline around the late nineteenth century [2]. The main assumption was that, as is the case with other animals, our sexual organs are primarily there for reproduction, and this view was given legitimacy after the ideas of Charles Darwin became widespread. Evolutionary theories replaced God's 'creation' with a process of 'natural selection', and thus positioned sexual reproduction at the centre of human development. At first regarded as heretical, Darwin's study on *The Origin of Species* (1859) gradually revolutionized the ways in which plant and animal life were understood, leading to the theories of evolution that are the basis of natural science to this day. Moreover, '[i]n *The Descent of Man, and Selection in Relation to Sex* (1871), Darwin extended these conclusions to humans, and further elaborated his theory of sexual selection: male characteristics (for example, strength, intelligence, virility) are evolutionarily favoured in the competition for females, who will be selected for beauty, health, and fecundity' (Rosario, 1997: 10). The idea of evolution provided a 'naturalist' reproductive blueprint that explained gender differences through 'sexual selection' and also therefore inevitably regarded non-procreative sexualities as perversions of the 'natural' process – and came to influence science more generally. Darwin's work is also an example of the expansion and institutionalization of natural science during this era – granting it a social legitimacy which benefited medicine and the emerging 'science' of sexology. Sciences are seen as part of a neutral uncovering of 'true' facts, part of the progress towards universal knowledge, which began during the eighteenth-century Enlightenment and has continued to this day (Callinicos, 1999). The premise and promise of 'science' are that its knowledge derived from value-free methods of inquiry – based primarily on neutral observation of naturally occurring facts. The problem with the application of science to the realm of the sexual is that these scientific studies developed in a historical and cultural context of increasing social concern around gender and sexuality, and are therefore influenced by these concerns, in both the terms of their inquiry and their scientific conclusions.

For example, the idea of asexual femininity was reflected in medical science, as in the gynaecologist William Acton's famous pronouncement (in a medical textbook that ran to several editions): 'Most women, happily for them, are not much troubled by sexual feelings of any kind' (Acton, 1857, in Laqueur, 1990: 196). Medieval female lusts had, it seems, vanished, defined out of existence by medical science. Autonomous sexual desire in women came to be pathologized as either a cause or a symptom of gynaecological disorder, and this sometimes, in the mid-nineteenth century, led to surgical removal of the clitoris or ovaries in an attempt to effect a 'cure'. Men did not, however, escape medical scrutiny. Male lust, increasingly reconceptualized in terms of urges or drives, continued to be seen as problematic, and the medical profession expended much energy in debating how frequently a man should allow himself to ejaculate to maintain optimal health. The manly bourgeois man was expected to 'master' his 'natural' sexual urges – often represented as a spirited horse reined in by a strong rider. Failure to do so was seen as a sign of weakness and degeneracy and the cause of all manner of physical ailments (Heath, 1982; Jackson and Scott, 1997, 2010).

In this era there were also public, religious and government concerns about population increases and concentrations due to industrialization and urbanization accompanied by a perceived decline of morality and increase in 'vice', such as prostitution and homosexuality. The prevailing morality of the time – anchored in Christian Victorian values – became the starting point for the first wave of sexological studies, which began to describe in great detail the varieties of human sexual behaviour, often with a focus on non-heterosexual, non-procreative acts, including homosexuality – often called sexual inversion. Studies such as Richard von Krafft-Ebing's *Psychopathia Sexualis* (1965 [1886]), Havelock Ellis's *Sexual Inversion* (1936 [1897]) (Volume 2 of his seven-volume *Studies in the Psychology of Sex*), along with numerous less famous works, focused both on describing and cataloguing varieties of 'abnormal' sexual behaviours, and/or on discussing how 'normal' sexual relations between men and women were driven by the biological urge to procreate. Whilst many of these writers regarded themselves as reformers, their work was based on pre-existing cultural assumptions around 'natural' gendered sexual behaviour, taking for granted the existing versions of femininity and masculinity as 'natural' and then defining other behaviours as perversions in relation to this norm:

> Krafft-Ebing premised his initial theory of sexual pathology on a comparatively small number of generally severe cases, such as lust murder and necrophilia, often derived from criminal proceedings. New categories of perversion were created and underpinned more or less by systematically collecting and publishing new case histories. . . . Although he also paid attention to voyeurism, exhibitionism, pedophilia, gerontophilia, bestiality, necrophilia, urolagnia, coprolagnia, and other sexual behaviours, Krafft-Ebing distinguished four main perversions: sadism, masochism, fetishism, and contrary sexual feeling (or inversion). (Oosterhuis, 1997: 72)

The dualist split between the body and soul evident in religious essentialism also became the framework within which the science of the mind – psychology – developed. Psychological pathologies or disorders therefore became the way to explain 'immoral' behaviour

– or the lack of control over impulses to 'base' lustful behaviours. However, the 'scientific' methods of inquiry in sexological research were haphazard and often based on anecdotal testimonies, medical records of 'pathological' cases and court records (accounts from other professionals who had already made a value judgement on the behaviour), and very seldom on systematic studies. Conclusions about the psychology of individuals were therefore based on very slim evidence – indeed, psychology itself was in its infancy as a science, based at this time on theories and inferences rather than data. Nonetheless, psychological rationalizations became widespread in the developing field of sexology as explanations for 'deviant' sexual behaviours, including heterosexual women's lust *and* their unresponsiveness to sex, children's interest in masturbation, and homosexual inclinations amongst both men and women. When used in studies of 'perversions' such as *Psychopathia Sexualis*, psychological theories facilitated explanations of such 'abnormalities' as 'pathological' conditions – mental disorders.

Even when medical or physiological evidence was brought into play, such as developing scientific studies of glands and secretions, the conclusions drawn from such work simply reinforced pre-existing assumptions about male and female differences. For example, the discovery of ovarian hormones in the early twentieth century led to the conclusion that women were so susceptible to these substances that their mental states were dependent on them (Weeks, 1989: 147), simply reflecting and confirming widely held beliefs about women's inferior mental capacities. What this tells us is that sexology began and developed in a climate where cultural definitions of the 'norm' and the 'deviant' already existed. This is not to say that the researchers themselves were necessarily 'patriarchal' or 'homophobic', but rather that the basic concepts with which they began already reflected contemporary cultural ideas of appropriate gendered and sexual behaviour and, moreover, were heavily based on the Darwinian and Christian idea that the 'sexual instinct' was primarily designed for reproduction and the survival of the species.

6.4 Essentialism and Bourgeois Victorian Culture

Perhaps the greatest impact of sexological 'science' is also its greatest flaw: its claim to have created a new scientific body of knowledge around sexuality and gender actually reproduced and legitimized existing patriarchal ideologies. In cataloguing and describing variations of human sexual behaviour, early sexologists drew upon their existing moral culture. Scientific theories that reduced gender and sexuality to the instinct for biological reproduction served only to confirm existing social understandings of gender and sexuality. Importing newly developed psychological theories to explain the link or, more often, the mismatch between biological function and actual behaviour added to the sexological mix of 'science' but rested on untested theories and actually continued the Christian emphasis on the mind as the ultimate arbiter of moral or 'normal' behaviour. Science may have gradually come to replace religion as a dominant cultural framework, but simply reproduced and elaborated upon essentialist patriarchal ideas.

Thus, there was continuity between religious essentialism and the emergent scientific emphasis on reproduction and psychology. In combination with the cultural morality inherited from religion, it is also important to note that science was patronized by the bourgeoisie, particularly through their funding of learned societies and universities, so that the authority and legitimacy of science and its practitioners became entwined with the growing pre-eminence of the capital-owning class, and thus made dominant intellectual culture a thoroughly bourgeois culture. Marx suggested that the dominant culture serves the needs of the dominant class. It can be argued therefore that scientific essentialism is part of the dominant culture, which in turn serves the interests of the capitalist class, which itself is patriarchal. The aim of social control thus became the 'definition of acceptable sexual behaviour within the context of changing class and power relations' (Weeks, 1989: 23), and central to this definition was the consolidation of the domestic ideology within the dominant bourgeois class, justified by *both* emerging sciences and reformed religious doctrines (see Ch. 3.2). Essentialist and moral constructions of masculinity and femininity were thus mobilized within the family ideal to reinforce heterosexual relations as moral and natural. The corollary of the privilege of heterosexuality is the stigmatization of non-heterosexual identities, manifested in many sexological studies and in the cultural and legal regulation of homosexuality. It was also evident in psychoanalysis.

6.5   From Sexology to Psychology: Freud and Psychoanalysis in the Twentieth Century

Freud's psychoanalytic approach to psychology followed on the heels of Kraft-Ebing's *Psychopathia Sexualis* and Ellis's *Studies in the Psychology of Sex*, with his *Three Essays on the Theory of Sexuality* (1995a [1905]), followed by numerous other essays in which he elaborated upon and modified his theories. His ideas became the basis of clinical intervention and therapy, therefore becoming a respectable way of *treating* perceived sexual disorders, including homosexuality. Again, it was the cultural climate that shaped Freudian ideas; these have, in turn, filtered into popular culture with the widespread use of such terms as sexual drives, the unconscious, repression and penis envy. As Connell argues, '[B]y the 1920s Freud's ideas had spread far beyond their original technical audience and had become a cultural force. It was clear that, whether right or wrong, Freud had put his finger on problems which were both troubling and important for modern Western societies. He laid bare, we might say, key crisis tendencies in the structure of emotional relationships' (2002: 120).

Freud insisted that the sexuality with which we are born is polymorphously perverse: neither masculine nor feminine and not intrinsically directed to any particular object or centred on any particular part of the body. Freud did not regard homosexuality as an illness, mental or physical. He *did* regard the moulding of sexuality into genitally focused heterosexuality as repressive and potentially damaging to psychic life. In these senses, Freud's arguments were revolutionary in that he posited a continuum between 'perverse' and 'normal' behaviour, which challenged prevailing scientific psychological/biological essentialism and the moral norms of the late Victorian age (Gay, 1995). However, as Stephen Heath says: 'The genuine originality of Freud's [work] should not hide the fact that his work is in many respects part of a whole context of investigation of the sexual and movement towards the conception of sexuality' (1982: 53). Heath locates Freud as part and parcel of the advent of scientific essentialism.

Although Freud suggests that we move from an infantile state of 'polymorphous perversity' into a heterosexual gendered and sexual identity, his theory is premised on the consequences of the 'anatomical distinction between the sexes' (Freud, 1995b [1925]) and, moreover, on a conflation of gender and sexuality. According to Freud, infants of both sexes are primarily oriented towards their mother as primary love object until they become aware, simultaneously, of the anatomical difference between the sexes and the power of the father. A little boy, noticing that girls 'lack' a penis, fears castration as punishment for his attachment to his mother. He thus represses his desire for his mother and identifies with the powerful father (his 'rival' for the mother's affection) but will remain attracted to women. A girl, meanwhile, 'realizing' that she 'lacks' a penis, blames her mother for this fate and turns her desire towards her father. It is as a result of this that the paths of boys and girls diverge – and, in desiring the 'other' sex, establish their own sexed (gendered) identity. As with biological sexology, the idea that anatomy distinguishes men from women is used to contain the social concepts of masculinity and femininity. But Freud goes further, equating masculinity and femininity with orientation towards the opposite sex/gender. Sexuality is reduced to gender, as gender is reduced ultimately to anatomical sex: '[T]he strongest force working against a permanent inversion of the sexual object is the attraction which the opposing sexual characters exercise upon one another' (Freud, quoted in Gay, 1995: 292). In assuming an inevitable connection between anatomical sex, gender and sexual attraction to the opposite sex, Freud is profoundly essentialist. This undermines the radical potential of his claims about an innate polymorphous sexuality. Freud also assumes, in common with early sexologists, that there is some innate or pre-social physical source of sexual desire – without establishing any scientific basis for this assumption.

6.6 The Persistence of Scientific Essentialism into the Twenty-First Century

Scientific essentialism remains a ubiquitous feature of contemporary culture and continues to give rise to 'research' purporting to demonstrate 'natural' differences between men and women – whether these are based on hormones, brains, genes or the supposed conduct of our evolutionary ancestors. Indeed, the power and legitimacy of science have increased so that it has now become almost like a religion: people may believe in its capacity to explain the world even if they have minimal scientific knowledge themselves. Thus it is not uncommon, for example, to hear someone with no understanding of genetics confidently claiming that homosexuality or the differences between men and women are 'in our genes'.

At present the most pervasive and influential form of biological determinism and the broadest in scope is evolutionary psychology, which developed from an earlier perspective known as socio-biology. These perspectives are based on Darwin's theory of evolution and have perpetuated his biases about gender relations into the twenty-first century – and extended them far more than Darwin himself ever did to human social relationships. Accounts of physical evolution

– how we developed opposable thumbs, large brains and the ability to walk upright – are based on reconstructions from fossil records. Evolutionary psychology, on the other hand, reconstructs our behavioural past without any such direct evidence. Rather, it bases 'scientific' claims on observations about current sexual practices and preferences, speculates about how they might have evolved and then claims that they are part of our evolutionary heritage and thus fixed in 'human nature'.

Evolutionary psychology is almost exclusively focused on sexual selection as opposed to natural selection more broadly. Thus gender and sexuality are not only presented as natural facts, but they occupy centre stage as the motor of evolution and the basis of all human conduct – which is reduced to the heterosexual, reproductive imperative to pass on our genes to the next generation. For evolutionary psychologists, all animal and human life is seen as a competitive race to reproduce and pass on genes to the next generation. They reason that any human traits identifiable today must be inherited from our pre-historic past, and that to have survived into the modern gene pool they must have been 'adaptive' in terms of maximizing past opportunities to produce offspring – a genetic inheritance that is seen as continuing to motivate sexual (and wider social) behaviour. They argue that men and women have different investments in reproduction because women must spend a long time gestating and feeding offspring while men can potentially impregnate many women. Thus men are motivated by the desire to spread their sperm as widely as possible, while women seek a long-term mate to protect them and their infants (see, for example, Dawkins, 1996 [1976]; Diamond, 1997). This is said to explain, for example, men's sexual infidelity, their attraction to very young women and the propensity to rape, and thus confirms widely held beliefs in the naturalness of gender divisions and current heterosexual relations (Jackson and Rees, 2007; McCaughey, 2008).

Evolutionary psychologists often directly contest sociological and feminist accounts of the social construction of gender and sexuality. One infamous example is Randy Thornhill and Craig Palmer's (2000) analysis of rape, which sees rape as common across many species and the inevitable outcome of the male competition to impregnate as many women as possible. They dismiss feminist and sociological accounts of rape (which see it as an outcome of social inequality between women and men) as failing to understand the powerful, innate sexual motivations underlying it. Thornhill and Palmer are not justifying rape; rather they see their work as providing an objective explanation of men's behaviour, which can offer better strategies for combating rape than what they view as the 'misguided' politically motivated accounts of feminists and sociologists.

Not surprisingly, many feminists have been critical of this perspective and have pointed out the methodological flaws in its reasoning (its reconstruction of the past from the point of view of the present) and its evident biases. They have also raised concerns about its wider cultural influence, which is evident in many aspects of popular culture, from television programmes about human and animal sexuality and reproduction to self-help books (see, for example, Jackson and Rees, 2007; McCaughey, 2008). These popular versions of evolutionary psychology can serve as rationalizations and justifications of certain aspects of male sexual conduct and are particularly evident in media aimed at male audiences (though they also appear in self-help books for women). McCaughey provides numerous examples. For instance, readers of *Men's Health* were told that men of all ages prefer 'young girls' because 'we were designed to get them pregnant and dominate their fertile years by keeping them that way', and tells them that once a man's 'first wife has lost the overt signals of reproductive viability' he will look for someone younger who 'still has them all' (quoted in McCaughey, 2008: 4). Popular self-help books offer similar accounts, though some advise men to control their primeval instincts, such as Jeff Hood's *The Silverback Gorilla Syndrome* (1999), which encourages men to get in touch with their 'inner gorilla', or 'Big G', who approaches every social situation with one of two questions: 'Fuck it?' or 'Kill it'? (in McCaughey, 2008: 79). McCaughey suggests that these popular versions of what she calls the 'caveman mystique' have a particular appeal to men in the context of the increasing erosion of traditional bases of male power and offer them explanations that resonate with how they see themselves.

7

Critical Perspectives on Knowledge

7.1 'Biology as Ideology': The Problem with 'Natural' Science

When scientists began to question the divine basis of social order and replaced faith with empirical knowledge, what they saw was that women were very different from men, in that they had wombs and menstruated. Such anatomical differences destined them for an entirely different social life from men.

(Lorber, 2008: 8)

The point that Lorber is making here is that the advent of scientific methods of inquiry became the basis for determining or justifying the *social* position of women. Lorber is therefore challenging the commonsense cultural perception that science is merely describing the natural differences of gender, or that 'biology is destiny'. As Beauvoir argued in her claim that 'one is not born a woman' (see Ch. 1.1), so feminist critics of scientific essentialism have directed our attention to the *causal* role that science has played in our culture in creating and sustaining the social divisions of gender and sexuality.

This critique has many different variants, challenging diverse forms of biological determinism such as those based on hormonal, brain or genetic differences, socio-biology and evolutionary psychology, but an overriding theme is that the methodologies and conclusions of such studies are fundamentally flawed – as we saw in the discussion of evolutionary psychology in the previous chapter. Whilst science equates biological sex with gender, sociologists ask us to consider that gender is socially and culturally produced and that socio-cultural gender affects how biological sex is understood and represented, rather than accepting 'sex' as an eternal, pre-given fact that determines gender and sexuality [3].

While the acceptance of 'natural' sexual divisions is central to biological explanations of gender and sexuality, historical analyses have demonstrated that the idea of two distinct sexes is a relatively recent one: a pre-Enlightenment understanding in most western cultures was of one sex which had variations along its scale, from masculinity at one end to femininity at the other, with many variations along the way (Lacqueur, 1990; Hird, 2004: 18). How scientists view human biology, then, is a product of the cultural climate in which they work. Thus they translate social identities and cultural values into eternal, biological facts. This is illustrated by the medical interventions practised to assign gender to intersexed people – those whose bodies do not fit neatly into a two-sex model. Many intersexed people are operated on, often as infants, to 'correct' their anatomy to fit into one of the two 'sexes' (Fausto-Sterling, 2000), legitimized through a psychological discourse that claims a core gender identity is a natural, internal 'fact' (Hird, 2004: 133). However, feminists have argued that such practices are not informed by conclusive scientific evidence but rather that *a prior assumption of gender is used to interpret 'biological' evidence*. Decisions about sex/gender assignment in intersexed infants are not made on the basis of physiological characteristics but on the basis of what is medically possible, thus physicians and surgeons literally 'construct' sex based on their assumptions of the meaning of gender (Kessler, 1998).

It is not only sex/gender difference that is pre-judged through the existing essentialist cultural framework; recent studies have also sought to explain sexual identities in this way, for example through the idea of 'gay brains'. Beginning in the early 1990s, there was widespread media and popular interest in a study conducted by Simon LeVay on the hypothalamus region of the brain, in which he concluded that one out of the four anterior regions of the hypothalamus was smaller in gay men than in straight men – in fact, gay men's brains showed similarities to those of women (LeVay, 1993). Despite its small scale (nineteen 'gay' brains, sixteen 'straight male', six 'female'), the impact of this study was widespread. Media claims that this (gay) scientist had found a potential cause for homosexuality were welcomed both by those opposed to homosexuality (since a potential cure might be found) and homosexuals themselves, who used the 'natural' cause to argue that they were like any other natural minority and thus deserving of minority rights protection. The straight brains, however, were from men and women *presumed* to be heterosexual. This assumption of heterosexuality was based on the lack of *identification* as homosexual, either by the man or woman concerned (on their medical records), or by the medical authorities. It was simply assumed that homosexual behaviour cannot have been part of the subjects' lifestyles or experience (whereas contemporary research around HIV transmission was indicating that there were significant numbers of men who had sex with men but did not identify as gay, and indeed many of them were in sexual relationships with women). In a classically essentialist mode of thinking, LeVay conflates identity with behaviour, without knowing anything about the actual behaviour exhibited by these subjects.

Moreover, the 'gay' brains were from men who had died of AIDS-related illnesses and whose patterns of sexual behaviour were unknown, and therefore it was not possible to tell if the brain differences found were caused by HIV, AIDS or sexual behaviour, or had actually caused the assumed behaviour. The central flaw in this and similar research – on 'gay' genes, for example – is that it accepts the cultural framework of gender and sexual binaries without question, assuming that sexuality is divided rigidly by gender, eternally and exclusively focused on one gendered object or the other. Thus LeVay can make a claim that gay men have feminine brains and we can all understand what he is trying to get at or explain. But do we stop to think whether brains can be 'masculine' or 'feminine', or indeed whether sex is a relevant distinction at the level of the brain? That we do not is, perhaps, unsurprising, since essentialism is so culturally pervasive, but it is more evidence that 'the scientific community . . . picks up these cultural ideas and plays them back to us, now vested with scientific authority, as facts of nature' (Vines, 1993: 117).

Along with gender difference and sexual identities, sexual acts have also been 'explained' scientifically. In 1972, Anne Koedt published a now classic essay on 'The Myth of the Vaginal Orgasm'. She argued that sexology and medical science, heavily influenced by Freudian ideas, had promoted a version of sex that was focused exclusively on penetration of the vagina as the route to orgasm and thus had created a discourse that defined women who did not achieve orgasm through penetrative sex as 'frigid':

All this leads to some interesting questions about conventional sex and our role in it. Men have orgasms essentially by friction with the vagina not the clitoral area, which is external and not able to cause friction the way penetration does. Women have thus been defined sexually in terms of what pleases men; our own biology has not been properly analysed.

> Instead, we are fed the myth of the liberated woman and her vaginal orgasm – an orgasm that in fact does not exist. (Koedt, 1996 [1972]: 112)

Evidence from the sexual studies of William Masters and Virginia E. Johnson, which had been published in the USA in the 1960s, showed that the clitoris and not the vagina was the seat of women's orgasm, and Koedt cites anatomical studies that demonstrate the importance of the clitoris. Despite such evidence, Koedt points out that the 'myth' of the vaginal orgasm persisted, focusing thus on the influence of science, medicine and psychology, which serve the interests of 'a male society that has not sought change in women's role' (1996 [1972]: 113). Koedt is not only criticizing the dominant discourse that – without any accurate anatomical evidence – prioritizes penile penetration as the proper form of sex, but she also argues that this 'myth' has a direct effect on the actions and identities of women: '[T]he worst damage was done to the mental health of women, who either suffered silently with self-blame, or flocked to psychologists looking desperately for the hidden and terrible repression that had kept them from their vaginal destiny' (1996 [1972]: 113). In contemporary times, science continues to prioritize the penis in sexual performance through the production of drugs such as Viagra (see Ch. 11.1).

Theorists of gender have therefore illuminated scientific culture's uncritical acceptance of the essentialist ideology that legitimizes 'findings' about sexual difference. The implication is that science cannot produce neutral knowledge, precisely because its biases include accepting social categories – such as masculine, feminine, homosexual, heterosexual – as natural, biological facts and then seeks out differences to justify this categorization. It is not to say that there are no differences, but why would we look for them in the first place? What categories do we begin with, and are they natural or social? What frameworks of meaning do we use to interpret results? In the realm of gender and sexuality, biological explanations replay contemporary cultural ideologies rather than presenting neutral evidence.

7.2　Science as One of Many 'Knowledges': From Ideology to Discourse

Recent critiques of scientific accounts of sexuality have been heavily influenced by the work of Michel Foucault. Foucault identifies a contradiction between the accepted wisdom that the Victorian era was one of repression around sexuality and the historical evidence that shows a massive production of knowledge around gender and sexuality (see Ch. 6.3). He argues that medicine, psychology and the law produced discourses, or frameworks of knowledge, around gender and sexuality. According to Foucault, discourses construct their objects: rather than simply *describing* pre-existing facts and phenomena (such as the 'invert' homosexual), they bring them into being through defining and classifying them (see Ch. 2.9). He thus challenges the objectivity of science as feminist critics have done, and also argues that the way knowledge operates in society is more complex than the traditional, Marxist-inspired explanation of ideology.

Whereas the concept of ideology implies the distortion or concealment of truth in the interests of the powerful, Foucault argues that there is no truth outside discourse. Discourses produce 'regimes of truth' – they define the truth of our sexualities by virtue of the legitimacy and authority accorded to expert knowledge. Knowledge thereby becomes inextricably bound up with power – thus often written as power/knowledge. This power to name, classify and thus regulate is highly effective precisely because it works not through repression but through *producing* sexuality and defining and categorizing its normative and perverse forms. Since there is no 'truth' that ideology mystifies, the regulation of sexuality cannot be reduced to an ideological effect of bourgeois capitalism. What is radical and insightful about Foucault's ideas is that he identifies the discourses through which sexology gradually shifts our attention away from the moral regulation of sexual behaviour (deemed to be motivated by sinful impulses) to the construction of human 'types' or categories. Where previously sodomy had been considered a sinful and criminal act, the science of sex created homosexuality as a pathological condition of particular types of people: 'The sodomite had been a temporary aberration; the homosexual was now a species' (Foucault, 1981: 43).

Foucault also connects this focus on sex and the emergence of sexological 'types' to a longer tradition of social control of thoughts and desires through the church: he argues that from the Reformation onwards the Catholic Church had shifted its focus from the immoral or sinful acts committed by individuals, towards their immoral or sinful thoughts, thus laying the groundwork for western conceptualizations of the mind/body duality, which we have already suggested provided the basis for psychological premises (see Ch. 6.2). There was an incitement by the church 'to transform your desire, your every desire, into discourse' (Foucault, 1980: 12). Foucault therefore suggests a radical reconceptualization of power as *producing* particular kinds of sexual identity – through religious, medical and psychological claims to knowledge about these 'types' – rather than power as simply regulating 'natural' forms of sexuality.

TASK: Evolutionary psychology as discourse.

Consider the following BBC news report from 2006 on the findings of evolutionary psychologists:

> Researchers from Germany found that four years into a relationship, less than half of 30-year-old women wanted regular sex. Conversely, the team found a man's libido remained the same regardless of how long he had been in a relationship. Writing in the journal *Human Nature*, the scientists said the differences resulted from how humans had evolved. Dr Dietrich Klusmann, lead author of the study and a psychologist from Hamburg-Eppendorf University Hospital, . . . said: 'For men, a good reason [for] their sexual motivation to remain constant would be to guard against being cuckolded by another male.' But women, he said, have evolved to have a high sex drive when they are initially in a relationship in order to form a 'pair bond' with their partner. But, once this bond is sealed a woman's sexual appetite declines, he added. He said animal behaviour studies suggest this could be because females may be diverting their sexual interest towards other men, in order to secure the best combinations of genetic material for their offspring. Or, he said, this could be because limiting sex may boost their partner's interest in it. ('Security "Bad News for Sex Drive"', BBC News online, 14 August 2006, *http://news.bbc.co.uk/2/hi/health/4790313.stm*)

What do you notice about the knowledge being constructed here?
What identities are being discursively constructed?
What discursive strategies are used to make it seem authoritative?
How is it constructing a 'regime of truth'?

7.3   The Challenge of the 'Cultural Turn' in Social Theory

Foucault is one of the theorists associated with the theoretical tendencies known as poststructuralism and postmodernism, which became increasingly influential from the 1980s in the context of the 'cultural turn' in feminist and wider social theory (see Ch. 4.6). Although culture has featured in sociological theory from the founding fathers onwards, there was often a reduction of the cultural to the structural, as in the Marxist conceptualization of ideology. As Bryan Turner puts it: 'The weakness of traditional sociology has been its inability adequately to analyse culture. Postmodernism as a style of analysis can be seen as an attempt to provide an analysis of culture in late capitalism' (1993: 74).

Postmodernism in this sense is to be distinguished from the idea of *postmodernity* – a characterization of the era in which we live today. The postmodern era is seen as one in which new technologies and new working practices have radically altered the relations between classes so that social divisions are now based around the sphere of consumption rather than production (see Introduction to Part III and Ch. 8.6). The overall picture is of a more fragmented, fluid and diverse society. Postmodernism as a theory is concerned less with how the world *is* than how we know about it. The term 'postmodernism' is often used interchangeably with poststructuralism – and different writers will use either one of these terms to refer to the same body of theory. The structuralism to which this theory is 'post' is a body of ideas about the structures underlying human language and culture, which were seen as shaping human thought and action. It can also be seen as being 'post' structural sociology, such as Marxism. The 'modernism' to which this body of theory is 'post', and from which it distances itself, is usually defined in terms of the philosophical, scientific and social thought that emerged from the eighteenth-century period known as the Enlightenment. Postmodernism challenges ideas about language, truth and the self derived from this period – a time when there was an increasing confidence in the rational pursuit of objective knowledge. The basic tenets of postmodernism can thus be outlined as follows (see Jackson, 2010a [1997]):

- Language does not simply *transmit* thoughts or meaning; rather thought and meaning are *constructed through* language, and there can be no meaning outside language. Meaning is also *relational*: a word means something only in relation to other words. Hence categories such as 'women' or 'homosexual' only have meaning in relation to other terms – 'men' or 'heterosexual'. Meaning also shifts over time and from one context to another, and is also a product of wider linguistic processes – discourses in Foucault's terms – so no meaning is ever fixed.
- There is no essential self that exists outside language and culture. Our identities are products of the ways in which we are positioned by language and discourse, as in Foucault's account of the

homosexual. Subjectivity is also fluid and fragmented – there is no inner essential core self capable of rationally 'knowing' the world.
- There is no possibility of objective 'truth' – as we have seen with Foucault, knowledge is discursively produced from particular social locations. Knowledges and discourses, and the language through which they are constituted, can be deconstructed – taken apart – so as to reveal that they are not universal truths but constructions. There is, therefore, a rejection of grand theoretical 'metanarratives', like Marxism, which claim to explain the world (Lyotard, 1984). Postmodernists see any perspective that posits the existence of social groups (such as women) or structures (such as patriarchy) existing independently of our understandings of them as essentialist and foundationalist.

While these ideas posed a major challenge to earlier sociological, feminist and gay critiques of the social ordering of gender and sexuality, it is evident that cultural aspects of gender and sexuality were already being consistently addressed before the cultural turn and a questioning of language, truth and essentialist notions of self and identity pre-dated advent of postmodernism (see section 1 of this chapter and Ch. 2 throughout). Indeed it could be argued that sociology and especially feminism contributed to the theoretical development of postmodern analysis (Flax, 1990) – and it is certainly the case that critiques of essentialism are not exclusively a product of postmodern theory. Nonetheless, postmodernist theory has become an important strand within gender and sexuality studies, for two reasons. First, critiques of essentialist constructions of gender and sexuality have drawn upon postmodernist analyses of knowledge as historically and culturally specific, in particular on Foucault's work. Second, postmodernists have disputed some of the theories, concepts and methodologies characteristic of second wave feminist and gay studies. In this sense, postmodernist theory has been turned on feminism and gay theory as dominant knowledges. We discuss these challenges below in relation to 'queer theory', which drew upon Foucault's analysis of the cultural provenance of sexual categories.

Not all critiques of second wave feminism and gay liberation theory derive from postmodernism. There are other questions being raised about the limitations of earlier perspectives, which we will also consider later in the chapter: the question of gendered and sexual embodiment and the ways in which feminist and gay knowledge claims have been produced from white, western perspectives, excluding those of other ethnicities and nationalities. Where postmodernism has made a major impact is in the development of queer theory.

7.4   Queer Theory: Deconstructing Identity

Queer theory emerged in the late 1980s and constituted a radical reorientation of earlier lesbian and gay scholarship. Queer theorists draw on Foucault to explore the potential for the transgression and subversion of dominant discourses. This is made possible by Foucault's ideas on the generative or *productive* operation of power: 'Discourse transmits and produces power; it reinforces it, but also undermines and exposes it, rendering it fragile and makes it possible to thwart it' (Foucault, 1980: 101). Not only is this radically anti-essentialist but it represents a potentially transformative idea of power: we may turn the tables, so to speak, reversing the effects of power. Gay liberation was an example of resistance through which the 'deviant' social identity – 'homosexual' – is appropriated as an alternative, oppositional 'truth' of identity – 'gay is good'. As Bristow puts it: 'The very discourse which sought to produce a regulative order managed to empower those it sought to subjugate. In other words, sexological categories could cut either way, depending on who was deploying them' (1997: 178).

This resistance through a 'reverse discourse' (turning the tables) is, however, limited because it was achieved, in Foucauldian terms, within the same discourse that generated the sexological type 'the homosexual'. Queer theory, in keeping with its postmodern roots, brings into question *any* essentialized identity – including such identities as lesbian and gay. There is, therefore, no such thing as an 'authentic' identity. As David Halperin puts it: 'Those who knowingly occupy . . . a marginal location, who assume a de-essentialized identity that is purely positional in character, are properly speaking not gay but *queer*' (1995: 62, emphasis in the original). Rather than affirming oppositional identities such as 'gay', queer theorists seek to interrogate the binary oppositions of gay/straight or male/female through which identities are discursively constituted. In particular they seek to trouble the privileged and normative status of heterosexuality, or what has come to be called heteronormativity. We can think of queer analysis as focusing on what Diana Fuss describes as the dynamic of the norm and the other, or how normative forms of identity achieve their disciplinary dominance by both containing and externalizing ambiguity through an 'inside/out' process:

'[H]eterosexuality secures its self-identity and shores up its ontological boundaries by protecting itself from what it sees as the continual
predatory encroachments of its contaminated other, homosexuality'
(Fuss 1991: 2).

One of the foundational texts of queer theory is Judith Butler's
Gender Trouble (1990a). Butler is best known for contesting the
ontological basis of sex/gender categories, arguing that it is the heterosexual matrix that serves to instate these categories as exclusive,
natural and interdependent. She uses the example of 'drag' to argue
that gender is constructed through repeated performance and to
develop the concept of performativity.

> Drag constitutes the mundane ways in which genders are appropriated,
> theatricalized, worn, and done; it implies that all gendering is a kind
> of impersonation and approximation. If this is true, it seems, there is
> no original or primary gender that drag imitates, but *gender is a kind of
> imitation for which there is no original;* in fact, it is a kind of imitation that
> produces the very notion of the original as an *effect* and consequence of
> the imitation itself. . . . In this sense, the 'reality' of heterosexual identi-
> ties is performatively constituted through an imitation that sets itself
> up as the origin and the ground of all imitations. (Butler, 1993a: 313,
> emphasis in the original)

Butler envisages the possibility of resistance to the normative performance of gender in terms of the Foucauldian insight that discourses
contain within them the potential for destabilization. However, she
extends this argument by pointing out that 'heterosexuality is always
in the process of imitating and approximating its own phantasmatic
idealization of itself – and *failing*' (1993a: 313, emphasis in the
original). Precisely because heterosexuality's discursive constitution
depends on the constant enactment of its gendered identities, these
'perfomances' are constantly being replayed over and over, becoming 'performative' in that they are reiterating gender norms, but
often they will fail to live up to perfect copies of the ideal, and it is in
these failures that resistance becomes possible – choosing to be gay,
for example. Furthermore, these resistances reveal that there is no
original gender from which homosexuals deviate, but rather that the
heterosexual matrix itself is a 'regulatory fiction'.

Queer theory, then, presents a challenge to the foundational categories of second wave feminist and gay theory – 'women', 'lesbian'
and 'gay' – since these categories derive from the binary divides
constituted through heteronormative discourse (even though they
have served as the political basis for many of the advances made

by women, lesbians and gays). From a sociological perspective this radical rejection of identity categories can be problematic. Some sociologists are critical of queer theory's inability to account for the evident social structural foundations of gender and sexuality and the lack of attention to the ways in which identity categories give meaning to everyday practices and experiences. Materialist feminists in particular have provided consistent critiques of the dangers of a queer analytics that is divorced from understandings of patriarchy and capitalism as social systems that anchor discursive regimes (Hennessy, 2000; Jackson, 2001). Moreover, while the focus on deconstructing and resisting cultural knowledge has produced a wealth of research in the academy, particularly in North America, Britain and Australia, the subversion of heteronormativity outside these academic debates seems a long way off. Take for example, our introductory discussion of the television programme *Queer Eye for the Straight Guy* (see Introduction to Part III). The identities of its hosts and public participants are absolutely essentialist versions of both homosexuality (with the various 'types' of gay men there to provide 'gay' skills usually associated with femininity, such as grooming and cooking) and heterosexuality (the independent women still require heterosexual coupling for personal fulfilment). Despite the attractions of the theoretical explorations of identity and resistance, it is difficult to see how we have moved beyond either identity categories or the politics of liberation in our not so queer world.

TASK: Queer culture – when do you do drag?

Discuss amongst your group whether any of you have done drag: dressed up as your opposite gender.

Discuss the images and clothes used and what environment this was done in.

Did it challenge heteronormativity in the way that Butler describes in her account of performativity?

How common are such 'queer' challenges in your everyday experience?

7.5   Embodied Sociology

Sociological conceptualizations of gender and sexuality have, for the most part, rejected any biologically based arguments in favour of the social structural and cultural bases of gender differences and inequalities. More recently, there has been a resurgence of interest in how the body figures in theories of gender and sexuality, challenging both the radical deconstructionism of postmodernist theories such as queer, and the wider absence of the body from the sociology of gender and sexuality. Butler (1993b) is one queer theorist who has responded to the first challenge, and she attempts to think through the question of whether her influential theory of discursive performativity ignores the reality of 'sex' or 'the body' (see section 7.4 above). Butler does not see the body as intelligible without the cultural construction of gender. In *Gender Trouble* she had claimed that bodies 'cannot be said to have a signifiable existence prior to the mark of their gender' (Butler, 1990a: 8). In *Bodies That Matter* she defends and further develops her position. The body cannot, she argues, simply be regarded as pre-existing physical matter; rather, sexed bodies are materialized, brought into being as intelligible and 'real', through the operation of regulatory power.

> What I would propose in place of these conceptions of construction is a return to the notion of matter, not as site or surface, but as a process of materialization that stabilizes over time to produce the effect of boundary, fixity, and surface we call matter. That matter is always materialized has, I think, to be thought in relation to the productive and, indeed, materializing effects of regulatory power in the Foucauldian sense. Thus, the question is no longer, How is gender constituted as and through a certain interpretation of sex? (a question that leaves the 'matter' of sex untheorized), but rather, through what regulatory norms is sex itself materialized? And how is it that treating the materiality of sex as a given presupposes and consolidates the normative conditions of its own emergence? (Butler, 1993b: 9–10)

Some feminists contest this move away from any residual sense of the physical, suggesting that there is indeed a realm of embodied experience that is lost through many social constructionist approaches to gender and sexuality (Bordo, 1993, 1998) and that there remain 'material bases of our bodily selves . . . that complex of matter that constitutes our sensuous, cultural, kinetic and physical place in the world' (Rothfield, 1996: 33). Iris Marion Young (1994) argues that gendered bodies are constituted through vectors of *action* and meaning – that doing gender is irreducible to being gendered – while others have argued that gendered bodily experiences are mediated through meanings deriving from interaction with others in specific socio-cultural settings (Jackson and Scott, 2007) (see also Part IV). These feminists deny neither the physical materiality of bodies, nor the cultural processes through which bodies are made meaningful, and they continue to locate embodied experience and practice within the social.

By contrast there is another tradition within feminist theory that valorizes women's embodied specificity. Luce Irigaray (1985), for example, sees western knowledge and culture as 'phallogocentric', symbolically privileging all that is masculine and defining women only in relation to men as 'the other of the same' and suppressing women's radical alterity (otherness), which she locates in the female body, in its complex and diffuse capacities for sexual pleasure. There are other 'corporeal feminists' who privilege the body. Elizabeth Grosz, for example, argues against the use of the term 'gender'. Drawing on Foucault, she defines 'sex' as referring 'to the domain of sexual difference, to questions of the *morphologies of bodies*' (her emphasis) as distinct from sexuality: erotic desires, pleasures and practices. She maintains that the term 'gender' is redundant because everything it designates is 'covered by the integration of and sometimes the discord between sexuality and sex' (1995: 213). Grosz's line of argument risks conflating social differences between women and men with bodily difference. This, as Anne Witz points out, bequeaths us an impoverished concept of sexual difference from which the social disappears (Witz, 2000: 8). The challenge for feminist thought today is to retain a grasp of both embodied experience and the ways in which it is always mediated through society and culture.

7.6   Differences of Race: Intersectionality Theory and the Critique of White Feminist Knowledge

Many have argued that differences of race and class were ignored in both conceptualizations of gender and theories of gender inequalities developed in second wave feminism and early gay studies. There was some recognition of gender as differentiated by race in early second wave engagements with black liberation politics and activism, identifying the 'double jeopardy' of being black and female (Beal, 1970) and arguing for theory that could account for systems of racism, sexism and capitalism (Combahee River Collective, 1983 [1977]). It was not until the 1980s and 1990s, however, that a critical mass of writings on this issue accumulated and began to influence academic feminism (see Chs 3.7 and 5.4). The African-American theorist Patricia Hill Collins has made a major contribution to the development of intersectional analysis as a theoretical and methodological framework. In *Black Feminist Thought* (2000) Collins challenges the exclusions of white feminism and presents an alternative perspective on feminist politics and knowledge. She argues for an intersectional paradigm as the only way fully to understand the qualitatively different experiences of being gendered that are constituted through the complexities of American black women's experiences. In the second edition of her book, she reflects on the development of intersectional perspectives in the decade since the first edition, observing that by 'rejecting additive models of oppression, race, class and gender studies have progressed considerably since the 1980s. During that decade, African-American scholar-activists, among others, called for a new approach to analyzing Black women's experiences. . . . Intersectional paradigms remind us that oppression cannot be reduced to one fundamental type, and that oppressions work together in producing injustice . . .' (2000: 18).

An important aspect of intersectional theory and methodology is its rejection of dominant knowledge, whether from mainstream white, patriarchal society, or from white feminism. The *standpoint* perspective has been identified with the work of Dorothy Smith, a white Canadian feminist, but it is useful to Collins because it takes all knowledge as relative, arguing that a group's location in social hierarchies of difference reflects their relative power and thus affects their ability to make their knowledge (of their particular experience) both heard and legitimate:

> Oppressed groups are frequently placed in the situation of being listened to only if we frame our ideas in the language that is familiar to and comfortable for a dominant group. This requirement often changes the meaning of our ideas and works to elevate the ideas of dominant groups. In this volume, by placing African-American women's ideas in the center of analysis, I not only privilege those ideas, but encourage White feminists, African-American men, and all others to investigate the similarities and differences among their own standpoints and those of African-American women. (Collins, 2000: vii)

'All feminist positions are founded on the belief that women suffer from systematic social injustices because of their sex' (Whelehan, 1995: 25), but the challenge of difference has been to force a recognition

that women are not a homogeneous category. Universalistic characterizations of women within feminism have, in fact, been based on
specific women: those who are white, middle-class and heterosexual.
The same can be said of the lack of attention to differences of race/
ethnicity and class in lesbian and gay politics and activism (Jackson
and Scott, 1996a; Seidman, 1996: 10–11). Research on the intersections of gender and sexuality with other hierarchies and differences
has been relatively recent, emerging only over the last two decades.
Now it has become widely accepted that analyses of gender should
factor in race, class and sexuality into the framework of study. This
challenge to identity categories is often taken as part of the general
postmodern challenge to dominant forms of knowledge, whereby
gender as a concept is seen as part of a white, Eurocentric tradition
of knowledge production. Kathy Davis identifies the affinity between
intersectionality and postmodernism, describing the former as a
'welcome helpmeet' in the postmodernist project of deconstructing
'binary oppositions' and 'universalisms' in identity categories (2008:
71). However, partly because of its emphasis on standpoint knowledge, we think it is more useful to understand intersectionality theories as insisting upon the realities of 'differences' amongst women
rather than simply as a call to deconstruct the concepts of woman
and gender.

Deconstruction is an analytical strategy identified with postmodernism, and it is a useful method in highlighting the assumptions
that are coded into language and culture, but recognizing differences is not simply a matter of deconstructing dominant identities,
but requires locating these differences within complex matrices
of intersecting *inequalities* (see Chs 4.7 and 5.4). This brings into
focus race and class as specific structural features of modernity that
affect the construction of gender categories and renders visible the
complex ways in which colonization has operated, and continues
to operate, as central to modernity, *not only within dominant culture
but also within feminism as a 'knowledge' project.* In common with
black feminism in North America and Britain, we have seen inter-
rogations of 'western' white feminist thought from post-colonial
feminism, detailing not only the historical exclusions of non-white,
non-western women (Spivak, 1988); Mohanty, 1991b), but the
necessary inclusion of such perspectives in the context of contemporary global divisions and the complex challenges they raise for feminist theorizing and political strategies (see Alexander and Mohanty,
1997a: xvii–xviii).

TASK: Identifying intersectionality – lesbian and gay Muslim Westerners.

In a study from Australia on lesbian and gay Muslims, Ibrahim Abraham uses the term cultural 'hybridity' to describe the intersectional location of his subjects (referring to them as queer in the everyday sense): '[W]hereas for conservative Muslims a *queer* Muslim becomes the unviable subject, for some in the queer community, a queer *Muslim* is an impossible – or at least dubious – subject' (2009: 88–9, emphasis in the original).

Try to identify the different social hierarchies that intersect to create the location of lesbian or gay Muslims living in the West.

Think about the intersections of national identity, race, religion, sexuality and politics.

8

The Complexity of Contemporary Culture

8.1 Everyday Culture: Language and Meaning

In contrast to the previous chapter, we focus here on everyday culture as an important means by which we make sense of the world around us. Everyday culture is *meaningful* and includes language to beliefs and attitudes; popular culture such as advertising, music, movies and television; and cultural practices, like modes of dress, behaviours and lifestyles. How humans act is not 'natural' but based on social norms (or expectations) of behaviour according to our place within social structures and our identities. Like the powerful knowledges discussed in the previous chapter, everyday culture encodes meanings about gender and sexuality that not only reflect society but also construct it and affect how we can take action.

Feminists have argued that language is a key early component in shaping our understandings of the world as gendered. For example, Kate Millett's work on literature – credited with identifying patriarchy as an analytical concept (see Ch. 2.2) – argues that language is not simply a neutral description of 'things' but institutionalizes meanings of hierarchy and subordination in the case of femininity. Subsequent feminist research has developed these ideas, both in looking at literary representations of society (Moi, 1985) and in arguing that language itself encodes gender and sexual division (Spender, 1985; Cameron, 1998). These analyses have illuminated the ways in which language codes men as active agents and as the generic subject for all humanity, thus either rendering women invisible or specifically identifying them in negative ways. In many institutions, these analyses have had an impact that has led to a widespread cultural shift towards the use of gender-neutral language.

Your World: Research whether the institution where you study has a policy on non-sexist language. How does the policy compare to your everyday experiences of the use of male and female nouns and pronouns? Are words for men still taken to refer to all of humanity?

Many languages do not have gendered pronouns. If this is true for your culture, reflect upon whether written or spoken sexism still exists.

Language is not the only source of meaning, however. While we always use language to explain our experiences and understanding (using culturally available discourses), we are exposed to a wide range of visual cultures (such as advertising) and engage in an equally wide variety of cultural practices in everyday life (putting on make-up, for example). We must also recognize that everyday culture – like the forms of dominant knowledge discussed in the previous chapter – is similarly linked to social structures, identities and action (see Parts II and IV).

8.2   Sexual Objectification in Popular Culture

Back in 1968, a range of women's liberation movement groups protested the annual Miss America contest. In a ten-point manifesto they focused on how the 'beauty' contest represented and contributed to the objectification of women, which they labelled the 'Degrading Mindless-Boob-Girlie Syndrome'. They also drew attention to the racism of the contest, which had never had a native or black finalist, and the white version of America that it promoted (Morgan, 1970: 522). The contest, which still runs annually (although it was dropped from network US television in 2004), has since adapted somewhat. Vanessa Williams (currently in the TV show *Ugly Betty*) became the first black winner in 1984, and the contest is now framed as an educational scholarship programme, again indicating some decline in the marketability of women as sexual objects. However, considering the range of popular culture, from books, film, television, advertising and related material on the world wide web, it is evident that the sexuality of women remains a central mode of constructing meanings in contemporary times [4].

There have been two central analytical concerns here: the first is that women are represented as passive (as in the critique of language), without agency and as sexual objects for the pleasure of men; and, related to this, the second is the way in which this affects the development of self-identity. In his classic text on art and visual culture, *Ways of Seeing* (1972), John Berger pointed out that the dominant ways of positioning women is to portray them as subordinate and passive:

Your World: Consider the Barbie Doll, produced by Mattel toy corporation for fifty years by 2009 and still going strong. What does its popularity say about culture, from the way children might learn about gender through to how corporations might reinforce gender essentialism?

[*M*]*en act* and *women appear*. Men look at women. Women watch themselves being looked at. This determines not only most relations between men and women but also the relation of women to themselves. The surveyor of woman in herself is male: the surveyed female. Thus she turns herself into an object – and most particularly an object of vision: a sight. (1972: 47, emphasis in original)

Berger identifies this convention in the overwhelming majority of European paintings of nudes and illustrates how it continues in the contemporary visual cultures of advertising, journalism and television (1972: 64). Moreover, this positioning of women as passive is central to another form of visual representation: pornography. Government regulation of pornography was in force from the late nineteenth century in both the UK and the USA. Pornography was legislated against as being morally obscene, but there was also an implicit assumption behind the laws that, as with prostitution, men might be easily aroused and thus led into 'temptation' by pornographic images and texts. Just as the 'double standard' of morality was applied in the regulation of prostitution (see Ch. 1.2), the initial regulation of obscenity both encoded Victorian morality and accepted the essentialist idea of men's powerful sexual drives.

Second wave feminist anti-pornography campaigns were, however, informed by a more sociological understanding of the link between culture and patriarchal social structures, arguing that the sexual objectification of women was a reflection of gendered power relations in society. Perhaps the best-known critique is Andrea Dworkin's *Pornography: Men Possessing Women* (1981). Like many other feminists, Dworkin characterized male power as a social system, and prostitution and pornography as examples of the exploitation of and violence against women. She pointed out that the historical meaning of 'pornography' derived from Greek and meant 'writing about whores', *'porne'* referring to the lowest social status prostitutes. She detailed the huge amount of visual imagery in pornography that depicted women being dominated, beaten and raped. The point that Dworkin and others such as MacKinnon were making was that the existence of pornography reflected structural inequalities, with the subordinate feminine represented as a sexual object for the gratification of men: '[M]ale dominance is sexual . . . male power takes the social form of what men as a gender want sexually, which centres on power itself as socially defined' (MacKinnon, 2002: 33–5). This work therefore linked structural gender divisions to the production of cultural discourses that created the resources for self-identities and, crucially, for action, which overall 'developed a theory linking pornography to criminal violence against women and the patriarchal culture of male domination and oppression. "Pornography is the theory, and rape is the practice," wrote Robin Morgan (1977)' (McBride-Stetson, 2004: 333).

Subsequent developments in the 1980s and 1990s have led to a re-evaluation of the potential for pleasure in sex. Some feminists felt that too much emphasis was being placed on the 'dangers' of sex for women at the expense of pleasure (see Vance, 1984) and worried that campaigns against pornography created an unholy alliance between feminists and the Moral Right that might result in unwanted censorship – as well as endorsing essentialist ideas of men as inherently sexually predatory. These debates, which centred on pornography and prostitution, became known as the 'sex wars', with libertarians or 'sex positive' feminists on one side and anti-violence feminists (dubbed by their opponents as 'sex negative') on the other. Some of the former experimented with erotic writings of their own, which included a rethinking of the role of power in sex, suggesting that power had erotic potential – and sometimes this included an explicit defence of sadomasochism (Califia, 1981). This occurred primarily in the context of lesbian relationships, which were argued to be free of the institutionalized gender hierarchy of heterosexuality. For some this resulted in a shift of emphasis from gender oppression to sexual oppression. Gayle Rubin (1984), for example, maintained that the analyses of gender and sexuality should be separated, and she focused on the exclusion of sexual minorities from the 'charmed circle' of monogamous heterosexuality. She also implicitly championed the cause of those furthest from the charmed circle, including those engaged in pornography, prostitution and 'cross-generational relationships' (what is commonly termed paedophilia). While such writers always claimed to be defending only consensual sexual practices and placed a great deal of emphasis on the role of fantasy and play in sexuality, they could be seen as ignoring the origins of the eroticization of power and the extent to which fantasies, games and desires often replicate themes from the dominant culture. In failing to address where, for example, sadistic or masochistic desires came from, they could themselves be seen as guilty of essentialism (Cameron and Frazer, 1987).

Since the time of the 'sex wars', there has been a sexualization of popular culture in general beyond specifically pornographic material, particularly in advertising (Gill, 2007) and other promotional cultures that focus on sexuality, such as celebrity culture (Turner, 2004). This is more complex than in previous eras, often with an assertive sexualized femininity on display (Gill, 2007), with heterosexual men now represented as sexual objects as well (Nixon, 1996; Bordo, 1999) and with more common portrayals of lesbian and gay sexuality. What this means for gender and sexual politics is an open question but one that we address in sections 8.4–8.6 below.

TASK: Where does desire come from?

Bring in a range of lifestyle magazines for class discussion – those aimed at heterosexual women, heterosexual men, gay men, and lesbians.

Analyse and compare the images within to identify the main discourses of sexuality being deployed. How many of these images are 'pornographic'?

Next, think about whether these images directly condition our beliefs and actions about our own sexualities and how far we are able to interpret and negotiate our own meanings from cultural resources.

8.3   Racialized Gender and Sexualized Race

In their critiques of pornography, feminists such as Dworkin pointed out that the women depicted as the sexual objects of men were often from minority groups within white majority western society. This racialization is not accidental, or merely another variable in addition to gender inequalities, but can be traced to the period of industrialization and urbanization that resulted in the current essentialist understandings of gender and sexuality. Imperialism and colonialism were very much a part of the rise and development of industrial capitalism. The subjugation of other peoples and nations facilitated the extraction of natural resources, cheap labour in the colonies and the creation of controlled markets for industrial commodities mass produced in the 'home' (colonizing) nation (see Ch. 5.4 and 5.5). Moreover, although slavery was made illegal in most European countries and their colonies by the early nineteenth century, the devaluation of Africans as sub-human remained a constant theme in the cultural values of both Europe and the Americas. The historical objectification of black women as slaves meant that their bodies were always on display, for potential owners, and this mode of representation of black women's bodies continues in the use of black women in pornography (Collins, 2000) and in the identification of black women as sexual objects in general (hooks, 1982). Moreover, wider cultural images of US black women as 'mammies, matriarchs, welfare recipients and hot mammas helps justify US black women's oppression' (Collins, 2000: 69) by producing stereotypical images that define black women as powerless, passive or reduced to sex. Women from other parts of the world are also represented in highly sexualized, racialized terms, such as the Thai sex workers discussed in the Introduction to Part II.

In a period when nations were competing for empires, national identities were defined in racial terms, as superior or inferior to each other. Masculinity and femininity thus inevitably became not only markers of a 'natural' division, but also ones of national and racial character (Seidler, 1989). A consequence of this alliance of gender with nation was that the various dimensions of essentialism, both scientific and psychological, developed in a context in which *western superiority* was being asserted and justified as the basis for colonial expansion and control of 'native', overwhelmingly non-western peoples. Thus the idea of 'race' developed during this time, with attempts to provide 'scientific' explanations for the physical and mental superiority of the white European over the rest of the world. This resulted in the 'exoticization' of other races, rendering them not only different from the West, but overwhelmingly inferior, with cultural ideas circulating about the inherent animalistic savagery of African peoples (hooks, 1982), the mystical irrationality of Asiatic peoples (Yuval-Davis, 1997) or the uncivilized immorality of Native Americans (Blackwood, 2000). Identified as less mentally developed and less culturally civilized, these non-western 'races' were relegated to the realm of the impulse-driven, untamed, uncivilized sexuality associated with the working classes in Europe or with the sexuality of animals.

Gender and sexuality therefore became racialized, with white women in general placed only slightly above non-white 'others' in the hierarchy of mental capacity: 'In the nineteenth century racial categories were viewed as natural kinds, with distinct physiological and psychological characteristics. . . . Analogies were drawn between women and non-European peoples in term of physiological characteristics such as the shape of their skull, and psychological characteristics' (Alsop et al., 2002: 19). This intersection of gender and race is a key dimension of essentialist cultural constructions of gender and sexuality. We have already discussed (Chs 1.2 and 2.6) how the emergence of new ideological forms of gender in the West during modernity were overwhelmingly based on a bourgeois standard that positioned the working classes as essentially less able to achieve these ideals because they were more prone to physical instincts (biological essentialism) and less able to exert moral mental control (psychological essentialism) (Mort, 1987; Weeks, 1989). This colonialization of the working classes by new forms of ideal gender was repeated by the European bourgeoisie as they became colonizers of different ethnic groups, or what they termed 'races'. For example, there has been a wealth of anthropological research on Native American tribes and bands that demonstrates that a significant number had gender categories consisting of people (usually men) who 'crossed' over to live as the other gender (Whitehead, 1981; Blackwood, 2002). As Evelyn Blackwood argues in her research on the issue, the presence of such identities and categories was problematic for imperialists because the 'Native American cross-gender role confounded Western concepts of gender. Cross-gender individuals typically acted, sat, dressed, talked like, and did the work of the other sex' (2002: 114). However, by the late nineteenth century, European dominance was so complete that '[i]deological pressures of white culture encouraged Native American peoples to reject the validity of the cross-gender role and to invoke notions of "proper" sexuality that supported men's possession of sexual rights to women. . . . In effect, variations in sexual behaviour that had previously been acceptable were now repudiated in favor of heterosexual practices' (Blackwood, 2002: 120).

A contemporary example of the racialization of gender and sexuality is the characterization of Muslim women. The political rhetoric of the 'War on Terror' has its origins in academic thought: historian Bernard Lewis proposed that Islam and western modernity are incompatible, because the West surpassed Islamic culture through modernization and Islamic cultures now reject modernization when it is seen as westernization. He cites gender equality as the key example of his distinction: 'The emancipation of women, more than any other single issue, is the touchstone of difference between modernization and Westernization. . . . The emancipation of women is Westernization; both for traditional conservatives and radical fundamentalists it is neither necessary nor useful but noxious, a betrayal of true Islamic values' (2002: 73). Within this discourse, the impact of the gender equality issue has been significant. Sherene Razack presents a compelling argument that 'the policing of Muslim communities in the name of gender equality is now a globally organized phenomenon' (2008: 20), in large part because 'three allegorical figures have come to dominate the social landscape of the "war on terror" and its ideological underpinning of a clash of civilizations: the dangerous Muslim man, the imperilled Muslim woman, and the civilized European' (2008: 5). Razack locates these current discourses on gender as part of a longer tradition of colonialist thinking, both historically from western societies and also within more recent feminist thought that sees women's liberation in western terms (see Ch. 7.6). She provides case studies that range from Norway to Canada, illustrating her contention that 'race thinking' now operates when western states are dealing with Muslim populations – including those who are their own citizens – and citing the involvement of many feminist organizations in such policies. In her analysis of immigration policy prescriptions and public debates around multiculturalism in Europe since 9/11, Liz Fekete describes a re-emergence of anti-immigrant right-wing politics, and comments that:

> Most alarmingly, even some feminists and gay activists are now part of an overtly right-wing consensus that calls for immigration controls specifically targeted at immigrants from the Muslim world. Central to such a process is a generalised suspicion of Muslims, who are characterised as holding on to an alien culture that, in its opposition to homosexuality and gender equality, threatens core European values. (2006: 2)

White western feminism is challenged when we study the realities of the intersecting oppressions experienced by Muslim women. For example, there is an emerging body of work centred on Muslim women, particularly those who choose to wear the *hijab* or head-covering, which indicates that this has become a positive statement of female identity within Muslim communities *and* a resistance to 'immodest' western cultures in which they are immigrants (Ruby, 2008). Tabssum Ruby draws on qualitative interviews with both women who choose to adopt the *hijab* and those who reject it, but notes that even those who reject it adopt the modest behaviours expected of them within their religious/ethnic cultures, whilst choosing to avoid the direct racism that wearing the *hijab* might provoke. As Stewart Motha (2007) points out, veiling presents a challenge to feminism and its ideas of women's rights. Research such as Ruby's, however, at least demonstrates that women's agency and self-identity within their specific ethnic/religious cultures may be *enhanced* through their adoption of practices that western feminists may have identified as patriarchal.

8.4   Lesbian and Gay Stereotypes

Throughout this book we have seen how the categorization and identification of 'abnormal' desires by early sexologists, combined with pre-existing moral injunctions, created the understanding of the homosexual as a psychologically abnormal *type of person*: a new 'species' of humanity in the form of the 'perverse' adult. 'Perversion' was defined in relation to normatively gendered heterosexuals, so that the emergence of a stigmatized homosexual identity was a direct consequence of the cultural dominance of heterosexuality. Although there is historical evidence showing that homosexuals did manage to create spaces for meeting and/or sex, with the exception of some visible sub-cultures in specific urban locations such as New York (Chauncey, 1994) these usually remained covert, private and hidden (Weeks, 1989) because of their criminalized and socially stigmatized status. On the whole, homosexuals emerged into the public realm only in negative ways, either through court cases, such as the infamous trial of Oscar Wilde in England in 1895, or as pathological cases of 'inversion' in sexological studies, such as those of Havelock Ellis around the same era. In popular culture, homosexuals remained invisible. As one American gay activist writes at the very beginnings of gay liberation in the 1970s: 'Inasmuch as they reflect society, mass media pretend that homosexuality does not exist', even though 'there has been, let us remember, a gay sub-culture and life-style long before there was a gay liberation movement' (Byron, 1972: 59–61). Of course, public culture has now changed, but what is noticeable is that the change to more positive representations of lesbians and gays has been very recent and remains uneven.

In his study of the representation of gays and lesbians in American popular culture, Rodger Streitmatter argues that there have been three distinct phases. From the 1950s to the late 1970s, including the Stonewall riots of 1969, the coverage was 'unremittingly negative' (2009: 179), reflecting the essentialist discourse of homosexuals as perverts and psychologically damaged. From the 1980s to the 1990s, he argues that there was a more neutral portrayal, with a balance of positive and negative images, but significantly weighted towards the latter in discussion of the AIDS epidemic, which had been initially associated with gay men. Streitmatter concludes relatively positively, arguing that the 1990s and early twenty-first century produced a critical mass of media outputs that portrayed homosexuals in a positive light – citing movies such as the AIDS drama *Philadelphia* (1993), *Brokeback Mountain* (2005) and the television series *Queer as Folk*, *Will and Grace*, *The L Word* and *Queer Eye for the Straight Guy*. However, he acknowledges that the 'types' of gay and lesbian people portrayed – however positively – are very narrow, mostly white and wealthy, and that on the whole sex is very rarely portrayed – in contrast to heterosexual sex:

> The Powers That Be had decided to take the sex out of homo*sex*ual. . . . TV executives learned the benefits of creating de-sexed gays through the *Ellen* phenomenon. After the Ellen de Generes character came out as a Sapphic woman on her ABC sitcom and then had the audacity to become romantically involved with another woman, she was *tout suite* declared 'too gay'. So executives at NBC decided to build a sitcom around a handsome gay lawyer who was virtually sexless, not shown even kissing a beau – much less 'doin' the nasty.' When *Will & Grace* triumphed in the ratings like no gay-oriented series before it, Bravo followed in the show's footsteps and offered viewers *Queer Eye* and its whole quintet of charming eunuchs. (Streitmatter, 2009: 187)

8.5 Masculinities in Crisis?

Most second wave feminism and lesbian and gay theory has high-lighted the power and privilege of a particular social group: hetero-sexual men. There has, however, been a developing body of research and theory over the last twenty years or so that looks more critically at the diversity of masculinities, particularly along the dimensions of class, race and sexuality. Socio-historical analyses of the development of essentialism in western culture had already identified the ways in which the dominant ideological constructions of femininity and masculinity were based on white western middle-class life and, furthermore, entwined with ideas of national, racial 'character' (Weeks, 1989). These differences were taken up only gradually within the sociological studies of gender and sexuality, but the issue of different masculinities and the implications this has for understanding patriarchal culture and its intersecting hierarchies is now established. Raewyn Connell's work is an excellent introduction and guide to the research on masculinities including concerns around work, the impact of feminism, male violence and the consequential remaking and remarking of identities. Her concept of 'hegemonic' masculinity has proven to be a key analytic for the exploration of the complexities of masculine experience and dominant symbolic expectations of men. Central to her theory is that a culturally dominant or 'hegemonic' form of masculinity is promoted by the law, politics, cultural institutions such as education, popular culture, workplaces and the family (Connell, 1987). However, not all men can (or wish to) achieve this status or participate in its benefits, precisely because of other dimensions of their social identities or locations, which complicate or undermine the exercise of male privilege.

Numerous examples of exclusion through sexuality exist in sport – one of the main cultural arenas in which hegemonic masculinity is organized, practised and represented. Eric Anderson's research on openly gay athletes in a variety of sports in the USA suggests that once they have 'come out', these men are treated relatively well, with few reporting any verbal abuse, and none reporting physical abuse or intimidation. They are therefore able to participate and share in the overwhelming heterosexual male culture that is sport, despite their identities as 'gay' – which has historically been defined as the antithesis of 'real' masculinity. However, homophobia appeared in different ways, 'including the presence of a don't ask, don't tell policy in which gay athletes' sexual identities were not treated on par with that of heterosexual athletes' (Anderson, 2002: 874). Anderson also illustrates the continued maintenance of a hegemonic masculinity through the use of homophobic discourse as the common currency of insult, supporting analyses that position homophobia as pivotal to the achievement of heterosexual masculinity (Kimmel, 2004). He concludes negatively on the issue of whether the presence of gay athletes will ultimately help to 'soften' hegemonic masculinity by providing a new association of sporting masculinity with gay identity, thus also opening up the acceptance of female athleticism. Yet there is some contradiction here in that many of these athletes feel able to 'come out' whilst they are relatively young, whilst at the same time the cultural association of sport as one key bulwark of hegemonic masculinity remains.

Moreover, the boundaries between homo- and hetero-masculinity do not seem to have disappeared, although some suggest they have become more porous. Studies on one of the world's most famous 'metrosexuals' illustrate this tension. Garry Whannel's view of footballer David Beckham is that he represents the ultimate in 'post-modern' sports celebrity because '[h]is image has become the dominant icon of British sports representation, yet it is a strangely elusive and anchorless image – a floating signifier that can become attached to a range of discursive elements with equal plausibility' (2002: 202). Ellis Cashmore and Andrew Parker (2003) have similarly taken this position. However, on the basis of a six-month study of media outputs in the UK, it was suggested that Beckham is not a free-floating signifier, but rather one that can be manipulated precisely because it is so consistently and thoroughly mired in a heterosexual discourse (Rahman, 2004). There was a confirmation of traditional masculinity in the dominant modes of Beckham's representation, but there was also some ambiguity – or queerness – in the confirmation that a more rounded heterosexual masculinity is acceptable, particularly a narcissistic fashion sense, and, more unusually, his status as an object of desire for both men and women.

> Whilst there are codes to establish Beckham's credentials as an icon, these are mostly related to an established understanding of hetero-sexual masculinity as a concept which includes his footballing prowess, family life, and matrimonial status. The 'style icon' code expands these conventional properties to include an interest in fashion as a legitimate and endorsed part of his rounded masculinity, much in the same way that his comfort with being a gay object of desire is presented as the same. However, these expansions are interesting precisely because they are always presented within the context of confirmed heterosexual masculinity, suggesting that there is a recognition that they may present a challenge to, or subversion of the dominant effective construction of masculinity which is used to render these representations meaningful to the reader/consumer. (Rahman, 2004: 227)

The author argues that 'there was an evident recuperation of the dissonance around [Beckham's] masculinity' (2004: 228) which was achieved through contextualizing codes of hetero-masculinity in the texts and images studied. The anchoring of Beckham in heterosexuality is constant and consistent, and it is precisely this recuperative strategy that allows the dissonant elements to exist within his 'discourse', again suggesting a not so queer world.

Whilst there is an abundance of research that documents the dislocation of masculinity from traditional class occupations, positions of public power and gendered positions within families and culture, one common theme in this academic scrutiny has been the retrenchment of traditional heterosexual masculinities in various ways: through the emergence of men's movements, the continuation of sexual violence and exploitation, and the commodification of hetero-masculinity along some very traditional lines. In a recent book on the current state of academic work on masculinity, Connell argues that we have a better understanding of the complexities of masculinities at present than was demonstrated in the earlier academic work, where 'most of the critics thought that masculinity was in crisis, and that the crisis itself would drive change forward' (2000: 201). She goes on to suggest that the current range of work which demonstrates the experiential and social complexities of masculinities, within and against hierarchies and hegemonic forms, does indicate social change in gender orders, but alerts us to the often contradictory nature of change with the remaking of masculinities going hand in hand with the persistence of traditional gender hierarchies and identities. For Connell, the contemporary 'historical moment' is unique, not because we are at a crisis point, but precisely because the reflexivity of knowledge about the fact that gender does change provides a context for speculations and explorations, whether these are academic, political or cultural.

8.6   Postmodern or Late Modern Culture?

Is it a postmodern world in terms of gender and sexuality? The increasing turn towards cultural analysis has produced a wealth of research that demonstrates the ambiguities and instabilities of gender categories, sexual identities and, overall, the ways in which knowledge about gender and sexuality is discursively constructed. Challenges to the dominant ideologies of sexuality and gender are clearly indicative of significant cultural change – brought about to a large extent by the production of sociological research and theories, as well as by political activism. One consequence has been the acceptance in many cultures around the world of the importance of equal rights for women and the possibility of achieving this through political intervention, rather than accepting women's subordination as a fact of nature. Of course, this is much less consistently the case where sexual diversity is concerned, and there are many countries where homosexuality is still illegal and some where it carries the death penalty. However, there has been a gradual expansion and internationalization of a human rights discourse around sexual diversity (Kollman and Waites, 2009) and there is no doubt that specific advances have been made in many nations, which may make individual lives better, and which are also suggestive of a symbolic cultural change. But just as we argued that there was an institutional and material basis for the enshrinement of essentialism in Chapter 6, so we want to consider the institutional and material basis of this apparently 'postmodern' culture.

In early modernity, industrialization and urbanization swept away traditional societies, with the growth of cities, the reordering of class and gender divisions, colonial and imperialist projects and the consolidation of the nation state. However, Anthony Giddens (1990) identifies the ongoing *momentum* of change as a key aspect of modernity and argues that it has accelerated in our contemporary technological times – describing the pace of social change as the 'juggernaut' of modernity. This late modern era brings with it ever more differentiated consumerist capitalism, locked to a sense of highly differentiated individuality expressed most consistently in the cultural discourses that exist around consumerism as a route to personal fulfilment. This momentum is now destabilizing even those structures consolidated during the earlier modern period and pushing us ever faster towards post-traditional individualization by 'disembedding' us from these traditional modernist structures that defined our identities through our social location within structures of class, race/nation and gender.

Late modern society, it is said, no longer provides these anchors to self-identity and so now it is up to the individual to produce continuity or ontological security, primarily through lifestyle consumption (Bauman, 2001). Thus, we are increasingly thrown back on the resources of the self – our bodies, pleasures and lifestyles – which requires that we self-consciously make decisions about our lives: 'The reflexivity of modernity extends into the core of the self. Put in another way, in the context of a post-traditional order, the self becomes a *reflexive project*. . . . In the settings of modernity, . . . the altered self has to be explored and constructed as part of a reflexive process of connecting personal and social change' (Giddens, 1991: 33, emphasis in original). Convergent with this, there has been an increasing tendency for social identity to be consciously constructed through consumption, and this has brought with it an emphasis on markets for both gay men (Evans, 1993; Hennessy, 2000) and heterosexual men (Nixon, 1996; Bordo, 1999) and the expansion of the already existing 'beauty industry' for women.

There is no question that there has been an ever-increasing sexualization of culture in contemporary capitalism (Gill, 2007; Heath, 1982). Importantly, *sexuality* has become ever more central to the consumer self; sexuality is regarded as an expression of lifestyle and character over and above simply an indicator of sexual desire (Evans, 1993; Jackson and Scott, 2010). Thus, the defining power of our location in relation to the means of production (class in gendered national/racial contexts) has shifted to a social location defined by our power to consume as individuals, and at the heart of this individuality is sexuality. Sexuality, in this sense, is not simply about sexual identity, but about the core of the self – how it defines the totality of our gendered, lifestyle, embodied, post-class identity. Moreover, this has not displaced gender categories, but reinforces them through its identification of sexuality with specific manifestations of or variations on gender. We suggest therefore that contemporary culture is marked by a *reflexive essentialism*: reflexivity combined with essentialist notions of sexual identity. The reflexivity expected of the self in a consumerist, post-traditional culture requires the widespread deployment of sexuality as the definitive aspect of our social identities. Therefore, instead of a postmodern culture, we think it is more accurate sociologically to think of contemporary gendered and sexual culture as late modern. Whilst the power of media-driven consumerism is now a global phenomenon, as is the discourse of women's and gay rights and identities, these are still dependent upon essentialist understandings of identity – a reformulated, reflexively produced essentialism organized primarily around sexuality, but nonetheless a continuation of modernity's emphasis on the innate origins of the sexual. Moreover, 'modern' biological and psychological essentialism is still the base-line cultural explanation for both gender and sexual behaviour (Hird, 2004), often popularized through media precisely because it presents a 'scientific' justification of current social arrangements – evolutionary psychology and its use in explanations of gender and sexuality is the latest such discourse that reinvents scientific essentialism (Jackson and Rees, 2007). Given the social power of such 'legitimate' discourses (see Ch. 7.2), and the imperative to consume as individualized gendered and sexual selves, it is no wonder that individual uses of this type of explanation are still culturally dominant, even as we are paradoxically self-consciously consuming and modifying ourselves to become suitably gendered and sexual. Indeed, we could argue that essentialist scientific discourse has become a resource for reflexive self construction and is therefore no longer merely regulatory (Jackson and Scott, 2010).

Of course this is contradictory, but there is no reason why culture should not be full of contradictions and in that sense it may exhibit aspects of postmodernity: a mass, globalized, technological, image-driven culture that cannot be accurately depicted as ideologically coherent. Rosalind Gill's work on recent media exemplifies these contradictions: she identifies new forms of sexual subjectification of women in advertising that – in direct opposition to the portrayal of women as passive sexual objects discussed earlier – suggest female empowerment and sexual agency through the figures of the fun, sexually fearless (heterosexual) female; the vengeful heterosexual woman punishing a male partner; and the sexually attractive (in heterosexual terms) lesbian couple (Gill, 2008). In the last case, Gill argues that the visibility of lesbianism is made possible because it is a continuation of representational paradigms that are focused on lesbian sex presented for a *male* heterosexual audience. Thus she questions the progressive nature of these new cultural modes of sexual subjectification, recognizing their contradictory nature, and asks us to think about what this means for feminist politics. Contemporary gendered and sexual cultures, then, must be thought of as complex and contradictory – as both progressive and oppressive:

> What is striking is the way in which advertisers have managed in these [new images of sexual subjectification] to recuperate and commodify a particular kind of feminist consciousness and offer it back to women shorn of its political critique of gender relations and heteronormativity. A new version of female sexual agency is on offer that breaks in important ways with the sexual objectification and silencing of female desire of earlier advertising. Yet in refiguring female sexual agency in these particular ways, it raises new problems and challenges. If this is empowerment, we might ask, then what does sexism look like? And if second-wave slogans such as 'THIS AD OBJECTIFIES WOMEN' are no longer effective in a mediascape populated by active sexual subjects, what kind of cultural politics is equal to the task of resisting contemporary representations? (Gill, 2008: 55)

Learning Outcomes

After reading the chapters in Part III you should:

- understand that our contemporary cultural beliefs and values around gender and sexuality are historically specific and were consolidated during modernity;
- understand how this essentialist model meshed with the reordering of gender relations within industrial capitalism and how it was legitimated through emergent scientific ideas on gender and sexuality;
- understand the consequences of this for the cultural construction of binary gender categories and the stigmatization of homosexuality;
- be able to demonstrate knowledge of feminist/lesbian/gay challenges to the objectivity of 'scientific' essentialism, including the critique of its methodologies and ideological purposes;
- understand Foucault's conceptualization of power as multi-relational and productive and how this contributes to understanding the construction of sexual 'types', particularly the homosexual;
- be aware of recent challenges to monolithic structural explanations of gender and sexuality from intersectionality and post-colonial theorists, postmodernist queer theorists, embodiment theorists and masculinity theorists;
- understand how we have used the concept of 'reflexive essentialism' in relation to the emphasis on fashioning the body and lifestyle within consumer culture;
- understand that contemporary gendered and sexual cultures are contradictory, incorporating both progressive and traditional elements, and why this indicates that it is more useful to think of a late modern rather than a postmodern sexual culture.

Notes and Resources for Further Study

1 Details of the show, episodes and history are available at *www.bravotv. com/Queer_Eye*.

2 For a chronology of sexology, see the resource at the Magnus Hirschfeld Institute at Humboldt University in Berlin: *www2.hu-berlin.de/sexology*. *Studies* by Havelock Ellis were published in Germany and the USA over the late 1890s and early 1900s, after the first volume was labelled obscene by an English court in 1897 (see Weeks, 1989: 142).

3 See Myra Hird's thorough sociological critique in *Sex, Gender and Science* (2004), particularly Chapter 1, which details the way that sexual difference has been historically created and sustained by scientific studies of anatomy, including those of 'skeletons, gametes, hormones and genes'. Anne-Fausto Sterling is a feminist biologist who has written similar critiques of science in *Myths of Gender: Biological Theories about Men and Women* (1992) and *Sexing the Body: Gender Politics and the Construction*

of Sexuality (2000), and see also Vernon A. Rosario (ed.) *Science and Homosexualities* (1997).

4 Rosalind Gill's recent studies on a range of media highlight the ways in which feminist critiques have been incorporated into many contemporary advertising and promotional products that now include sexually assertive female discourses and depend on a reflexive, knowing audience, but she questions whether this is progressive given that this sexualization is still intersected by class, race and sexuality (Gill, 2007, 2009). See Sean Nixon's 1996 study on the first wave of heterosexual men being represented as sexual objects and Susan Bordo's later (1999) study on this issue. See Adie Nelson's 'Symbolic Representations of Gender' (2010: Ch. 5) for a good overview of research on gender, language and media in Canada.

Part IV

Self, Identity and Agency

Part IV explores the ways in which our gendered and sexual selves and identities are socially constituted yet actively constructed and negotiated by us as we go about our daily lives. The sociological perspectives we cover here tend to take a 'bottom-up' rather than 'top-down' view of social relations, emphasizing the meaningful nature of social life and the human capacity to make sense of the social world and act intentionally in it. In Chapter 9 we consider how these 'interpretive' sociologies challenge the conventional socialization paradigm, and in Chapter 10 we suggest how they illuminate the processes of becoming gendered and sexual. In Chapter 11 we discuss how changing gender and sexual relations in these late modern times may be affecting constructions of self-hood and opening up new forms of gendered and sexual identity. We also consider the extent to which these changes are global phenomena.

Introduction: Living with Multiple Identities

A young Asian woman lives her life between Britain and her native South Korea. In Britain she lives openly with her woman partner and has come to feel reasonably comfortable with being 'out' as a lesbian. There is still some hostility towards lesbians and gays in the UK, but she is more conscious of the racist hostility of local youths who hurl abuse at her in the streets – generally misidentifying her as Chinese and calling her a 'chink' (a term of racist abuse in Britain). In Korea her ethnic identity is not an issue, but she is no longer at home with her lesbian identity. Here it must remain hidden from family, friends and colleagues, acknowledged only in the underground community that Korean lesbians have created for themselves. Like others in this community, she has a secret name known only to other trusted lesbians who neither know her real name nor expect her to reveal it. Her two names mark the boundaries of her separate Korean lives and identities. Under her real name she is taken to be heterosexual and would risk her social ties to others if her lesbian identity were revealed. Under her assumed name she is known, to a few others, as a lesbian. She thus moves between multiple worlds and identities: in Britain she lives as an acknowledged lesbian under her real name but as a racialized other; in Korea she can 'be' a lesbian only by leaving behind her name.

This story, which is based on an autobiographical account (Woo 2007), tells us something about the construction of self and identity in an increasingly complex modern world. First, it is clear that identities are shaped by the societies we inhabit and that we face constraints on what is possible imposed by local social conditions. Moreover, the identities ascribed to us by others may not match who *we* think we are: our Korean woman is at times misidentified as Chinese or as heterosexual. Nonetheless, it is equally evident that the individual is not passive in this process: she actively negotiates her way around her multiple social locations, exercises a degree of agency in the identity choices she makes and is able to live, albeit sometimes painfully, with conflicting identities.

Throughout this book we have emphasized that gender and sexuality are social and cultural, rather than 'natural'. This can give the impression that we are in some way 'programmed' into particular identities and ways of being. As people go about their daily lives, however, they interpret what is going on around them, negotiate relationships with others and reflect on their own actions and experiences. This allows for variability and change in what it means to be a man or a woman, gay, lesbian or straight. To account for this active engagement in the social, while simultaneously acknowledging the sociality of gender and sexuality, we need to introduce the concepts of agency, self, subjectivity and identity.

Agency is the capacity for intentional action and presupposes the human ability to reflect upon situations that confront us and to decide on appropriate courses of action. Without agency we would not be able to resist, subvert or change oppressive social relationships. The concept of agency, however, is important not only for explaining non-conformity and resistance, but also to understand the mundane conditions of our everyday gendered and sexual lives. Without a degree of agency we would lack the ability to interpret situations in which we find ourselves and interact and cooperate (or refuse to cooperate) with others. Agency is thus fundamental to being a competent member of society, but opportunities for exercising agency are not necessarily distributed equally, since there are always constraints upon it. It does not, therefore, imply 'free will': individual agency arises from, and is bounded by, what is possible within any given social situation.

The self and **subjectivity** refer to our sense of ourselves, along with our inner thoughts and desires. These two terms, though similar in meaning, derive from different theoretical traditions. 'The self' is associated with interactionist sociology, where it is seen as social in origin, arising from interaction with others, and reflexive – capable of reflecting back on itself. **Subjectivity** is more widely used in post-structuralist and postmodernist theory, where it is conceived as a product of language and discourse, through which we are positioned within the social. From both perspectives our subjective selves are seen as fluid rather than fixed, but the interactionist perspective has a more developed understanding of agency, which is related to the self's **reflexivity:** the ability to think about, act upon and engage in internal conversations with ourselves [1].

Identity is sometimes taken as synonymous with subjectivity or self but it is generally rather more narrowly conceived as our sense of who we are and who we perceive others to be, which is translated into labels with which we *identify* ourselves or others. For example, to say 'I am Scottish/Chinese/Canadian' or 'I am a doctor/student/ bus driver' is to claim a national identity or an occupational one. Gendered and sexual identities are particularly significant for our sense of self, but we must remember that being a man or a woman, gay or straight, is not all of who we are; we each have several intersecting identities that we embody simultaneously. Some connect us to larger social groupings such as class, ethnic and national identities; others will be more personal, located in our immediate social connections. There are also many aspects of the subjective self not necessarily reducible to any identity or to the sum total of our identities, such as emotions and desires, or personal attributes that might be part of our sense of self but which do not necessarily give rise to enduring identity labels. Thus it is sometimes useful to distinguish between self and subjectivity, on the one hand, and identity, on the other.

In *Gender and Agency* (2000), Lois McNay argues that much recent theory of subjectivity has rested upon 'a negative paradigm of subject formation', where subjectivity is the product of constraint and subjection, leaving little room for agency. Her critique is directed towards postmodernist theory, but the problem she identifies also has a long history in sociology. The dominance of functionalist perspectives in the 1950s led to human conduct being thought of as governed by external norms, internalized through socialization and enacted through pre-existing socially prescribed roles. Marxism did not really challenge this view of the relationship between the social and the individual, except that ideology was substituted for norms, for example in Althusser's (1971) argument that ideology constitutes us as subjects.

There are, however, alternative forms of social theory usually grouped together as interpretive sociologies or sociologies of social action: phenomenological sociology, ethnomethodology and interactionism. Some of the earliest accounts of the social construction of gender and sexuality derived from these traditions of thought and they continue to be useful in understanding agency, identity, self and subjectivity. While differing in their emphases, these perspectives enable us to envisage social life as a product of meaningful interaction, where human action is guided by how situations are collectively and individually defined rather than by norms or ideologies deriving from a social system. They can therefore help us to understand how we become gendered, sexual beings without denying diversity in the ways gender and sexuality are lived and the complex ways in which gendered and sexual identities intersect with other possible identities.

9

The Socialization Paradigm and Its Critics

9.1 Socialized Selves

Becoming a woman or a man was once seen by sociologists as a relatively straightforward matter: it was the outcome of 'socialization'. Even before the concept of gender entered the vocabulary of social scientists, it was accepted that 'sex roles' varied historically and culturally and were therefore learned rather than innate. Socialization theorists did not necessarily think of children as entirely passive in the process. Even the functionalist theorist Talcott Parsons, who argued that polarized masculine and feminine roles were necessary for the smooth running of society, believed that children were active in socializing themselves, in part through identification with the same-sex parent. However, he assumed that because sex roles were 'ascribed', assigned at birth, socialization into them began in infancy and became integrated into the child's 'personality structure' early in life (Parsons, 1951; Parsons and Bales, 1956). Thus it was generally thought that sex roles were thoroughly 'internalized' so that most people grew up to be well-adjusted masculine men or feminine women, ready to take their places in heterosexual family life.

When feminists first began to write and think about gender in the 1970s, many simply adopted the socialization paradigm, albeit from a more critical stance. Hence research focused on the institutional and informal settings in which socialization took place – the family, the school, the peer group – as well as the inculcation of gender (or sex role) 'stereotypes' through children's toys, books and the media (see, for example, Oakley, 1972). Soon, however, it became apparent that the socialization paradigm was flawed. One of the first and most thorough feminist critiques of the socialization paradigm was published by Liz Stanley and Sue Wise in *Breaking Out* (1983; see also Stanley and Wise, 1993). Stanley and Wise framed their argument from within interpretive sociology, pointing out that the socialization model could not explain those who did not conform to 'gender roles', for example feminists, gay men and lesbians. Indeed, very few women or men conform to the rigid definitions of femininity and masculinity that the concept of 'gender role' presupposes. Not only does the idea that we are socialized into 'gender roles' deny the variability and fluidity of gendered attributes and conduct, it also fails to allow for agency and reflexivity in the ways in which gender is lived and continually negotiated. Stanley and Wise propose an alternative perspective whereby we become social through the acquisition of a social self, which is reflexively constructed through everyday interaction with others. Rather than being socialized into predetermined norms and roles, self and social milieu are interdependent, both constructed through ongoing social interaction in which selves subtly evolve and change. Gender should not, therefore, be seen as fixed and immutable, but should be understood as 'situationally variable' (Stanley and Wise, 1993: 110).

Your World: Think about the experiences that might have contributed to your becoming gendered as a child. How were expectations about gender conveyed to you? Were you simply the passive recipient of these or did you actively make sense of them and resist/ modify them?

The interpretive sociologies on which Stanley and Wise draw, such as ethnomethodology and interactionism, provide an alternative to a 'top-down' view of society. They conceptualize human action as guided by meanings generated in everyday interaction, rather than through external norms. Ethnomethodology sees members of society as 'practical methodologists', actively engaged in constructing the shared social reality we inhabit. Interactionism, as the term implies, is concerned with wider processes of interaction, with the reflexive self at centre stage. Ethnomethodology allows us to see how we 'do' gender and sexuality, while interactionism has more to say about what it means to *be* gendered and sexual beings. The former has had more impact on the study of gender, while the latter has more often been used in exploring sexuality. Both, however, can be applied to gender *and* sexuality.

In recent years queer theorists and many feminists have favoured poststructuralist and postmodernist accounts of subjectivity. These perspectives conceptualize human subjects as constituted through discourse – as in Foucault's claim that it was not possible to *be* a homosexual until the category 'homosexual' was discursively constructed (see Ch. 7.2). This approach sometimes allows for agency by suggesting that we 'take up' subject positions or locate ourselves within discourses, but without any theorization of where this agency comes from (see McNay, 2000). Some use psychoanalytic theories of the unconscious to explain resistance to the social order, but since the unconscious is beyond our knowledge and control, it cannot be a source of agency. In this and the following chapters we therefore include poststructuralist work where it is useful, but will focus primarily on interpretive sociologies, particularly ethnomethodology and interactionism

9.2   Ethnomethodology: 'Doing' Gender and Sexuality

Ethnomethodologists see individuals as 'members' (of society) whose everyday interpretive practices collaboratively constitute the social. Members are 'practical methodologists' engaged in active sense-making, but as competent members of society we share basic assumptions, commonsense ideas about how things are and how things are done. Our shared social knowledge makes daily life intelligible to us, and we expect people's actions to be 'accountable', to be understandable in terms of accepted views of social reality. We usually only ask people to account for their actions when they are in some way unusual or unexpected – and such accounts can tell us something about the way social conduct is generally rendered intelligible and accountable. When we encounter unfamiliar situations where our taken-for-granted assumptions do not hold, we look for evidence to help us make sense of what is going on, applying our general knowledge of the world in so doing (see, for example, Stanley and Wise 1993: 136–49). Thus, rather than being determined by a society external to us, we routinely contribute to the continual remaking of social reality.

This approach to social life enabled ethnomethodologists to make a major conceptual breakthrough in the study of gender, to demonstrate that the division between men and women, though it seems to be an objective 'fact of life', is actually a socially constructed division maintained through our everyday interpretive practices. The classic study here is Harold Garfinkel's essay 'Passing and the Managed

Achievement of Sex-Status in an "Intersexed" Person' (1967). Intersexed people, he suggests, cast light on the background assumptions about sex differences which permeate our lives, but which usually go unnoticed because they are so taken for granted. In focusing on the ways in which 'Agnes', a purportedly intersexed person, seeks to 'pass' as a 'real woman' despite having male genitals (preoperatively), and later 'artificial' female genitals, Garfinkel brings the presumed normality of sex difference into question.

Garfinkel links the problems that intersexed people have in negotiating their daily activities to the importance of 'sex-statuses' in ordinary life – note that he was writing before the term 'gender' became current. He discusses at some length the taken-for-granted beliefs held by adult members of society that constitute '"normally sexed persons" as cultural objects' (1967: 122). These include the following:

- There are 'two sexes and only two sexes' (1967: 122).
- Everyone *must* belong to one or the other.
- Normal people remain in their sex category for life.
- Certain insignia, particularly the possession of a penis or a vagina, are taken to be essential to identifying us as a man or a woman.
- We are all entitled to the 'correct' genitals – if something is 'wrong' with them this should be surgically rectified to provide the genitals '*that should have been there all along*' (1967: 127, emphasis in original).

It is because of the pervasiveness of such assumptions that Agnes is able to pass at all, since she can rely on others to take her feminine appearance as indicative of normal womanhood. Moreover, she is able to present herself, despite her 'anomalous genitals', as a 'naturally sexed person' and to persuade the doctors treating her that she is entitled to a vagina as her '*legitimate possession*' (Garfinkel 1967: 127, emphasis in original). Importantly, Garfinkel sees genitals as *cultural* insignia: they are taken as a 'sign' that someone is male or female, rather than intrinsically making us one or the other.

Passing, for Agnes, requires a carefully managed 'performance' of femininity. She secures for herself the status of a 'normal woman' through 'the efficacious display of female appearances and performances' (Garfinkel, 1967: 134). In fact the performance was even more skilled than Garfinkel himself initially appreciated: Agnes, as he later discovered, had 'faked' her intersexed condition by taking oestrogen since puberty and thus was not in medical terms intersexed at all, but rather a male-to-female transsexual (see Garfinkel, 1967: 285–8). This does not, of course, invalidate Garfinkel's argument. His point is that gender (or sex, in his terms) is *always*, and for *everyone*, a performance (see Ch. 7.4 for similar arguments from queer theory – a very different theoretical perspective). Agnes simply makes visible what is usually invisible – she reveals how we all accomplish or 'do' gender. This accomplishment is a two-way process, requiring a performance and an interpretation of that performance by others. Agnes learns to pass through reading other women's performances and constructing her own. 'Doing' gender is thus a continual process of action and interpretation. We 'do' gender as much by the interpretive processes by which we attribute gender to others as by our own actions. 'Normally sexed people', Garfinkel tells us, are 'cultural events' brought into being by 'members' recognition and production practices' (1967: 181).

Implicit in Garfinkel's analysis is the suggestion that sex differences themselves are social. Thus gender cannot be seen as simply a cultural overlay on biology. Garfinkel himself had no apparent feminist sympathies – he was not at all critical of the very traditional form of femininity to which Agnes sought to conform. Later ethnomethodologists, influenced by feminist analyses of gender, made the radical implications of Garfinkel's insights more explicit. For Candace West and Don Zimmerman, for example, gender is independent of any biological differentiation of sex: it is an 'emergent feature of social situations' (1987: 126). Doing gender means making it happen, 'creating' differences between men and women that have nothing to do with biology. Yet, once created, these differences 'reinforce the "essentialness" of gender' (1987: 137): we perceive as natural what, in effect, is our own collective social creation. Suzanne Kessler and Wendy McKenna (1978) went further in some respects in doing away with the idea of sex as a biological category of any kind. They use the term 'gender' in order to underline the social origins of differences between women and men – even when referring to differences assumed to be biological, such as hormones and chromosomes. They argue that the recognition of gender differences is always a social act, whether it happens within scientific research or everyday interaction. Scientists looking for biological differences between male and female, then, are doing gender.

Kessler and McKenna develop Garfinkel's concept of 'cultural genitals', pointing out that while we may assume that genitals are essential to gender, the practices of attributing gender to others in everyday life do not follow from an examination of their genitals, except in the case of newborn infants. We 'recognize' someone as male or female through interpreting other signs and thence infer that the essential, genital insignia *must* be there. We don't, in other words, ask people to remove their clothes before deciding whether they are 'really' men or women! Kessler and McKenna stress the primacy of gender attribution over all other aspects of gender: it is only because we make a gender distinction in the first place that we are able to talk about masculine or feminine characteristics or activities or order social activities and relationships around gender. Like Garfinkel, they see gender attribution as an interactive process, but suggest that it is androcentric. They point out that the categories 'male' and 'female' are defined in relation to each other: to be classified as the former is to be excluded from the latter. But these two categories, while mutually constitutive, are not equally significant, since to be male is the socially defined norm: to be female is to be not male. Here, the presumed presence or absence of a penis is the paradigmatic case – unlike Garfinkel, they suggest that the cultural genital that matters most is the penis (Kessler and McKenna, 1978: 155).

The process of gender attribution is a complex act, accomplished through 'practical reasoning', by interpreting a variety of gender insignia: how someone dresses, wears their hair, moves or speaks, as well as the discernible form of their body. Yet most of the time most of the population 'do' gender every day without reflecting critically on that doing; we become reflective about it only when faced with someone who is not immediately classifiable as male or female (see West and Zimmerman, 1987). This implies that gender cannot persist without our active collaboration in maintaining it, that it requires our continual reaffirmation for its continuance. This does not mean we can easily undo gender; doing gender, being able to mobilize the taken-for-granted assumptions that make gender happen, is integral to being a competent member of society. To challenge the ways this occurs in everyday life would not only be exhausting and socially disruptive, but would risk being seen as socially incompetent, eccentric or in need of psychiatric treatment.

TASK: How can you tell a woman from a man?

Work in pairs and write down all the clues that tell you whether the other person is a woman or a man. Do this anonymously. Collect the lists together and identify common markers of gender (and unusual ones). Discuss the assumptions you have all made in attributing gender and try to identify the social bases of these assumptions and how they contribute to the process of 'doing gender'.

In addition to doing gender we can also do sexuality, particularly through the attribution of homosexuality and heterosexuality. For example, a man who does not produce an accountable, intelligible performance of 'masculinity' is often assumed to be gay. Doing heterosexuality is often invisible, because it is a taken-for-granted feature of social life that the majority of people are heterosexual. This is one aspect of what is usually called 'heteronormativity': the ways in which heterosexuality is subtly normalized so that it is rarely questioned. Ethnomethodology, however, can potentially make this normalizing process visible through close attention to what actually goes on in everyday social practice.

This has been made apparent through conversation analysis (CA), a methodological approach deriving from ethnomethodology that examines how social reality is reproduced through everyday 'talk-in-interaction'. CA uses recordings of naturalistic talk that occurs in ordinary conversations and adopts rigorous transcription procedures that record every utterance (including 'ums' and 'ers'), the length of every pause, intakes of breath, intonation, overlaps in speech, and so on. In analysing the detail of how people actually talk to each other, basic shared assumptions can be revealed along with utterances that threaten to disrupt those assumptions and efforts made to restore 'normality' when this occurs. Celia Kitzinger (2005) has applied these techniques to displays of heterosexual identity. She demonstrates how heterosexuals continually produce themselves and others as heterosexual and reinforce the taken-for-granted normality of heterosexuality. This is most obvious where talk is about sexuality or relationships – where people talk about marital relationships as necessarily involving a man and a woman or engage in sexual banter that assumes that 'everyone' is attracted to 'the opposite sex'. But it also occurs in the course of ordinary, very mundane conversations about other things, where 'nothing special' is going on, but where heterosexuality is routinely and repeatedly displayed. This is achieved, for example, through heterosexually ordered relationship terms (for example, 'husband' or 'girlfriend') dropped into the conversation in passing and in the use of the pronoun 'we' to naturalize the heterosexual couple. All this passes without comment because it is seen as 'normal'; when lesbian or gay people use such devices, this can disrupt heterosexuals' sense of normalcy and therefore the flow of the interaction. This may be only momentary, as participants in the conversation are likely to engage in collective efforts to repair the situation, whether by including or excluding the unexpectedly non-heterosexual to achieve a reconstituted normality. CA, because of its attention to the detail of conversation, can detect these fleeting glitches in interaction and through them highlight what is, and is not, taken for granted by those involved in the conversation in question.

9.3   Doing, Being and the Reflexive Self

In everyday life we 'do' gender and sexuality in two senses. The first is the ethnomethodological sense, where gender and normative heterosexuality are produced as 'practical accomplishments' through everyday interpretive interaction (Kessler and McKenna, 1978; West and Zimmerman, 1987). The second sense of 'doing' refers to actual practical activities such as negotiating sexual relationships and practices, interacting with gendered others in the workplace, organizing domestic chores, and so on. Here, social interaction with others is essential to our ability to navigate through everyday life and fit ourselves into ongoing activities. Ethnomethodology has little to say about the doing of gender and sexuality in this sense, so here we must turn to interactionism.

Part of this everyday 'doing' entails producing appropriately gendered performances – here we are not too far from ethnomethodology, since we are still concerned with how performances of gender produce a sense of a gendered social world through which we collectively 'subscribe to the conventions of [gendered] display' (Goffman, 1979: 8). Erving Goffman notes, however, that these performances are variable and are situated within particular social contexts. Nonetheless, as he points out elsewhere (Goffman, 1977), gender is continually reproduced and naturalized in daily practices in a variety of interpersonal and public settings, from gendered acts of courtesy to the segregation of public lavatories (Goffman, 1977). One crucial aspect of interaction, however, is underdeveloped in Goffman. While he has a great deal to say about how we present ourselves to others and manage social interaction, he gives little attention to self-reflexivity.

Reflexivity is important not only for explaining agency (see Introduction to Part IV), but also for explaining how we come to be gendered and sexual subjects who take part in the interactive processes through which we produce a shared sense of reality and get the business of everyday life done. The idea of a reflexive social self derives from an American philosophical tradition known as pragmatism, particularly from the work of George Herbert Mead (1934), whose ideas became the foundation of symbolic interactionism (see Blumer, 1969). Mead argued that the self cannot exist outside the social and that human social action is founded on interpretive processes, mediated through language, in which self and society are interdependent. Society could not exist without reflexive human actors able to communicate and cooperate, while the self could not exist without social interaction. To have a sense of self is to be aware of ourselves as both separate from others and situated *in relation to* others. Through interaction we acquire and exercise the ability to see ourselves from the perspective of others and develop the capacity to engage in conversations with ourselves, to see ourselves as subject ('I') and object ('Me') – to reflect on and act on ourselves, to be *reflexive*. For example, we can think: 'I shouldn't have said that it made me look stupid' or ask ourselves 'If I do this what will they think of me?'

This subject/object relation within the self is a *process* in which the 'I' (self as subject) and the 'Me' (self as object to itself) are in ongoing dialogue or interplay. Failure to understand this has led to oversimplified and erroneous portrayals of Mead's distinction between the 'I' (self as subject) and 'Me' (self as object). Often it is said that the 'I' is the individual (unsocialized) part of the self and the 'Me' is the social part of the self (see, for example, Giddens, 1991). But Mead's self is *wholly* social: it does not have an individual component existing outside the social. As Nick Crossley puts it, the relationship between them is not a spatial one – two separate parts of the whole – 'but a temporal and reflexive self-relationship of an agent who chases her own shadow' (2001: 147). The 'I' only exists in the instantaneous present, and as soon as it is reflected upon, that moment has gone past, so the 'I' exists in memory as 'the self of the second, the minute or the day ago'; but because it is remembered, reflected on retrospectively, it has become an object, 'a "me", but it is a "me" which was the "I" at the earlier time' (Mead, 1934: 174).

Because we can be objects to ourselves, we are able to anticipate what others expect of us and thus interact and cooperate with them. We are also able to envisage how others are likely to interpret or react to particular circumstances: we can 'put ourselves in their shoes' or, in Mead's terms, 'take the attitude of the other'. We display this capacity in everyday conversations: for example, in gossiping about friends, we speculate about their motives and feelings, imagining how things seem from their point of view. It is through these reflexive processes that we come to take on as our own the commonsense assumptions – such as those about gender – shared by those around us. This is, then, an active process involving reflection and interpretation that goes on throughout life. The self changes not only over time but also contextually as we orient ourselves to a number of others in different situations, and it is therefore neither unitary nor fixed. We are, however, able to maintain a coherent sense of self through reflexively reconstructing our memories, bringing them into coherence with the present, weaving together the diverse strands of our experience (Mead, 1964 [1929], 2002 [1932]).

Unlike some other perspectives, notably psychoanalysis, the condition of social self-hood is not, in Mead's account, tied to gender; indeed he did not discuss gender. This gender-neutral approach, however, has advantages. As Stanley and Wise point out, there is no need to assume 'a different pattern of "psychological" development for women and men' (1993: 195). We can accept that our reflexive self-constructions are gendered, are the product of interacting with gendered others, without presupposing, as many psychological and psychoanalytic accounts do, that *how* we acquire our gender differs, that different psychic processes are at work. Because Mead specifies only the processes by which selves are formed (and not the 'content' of the 'psyche'), the details of individual self-hood are contingent upon the specific social conditions under which we lead our lives. This approach is therefore conducive to accounting for different forms of femininity and masculinity.

Efrat Tseëlon suggests one means by which we can extend Mead's conceptualization of the self–other relation to take account of gender asymmetry. She argues that while we all depend on the existence of others as a condition of self-hood, a woman has 'a *more heightened awareness* of her derivative nature than that which is common to all' as a result of 'her definition as spectacle' (1995: 5, emphasis in original) and a concomitant concern with how she *looks* (see Ch. 8.2 for discussion of this in popular culture). This interactionist account, as Tseëlon says, differs from conventional feminist positions whereby feminine subjectivity is constituted through objectification. From an interactionist stance, objectification 'is viewed not as a demeaning state exclusive to women, but a general state: the essence of reflexive consciousness' (1995: 75). Both women and men are objects to others but, Tseëlon argues, there are cultural reasons why women are more concerned specifically about their appearance and hence for their heightened perception of the gaze and judgement of others. This observation of women's heightened self-reflexivity could also be taken in another direction: insofar as it has been a conventional cultural expectation that women care for others, they are more socially practised in 'taking the attitude of the other', anticipating others' wants and needs and thinking of others in relation to themselves (see Jackson, forthcoming). Thus while the capacity for reflexivity is not gendered, the *practice* of reflexivity is affected by the gendered relationships within which it is deployed.

9.4   Sexual Selves and Sexual Scripts

The interactionist conceptualization of reflexive self-hood also finds expression in John Gagnon and William Simon's work, which provided the first fully sociological challenge to biological and essentialist accounts of sexuality. Beginning with a series of articles published in the 1960s and systematized in *Sexual Conduct* (1974), together and separately they developed a 'scripting' approach to sexuality, which enables us to link subjective, interactive and cultural aspects of sexuality (Gagnon and Simon, 1974, 1986; Simon, 1996; Gagnon, 2004; Simon and Gagnon, 2005). Gagnon and Simon contested drive-reduction models of sexuality, what Jeffrey Weeks (1989) has called the 'pressure cooker' model: the idea that we are all born with powerful sexual urges that would burst out if social forces did not keep the lid on. According to Gagnon and Simon, we are not born with innate sexual drives that are repressed and moulded by the effects of culture, but *become* sexual through interactive processes. In questioning the concept of repression, they allowed for a positive conceptualization of the social. They also emphasize the everydayness of sexual activity: it occurs in the context of ordinary lives and is embedded in wider patterns of social relations. Rather than sexual motives and desires governing much of our non-sexual lives (as in psychoanalytic accounts), they maintain that, on the contrary, sexual activity is often motivated by non-sexual goals and desires. Thus the desire for sex is not the same as sexual desire (Simon, 1996).

Your World: Think of some non-sexual reasons why you might have sex with someone. How are motives for having sex related to non-sexual aspects of our lives and relationships?

The basic premise of Gagnon and Simon's perspective is that sexual conduct is meaningful, that it is endowed with meaning by reflexive human actors. Nothing from their perspective is sexual in itself; what makes an act or a situation sexual is the application of 'sexual scripts': 'Scripts are involved in learning the meaning of internal states, organizing the sequences of specifically sexual acts, decoding novel situations, setting the limits on sexual responses, and linking meaning from non-sexual aspects of life to specifically sexual experience' (Gagnon and Simon, 1974: 19). Even in a situation where sexual activity is possible – for example two people who are attracted to each other alone in a room – nothing sexual is likely to happen 'until either one or both actors organize . . . [their] behaviour into an appropriate script' (1974: 19).

In later work Gagnon and Simon identify three distinct but inter-related dimensions of scripting: the cultural, interpersonal and intra-psychic (Simon and Gagnon, 1986; Laumann and Gagnon, 1995; Laumann et al., 1994; Simon, 1996). **Cultural scenarios** are the 'cultural narratives' constructed around sexuality that circulate within our society – what poststructuralists would call discourses. They define shared meanings of sexuality, 'what the intersubjective culture treats as sexuality' (Laumann et al., 1994: 6), and provide guides for sexual conduct. Representations of erotic acts in films and novels, public debates about sexual morality, scientific constructions of sexuality and commonsense assumptions about sex are all components of cultural scenarios. These scenarios do not *determine* sexual conduct, but are cultural resources on which we draw in making sense of the sexual. In late modern societies, moreover, there are competing sexual scenarios available – so not everyone will draw on the same cultural scripts.

Interpersonal scripting emerges from and is deployed within everyday interaction. In negotiating a sexual relationship with someone and engaging in sex with them, we draw on wider cultural scenarios but interactively shape them 'into scripts for behaviour in specific contexts' (Simon, 1996: 41). This might involve consider-able negotiation if sexual partners are mobilizing different variants or forms of cultural scenarios: in heterosexual relationships, for example, women and men bring gendered versions of cultural scripts into play. In interpersonal sexual interaction, partners co-construct their scripts for their relationships and practices. These might often be predictable variations on common cultural themes, but they are, nonetheless, locally, interactionally produced by the actors involved. It is impor-tant to note, however, that this does not, especially in heterosexual relationships, necessarily imply equal participation in any mutually agreed script. There are numerous studies, some of which we will consider in Chapters 10 and 11, which suggest that 'his' definition of sexual reality often takes precedence over 'hers'. Furthermore, think of the confusion when a homosexual is assumed to be heterosexual or when a lesbian or gay person might hit on someone who is straight.

While both are examples of incongruent scripts, the latter does not have the same validity as an expected cultural scenario.

Intrapsychic scripting occurs at the level of our individual desires and thoughts through the internal reflexive processes of the self. Such conversations with ourselves enable us to construct fantasies or reflect on sexual encounters. Unlike the psychoanalytic psyche, where desires are thought to originate largely in our unconscious, the intrapsychic is 'a socially based form of mental life' (Gagnon, 2004: 276) through which we reflexively process material from cultural scenarios and interpersonal experience and make sense of sexual desires and practices. Our personal intrapsychic scripts inform, in turn, our engagement with interpersonal scripting and our interpretation of cultural scenarios.

In everyday life, then, the three levels of scripting intersect, with each level informing the others. However, the analytical distinction between them is important as it avoids an over-determined view of the sexual subject and allows for individual agency without assuming voluntarism (Gagnon, 2004: 276). The idea of the three levels of scripting also answers one of the criticisms of Gagnon and Simon's earlier work: that it did not address where scripts come from (Walby, 1986). Through the elaboration of different forms of scripting we can begin to see how sexual scripts emerge, evolve and change and are sustained culturally, interpersonally and subjectively. It should be clear from this that in using the term 'scripts', Gagnon and Simon are not suggesting that there are pre-patterned ways of 'doing sex'. Scripts are more like improvisations on the sexual themes available to us through our culture and experience (Jackson and Scott, 2007) and mobilize 'a complicated set of layered symbolic meanings' (Gagnon and Simon, 1974: 23). 'Doing sex' involves active agency: participants are not simply performing sexual acts, they are making and modifying sexual meaning through the interplay between intrapsychic, interpersonal and cultural scripting.

Gagnon and Simon's approach allows for agency and change in the sexual self: it is not set on an irreversible course in infancy, as in psychoanalytic accounts (see Ch. 6.4), but is modified throughout life. How each of us changes and how much will, of course, depend on our individual biographies and social locations. Change in the self occurs in two ways: first, and most obviously, through reflexively ordered interaction in the course of life experience; and second through reflection back on the past. In commonsense terms we tend to think of the past's effects upon us as a one-way process: we are what we are today because of past experience. Once we take account of the interpretive, reflexive processes involved in self-construction, we can appreciate that there is a two-way relationship between past and present. While the past clearly affects what happens in the present, we reflect upon our past – and interpret it from the standpoint of the present (see Mead, 1964 [1929]). Thus 'the present significantly reshapes the past as we reconstruct our biographies to bring them into greater congruence with our current identities, roles, situations and available vocabularies' (Gagnon and Simon, 1974: 13).

This retrospective reinterpretation has implications for the ways in which we become sexual, because what is sexual is not intrinsic to any act, sensation or situation, but is a product of the meanings we invest in it. Gagnon and Simon insisted that children cannot become sexual without access to the sexual scripts through which acts, relationships and feelings (emotions and sensations) become sexually meaningful. When children engage in play that adults deem to be sexual (such as 'doctors and nurses') it may have no such meaning for the child. Similarly, when we reflect back on our own early 'sexual' memories we do so from the standpoint of the adult present, using sexual scripts retrospectively to reconstruct our own pasts. Gagnon and Simon are not saying that young children are intrinsically asexual, only that sexual self-hood depends on being able to make sense of oneself as sexual. Children are neither sexual nor asexual in any essential sense; whether or not and when they become sexual will depend on the sexual scripts available to them. For example, children today may have more and earlier access to sources of sexual information than they did when *Sexual Conduct* was written.

Gagnon and Simon suggest that the most significant aspect of early childhood for the shaping of our sexualities is the acquisition of gender. Here they challenge the psychoanalytic perspective, in which sexual and emotional and identifications determine gender. In psychoanalysis, gender and sexuality are conflated: to be one 'sex' is to desire the other, and the direction of this desire is established early in childhood. Gagnon and Simon, on the other hand, make an analytical distinction between gender and sexuality, although they see them as empirically interrelated. They argue that the gendered self is established before we become fully sexual and provides the framework within which a sense of sexual self-hood later develops. This is not a deterministic relationship: there are varied ways in which we become sexual women and men, and it is no longer necessary to assume that being masculine or feminine means becoming heterosexual. The association between femininity, masculinity and heterosexuality, from this perspective, is a consequence of social processes, not a product of the internal workings of the psyche.

10

Becoming Gendered and Sexual

10.1 From Gender Attribution to Gender Identity

The approaches we outlined in the previous chapter suggest that gendered selves and identities develop before sexuality becomes intermeshed with gender. The beginning of this process is gender attribution, which, according to Suzanne Kessler and Wendy McKenna (1978), is logically prior to all other aspects of gender. As Erving Goffman notes, '[A]ll infants at birth are placed in one or the other of two sex classes'; this is 'an exemplary instance, if not a prototype, of social classification' (1977: 302). The most frequently asked question on hearing the news of a baby's birth is whether it is a boy or a girl, and only when this question has been answered can the baby be thought of as fully human. Parents are generally insulted if their infant is referred to as 'it'. That it is so difficult to acknowledge a child's humanity without the ascription of gender tells us just how crucial this social distinction is.

The classification of babies into gender categories is accomplished on the basis of their genitals. This is a social act, not a mere 'recognition' of a natural fact. Remember that genitals are in Garfinkel's term's 'cultural insignia': what is important is what they signify. For example, when parents say they want a little boy or little girl, it is rarely genitals that are uppermost in their minds; rather it is what they represent in terms of culturally specific expectations about the characteristics of little girls and little boys. Nonetheless, the presence of these recognizable cultural insignia is regarded as essential because of the commonsense assumptions that there are two sexes and only two sexes and that everyone must be one or the other. Immense confusion is caused when a baby's genitals are not immediately

classifiable as those of one or the other, when a baby is born intersexed (Kessler, 1998; Fausto-Sterling, 2000). Generally the medical
profession steps in to 'correct' the genitals to make the child 'one or
the other', which involves extensive, dangerous and painful surgery
and follow-up treatment (a practice now vigorously opposed by
organizations of intersexed people) [2]. In her study of parents'
and doctors' responses to intersexed children, Kessler draws on her
earlier ethnomethodological work to question why the existence of
two sexes has to be sustained at all cost, why genitals are considered
so important in and of themselves, and why they cannot be left until
a child is old enough to choose whether to have them corrected:
'Accepting genital ambiguity as a natural option would require that
physicians also acknowledge that genital ambiguity is "corrected"
not because it threatens the infant's life, but because it threatens the
infant's culture' (1998: 32). For most of the population, however, the
cultural attribution of gender takes place routinely and without much
thought (though in intersex conditions that are not evident at birth,
'mistakes' are sometimes made). This initial act of classification, over
which infants have no control, is highly consequential. The simple
statement 'it's a boy' or 'it's a girl' effectively begins the process of
bringing the child into being as a boy or girl. A similar point is made,
from a postmodernist queer perspective, by Judith Butler. The statement 'it's a girl' is linguistically performative – a pronouncement that
brings what it names into being – and begins the process of 'girling
the girl', materializing a sexed body. Performativity works to produce
gender through the reiteration of norms, but performativity is more
than mere performance since it 'consists in a reiteration of norms that
precede, constrain and exceed the performer' (Butler, 1993b: 243).
Butler's account, however, says nothing about the everyday processes
involved in the production of gender and turns instead to psychoanalysis to explain how 'regulatory norms form a "sexed subject"
in terms that establish the indistinguishability of psychic and bodily
formation' (1993b: 22), how we come to identify with our bodily
identity. This conceptualization of regulatory norms that are external to us leaves little room for the child's own agency in becoming
gendered.

    Children are initially at the mercy of others' interpretive practices,
informed by their commonsense assumptions (or by discursively
constituted norms, in Butler's terminology). Interpretive sociologies, however, suggest that once children begin to interact with those
around them, they become active in the construction of their own
gendered self-hood. The formation of the self depends on becoming

an object to ourselves as a result of experiencing ourselves as the object of others' attention (Mead, 1934). This in turn is mediated through language. The gendered identifier 'girl' or 'boy' will be repeated to the child with great frequency, probably even more often than his or her name (and the name, in many cultures, is also likely to be gendered). In other words, this will be the term that children come to associate most closely with themselves in their interactions with others. Children are learning language through these interactions and are simultaneously being told how they are identified by others and are thus being prepared for the internal conversations entailed in self-reflexivity.

In order to become an object to her/himself, a child must not only learn the language through which this is accomplished, but must simultaneously be able to play at being self and other – to practise standing outside of her/himself. For example, children will play at being an adult telling a child off, thereby displaying their understanding of the position of the adult other. They are beginning to learn to 'take the attitude of the other', to see themselves and the world from another's point of view. In order to take their place in the social world, children must move on from this simple self–other 'play' stage to the 'game' stage (Mead, 1934), where they take several others into account at once in order to participate in the ongoing game. As children we must acquire the ability to take the attitude of the 'generalized other', to see ourselves and the world from the point of view of people in general, to share in the commonsense view of the world that is maintained and renegotiated in everyday interaction. We gradually become capable of orienting ourselves to numerous generalized others from specific groups of people we know to 'people in general'.

Gender attribution ensures that the child who enters into play or the game is already invested with gender by others. They are, however, subsequently active in making sense of gender. In the play stage, the other they 'play at' is gendered; when they engage in games, they are locating themselves within an interactional field of gendered others, beginning to make sense of the importance of gender categories. We should be wary, however, of assuming that when a child uses gender labels they have the same meaning for the child that they would have for an adult. What is apparently happening in the first few years of children's lives is that gender is becoming incorporated into their emerging and evolving sense of self, but that what gender means to them is likely to undergo significant revision and reinterpretation.

Your World: Do you remember when you first became consciously aware that the world was divided by gender?

Bronwyn Davies' ethnography of Australian pre-school children (1989), which was one of the earliest studies of young children to bring gender duality into question, illustrates the variable meanings that gender can have for this age-group. While she frames her research in poststructuralist terms, her account is consistent with interactionist and ethnomethodological interpretations. Her key finding is the importance of gender duality itself for children, such that they will do a great deal of interpretive work in order to keep that binary intact. Davies tried to disrupt the children's gender assumptions, suggesting, for example, that men could wear dresses and reading them feminist fairy tales in one of which the princess rescues the prince rather than vice versa. The children, however, resisted attempts to redraw gender boundaries and to challenge their ideas about the proper attributes of each gender. Nonetheless, the boundary between the two genders is, for these children, not entirely impermeable in that they will sometimes 'play at' being the other gender – as when a normally docile feminine girl put on a man's waistcoat and marched off assertively to reclaim a toy appropriated by one of the boys – and occasionally both boys and girls crossed the line to play with children of the other gender. Moreover, there was no single way of doing or being a little girl or a little boy. Gender duality permits variation within categories – more so for girls than for boys. Davies identified three varieties of pre-school femininity: the 'home corner girls' play house and are conventionally feminine; the 'rough tough princesses' are assertive, middle-class tomboys but retain typically feminine commitments to romance; the 'sirens', most of whom are working class, are already learning to present themselves as physically attractive and use flirtatious strategies to get what they want. For boys there are only two models: 'superhero' macho boys and 'articulate intellectuals' – and at pre-school the former is more highly valued. Hence, while gender is clearly a central factor in the social life and self-conception of these children, its precise content and meaning are by no means fixed. Moreover, some ways of being gendered and doing gender are class-variable, especially for girls.

An interactionist account, which presupposes a self constantly in process as a result of reflexive internal conversations, would lead us to expect the meanings of gender to undergo constant modification as we encounter and interpret new situations and experiences. Some examples can be found in Barrie Thorne's classic (1993) study of the ways in which American school children in their final years of elementary school construct, reconstruct and renegotiate gender boundaries. Thorne contests the notion that children at this age inhabit two entirely distinct gendered cultures, noting that there is far more ambiguity and ambivalence about gender than is usually acknowledged. Nonetheless, like Davies' pre-schoolers, these children were actively engaged in the construction and policing of the gender binary, and this was asymmetrical. Whereas a girl could be a tomboy and 'one of the lads' without losing status, a boy whose masculinity was in doubt risked being labelled a 'fag' (see also Renold, 2005). Thorne notes that younger children used this label without awareness of its sexual connotations – they simply took up a term that seemed to encapsulate failed masculinity – but older children were aware of its sexual import and it then became much more problematic and dangerous for any boy to be so identified.

10.2   From Gendered Selves to Sexual Selves

As Thorne notes, once children approach adolescence, gender as a whole becomes increasingly sexualized. Like Gagnon and Simon (1974), she argues that it is not the physical changes of puberty that bring this about, but the social meanings with which they are invested. Whether the children in her study embraced the more sexualized 'teenage' forms of gender or preferred to remain in the more asexual condition of childhood had nothing to do with their physical maturation: '[S]ocial practices shape the transition' (Thorne, 1993: 147). This is now even more evident as children gain access to aspects of sexual scripts earlier than was the case even a decade ago, and are often participating in a more sexualized teen culture well before the end of their primary or elementary schooling.

Asexuality is not a natural condition of childhood but a consequence of a social ideal of children as 'innocent'. Adults police children's access to sexual knowledge and worry about them becoming sexual too soon (Jackson and Scott, 1999, 2010). It is only the specifically erotic component of sexual scripts that adults attempt to conceal from children; other aspects of adult sexual scripts are more readily available and contribute to children's self-understanding and interpretation of the world around them. For example, adult ideas about bodily modesty and decorum are conveyed to children as part of the routines of child-care and are likely to affect the ways in which children make sense of their own bodies as they discover that certain body parts should not be displayed in public. These conventions are gendered: bodily modesty is more of an issue for small girls than for small boys, but at the same time to be a socially competent little girl also entails concern with appearance, and girls often construct a self-presentation as 'sexy' (like Davies' 'sirens') well before being aware of its *sexual* connotations.

Children of both sexes are also generally well aware that there are aspects of adult life from which they are excluded, that there are things that adults do not talk about in front of them or that adults avoid answering certain questions. Parents often express a desire to be open with their children about sexuality but find this difficult in practice (Solomon et al., 2002; Kirkman et al., 2005; Frankham, 2006). In a study of sexual communication within British families, Jo Frankham (2006) found that the most common parental strategy was only to talk about sexual matters when children asked direct questions and then only to provide answers that they think the child is 'ready' to hear. Parents see this as being 'honest', but the way they respond often forecloses the possibility of further questions and explanations so that children are left mystified rather than enlightened, once again learning that certain things cannot be discussed. Few parents, Frankham found, were willing to discuss sexual pleasure, even when children's questions could raise this. Most commonly, parental 'openness' was limited to answering questions about where babies come from, so that the information children receive is framed in terms of reproductive, heterosexual relations. It seems, then, that the idea that children are, and should be, asexual or 'innocent' colours parent–child interaction, making it difficult to talk about sex and marking it as different from other topics of conversation (and possibly taboo), so that children themselves can become too embarrassed to discuss sex with their parents.

The process of learning about sex is therefore made more problematic than it might otherwise be and has been likened to being given a jigsaw puzzle with important pieces missing and no picture on the box (see Jackson, 1982; Jackson and Scott, 2010). There is one crucial piece of the puzzle, however, to which children have access from an early age: the normality of heterosexual relationships. Children acquire a great deal of commonsense knowledge about heterosexual life simply by observing and participating in the social world around them and from representations of heterosexual relationships in the media. Only a minority of children grow up in alternative households where heterosexuality is dislodged from its central place. Most will learn, as a matter of course, that families are generally founded on a relationship between a man and a woman (even if they do not always stay together), that it is proper for them to have both a father and mother (even if they do not live together), and that it is normal to 'fall in love' with someone of the other gender. And these arrangements will come to seem 'normal' well before they are aware of the sexual activities these entail.

Emma Renold's (2005, 2006) research on 10- and 11-year-old schoolchildren in the UK illustrates the ubiquity of heteronormative assumptions and practices in children's lives. Children of this age in modern western societies are usually beginning to develop a sense of themselves as potential sexual actors, and in Britain it is usual for them to have received some rudimentary sex education by this time – generally limited to basic facts about puberty, conception and birth. The children Renold studied inhabited a world divided by gender and in which there were few friendships across gender lines unless a boy and girl were 'going out' with each other. These early boyfriend– girlfriend relationships were not highly sexual – physical intimacy was largely limited to holding hands and the occasional kiss – but they gave boys, and more especially girls, status within the peer group. Some aspects of this sub-teen culture were more sexualized. Girls were keen to dress and present themselves as 'sexy' or 'tarty' (slutty), but 'not too tarty', thus revealing their awareness of the importance of sexual attractiveness in maintaining a feminine identity and also of the fine line between acceptable and unacceptable manifestations of sexiness. Boys asserted their masculinity through playing football and through physical and verbal aggression directed towards each other and the girls – and sometimes through sexual harassment of the girls. Those who did not conform to this heterosexual culture – girls who were considered 'fat' or 'ugly' and boys who were insufficiently macho – were often stigmatized or bullied, and for boys this meant being labelled as 'benders' or as 'gay' (the latter intended as a term of abuse rather than a positive identity).

As they enter their teens, then, children have already begun to construct a gendered and increasingly sexualized sense of themselves and others. The physical changes of puberty are accorded gendered meanings: in her study of American adolescents, Karin Martin (1996) found that these changes gave boys a positive sense of maturity and agency, while girls were more ambivalent, concerned about body image and sexual objectification – and this had implications for their sexual selves. By this time the missing jigsaw pieces of sexual knowledge are acquired and begin to fall into place, enabling young people to create a picture of sexual life informed by the prevailing cultural scenarios. They do not simply 'internalize' aspects of the cultural scenarios available to them, but actively make sense of them as they reflexively incorporate sexual elements into their subjective sense of themselves. This process continues to be highly gendered (see Martin, 1996): '[G]ender is the dividing line along which sexual expression, desire and experience is organized' (Kimmel, 2005: 3). In the first place, heteronormative gender structures the contexts in which young people learn more about sexuality and the content of what is learned. Secondly, their established embodied gendered identity provides a framework for making sense of new knowledge and experience and plays a part in retrospective interpretation of past experience and their incorporation of it into an emerging sense of sexual self-hood.

Young people gain access to sexual information and to the wider sexual scenarios of their culture through a number of sources. Parental and school sex education provides some basic knowledge, but studies from the 1960s to the present suggest that this is limited (see, for example, Schofield, 1965; Thomson and Scott, 1991; Levine, 2002; Fine and McLelland 2006; Frankham, 2006). Because of public anxieties about the sexual conduct of young people, school sex education is often hedged around with restrictions that tend to reinforce its heterosexual, reproductive and conventionally gendered focus and places the emphasis on avoiding the 'dangers' of (hetero) sex: sexually transmitted infections and pregnancy (Levine, 2002; Wight et al., 2002; Pilcher, 2005). Little is said about desire and pleasure: even more liberal sex education tends to be characterized by what Michele Fine calls 'the missing discourse of desire' (1988; Fine and McLelland, 2006). Yet in order to become competent adult sexual actors, young people must somehow be able to make sense of sexual desire and pleasure and learn how to accomplish sexual acts. For this they must look elsewhere – most often to the media and their peers. These sources, too, are structured by gender.

TASK: How could sex education be improved?

In small groups discuss your own experience of sex education, its good and bad points. List what you think should be included in an ideal sex education programme, noting when and how it should be taught and what obstacles might be encountered in implementing your programme

Some media sources, such as mainstream movies, TV and the internet, are accessible to most young people. Others, however, are more differentiated by gender, such as girls' teen magazines and 'lads' mags'. The content of these media products often reproduces highly gendered assumptions about sexuality, most evident in objectifying images of women in young men's magazines and the assumption that all 'normal' men are excited by such images and motivated by innate unstoppable (hetero)sexual urges (see Ch. 8.2 and 8.5). Young women's magazines also purvey highly gendered messages about sexuality, though they are valued as a source of information not available elsewhere (Buckingham and Bragg, 2004; Allen, 2005). Sue Jackson's study of the problem pages of teen magazines in Australia and New Zealand (2005a, 2005b) reveals somewhat contradictory tendencies, which are also evident in similar publications in other western countries. On the one hand, the content of the magazines as a whole and the problem pages in particular give girls permission to discuss sexual desire and pleasure, but attempts to 'do' desire were often 'undone' in the response to the letters – especially in instances of lesbian desire. There was, she found, some recognition of sexual diversity, but on the whole the magazines assumed heterosexuality, and advice tended to reinforce the normality of heterosexual penetration and to emphasize the risks and dangers of sex (so defined) rather than its pleasures.

Young people do not, of course consume the media uncritically; they interpret what they read and see in terms of its relevance for them (Buckingham and Bragg, 2004). These interpretations are frequently mediated through interpersonal interaction with their friends, through which they collectively make sense of the sexual mores and practices deriving from wider cultural scenarios. This is not a matter of 'peer pressure', as if young people adopt a herd mentality, but rather a means of making sexual knowledge personally meaningful and developing a sense of sexual competence. Friends play a vital role in validating young people's own experience, but not everyone's experience is equally validated: the peer group can also regulate sexuality, stigmatizing and excluding those who do not conform to heterosexual norms – those who are perceived as gay, lesbian or, in the case of young women, 'too sexual' (Martin, 1996; Phoenix et al., 2003; Chambers et al., 2004). Young men can find that their peers act as 'gender police' (Kimmel, 2005: 36), threatening to unmask them as less than masculine, and will often present themselves as more macho in the peer group than when away from it (Phoenix et al., 2003), suggesting that there might be a disjunction between their self-presentation and their subjective sense of self. Peer groups can also exclude those who are different in terms of class or ethnicity. For example, the sexualized culture of young white femininity in the West can be alienating for young women of South Asian descent, though some become adept at moving between the cultures of home and peer group, adopting different identities in different settings. Those who are excluded must find other means of constructing gendered self-hood outwith the norms of the dominant peer group.

The construction of sexual self-hood is an ongoing process involving not only reflexive processing of novel information and situations but also retrospective reinterpretation as young people begin, in Gagnon and Simon's terms, to bring that past into greater congruity with their present understandings of themselves and their social world. Thus past experience is reconfigured as sexually meaningful – and this process, too, is gendered. Young women who had, as children, learned to play on their attractiveness can begin to manage and manipulate the erotic potential of being 'sexy'. Those who had, as children, not fitted into normative standards of masculinity or femininity might reconstruct themselves as potentially gay and lesbian (see Plummer's work on this in Ch. 2.5). Adult gay men and lesbians often tell a story of self in which they 'always knew' they were lesbian or gay or that they always were but only later came to 'realize' that this was the case – often because they felt 'different' as children, not quite normally (normatively) gendered (Whisman, 1996). The wider visibility of queer culture in recent times may make it easier to construct such an identity than it once was, since cultural scenarios other than normatively heterosexual ones are now more accessible, but the dominance of normative heterosexuality within teen culture continues to marginalize young lesbians and gay men (see Epstein et al., 2003; Savin-Williams, 2004). Ritch Savin-Williams summarizes research that suggests that those who have lesbian or gay relationships in adolescence are more likely subsequently to develop a positive sense of their own sexual identity. Such relationships, however, are difficult to establish while still at school and usually have to be hidden from peers and for many peer pressure makes it too risky to act upon same-sex desires (Savin-Williams, 2004).

10.3 Negotiating Gendered and Sexual Identities

Notably those who grow up to be heterosexual have no need to explain to themselves or others how they became heterosexual.

Heterosexuality is rarely adopted as an explicit identity; it is simply taken for granted as 'normal' and is a central feature of social life among young people. Gender, however, remains key to heterosexuals' sense of themselves as competent sexual actors and, conversely, heterosexual sexual competence helps validate their sense of gendered self-hood. Young western heterosexual women, however, find themselves faced with contradictory expectations. They are now expected to have aspirations beyond becoming wives and mothers, and, for the more privileged, educational and career opportunities have expanded a great deal since the 1970s (see Ch. 5.1). Nonetheless, success in sexual relationships continues to be a source of social esteem and self-worth and has arguably become trickier to negotiate. New sexual scripts are on offer validating female heterosexual pleasure and experimentation. For example, when young women graduate from teen magazines to those for young adults, they encounter exhortations to get in touch with the erotic potential of their bodies. Sexual passivity is no longer advocated: where advice on 'getting and keeping your man' was, not too long ago, confined to looking good and cooking well, now it routinely includes tips on techniques to guarantee him sexual ecstasy. At the same time, the double standard of morality, although considerably eroded, has not disappeared altogether and young women continue to be vulnerable to negative identification as 'sluts' or 'slags' if they are too sexual – and to equally negative labelling as frigid, uptight drags if they are not sexual enough.

The dominant cultural definition of what sex *is* has remained largely unchanged since feminists first challenged the myth of the vaginal orgasm in the 1970s (see Ch. 7.1). Sex is still defined in terms of the coital imperative (which also serves to define 'normal' sex as heterosexual), with a conventional sequence of sexual acts comprising foreplay, followed by vaginal penetration, followed by his orgasm (and hers if she's lucky). One single sexual activity among many – heterosexual, vaginal penetration – is equated with 'having sex', and this defines the boundary of virginity, the act needed to 'lose' it. Losing one's virginity is an important transition in the lives of young men and women, but with differently gendered consequences. It brings young men status in the peer group, it 'makes a boy a man'; but if young women's virginity is 'lost' too soon or without due care, it can negatively impact on their reputations (Holland et al., 1996; Martin, 1996). There are other ways of confirming manhood, such as through physical prowess, toughness and courage (Wight, 1996; Connell, 1995, 2000), but young men need to guard anything that might call their masculine identity into question in the eyes of other men. In many ways heterosexuality continues to define masculinity, and homophobia, as Michael Kimmel (2005) says, still serves to maintain its boundaries.

If masculinity is confirmed through being (hetero)sexually *active*, what confirms femininity is being sexually *attractive* to men – being 'sexy' but not too *sexual*. The traditional view that men want sex and women want love may now be widely challenged, but young women anxious for their reputations find it difficult to abandon it altogether (Allen, 2005). A number of studies have highlighted the constraints imposed on young women by double standards, male-defined views of sexuality and the difficulty of expressing their own desires (e.g. Holland et al., 1996; Martin, 1996; Tolman, 2002). Deborah Tolman, in her aptly titled *Dilemmas of Desire* (2002), presents case studies of young American women from varied class and ethnic backgrounds, few of whom seemed fully comfortable in acknowledging and acting on their own sexual desires and who often said that sex 'just happened' to them. A small minority denied their capacity for desire altogether, but most sought means of expressing it in ways that avoided its perceived dangers. Sexual violence and coercion is still an all too common experience, and awareness of it bounds young women's understanding of their own sexuality and limits their sexual practices (see Holland et al., 1996; Phillips, 2000). It is important to note, however, that these young women are by no means passive victims. They are actively navigating their way through a sexual landscape in which many potential obstacles stand in the way of reaching desirable destinations.

This is evident even where more casual forms of heterosexual encounter are the norm. In his study of 'hooking up' culture on American university campuses, Kimmel (2008) found that while both women and men seemed equally involved in recreational spontaneous sex, this practice was profoundly gendered. Women were far more careful about 'hooking up' than were the men and described it is as scripted and planned rather than fully spontaneous. Moreover, the double standard was still prevalent: 'Hooking up enhances his reputation; it damages her reputation.' He is a 'stud' who 'scores'; she is a 'slut' who 'gives it up' too easily (Kimmel, 2008: 55). Women are also more likely to try to turn casual sexual dalliances into a relationship – which men seek to avoid. Men's 'relationship phobia' is, Kimmel says, not a fear of romantic entanglement. Hooking up is less about 'relationships with women and a lot more to do with guys' relationships with other guys' (2008: 57). By hooking up, a man confirms his masculinity; he proves 'that he is a man among men, able to hold his head high . . . among the other guys, having scored the night before' (2008: 63) [3].

It should be clear from this discussion that gendered sexual self-hood derives not from within ourselves but from interaction with others and from anticipating and imagining others' views of us through 'taking the attitude of the other'. Moreover, how we might identify ourselves does not always coincide with how we might be identified by others. This creates the possibility of 'misidentification' and also dis-identification: distancing oneself from an undesired identity. These processes are particularly evident in relation to the 'othering' of racialized minorities or those from lower classes. Our sense of self is formed in part through the way others see us, but it is possible to resist negative identifications, especially if there is a community to which we can look for more positive sources of identity.

Women from the poorer segments of the working classes are often branded as improperly feminine: for example, as overly fecund, promiscuous welfare mothers. Certain styles of working-class dress and conduct are read as indicative of deficient femininity, lacking in the decorum or sophistication of its middle-class (or more respectable working-class) equivalent. When such women express their active agency, especially collectively, this is likely to be read from a middle-class standpoint as inappropriate conduct. In the UK in the 1990s a popular stereotype of disreputable white femininity was the 'Essex girl' (the US equivalent would be white trash), described by Germaine Greer (2001) in the following terms:

> She used to be conspicuous, as she clacked along the pavements in her white plastic stilettos, her bare legs mottled patriotic red, white and blue with cold, and her big bottom barely covered by her denim miniskirt. Essex girls usually come in twos, both behind pushchairs with large infants in them. Sometimes you hear them before you see them, cackling shrilly or yelling to each other from one end of the street to the other, or berating those infants in blood-curdling fashion. . . . The Essex girl is tough, loud, vulgar and unashamed. Her hair is badly dyed not because she can't afford a hairdresser, but because she wants it to look brassy. Nobody makes her wear her ankle chain; she likes the message it sends . . . she is not ashamed to admit what she puts behind her ears to make her more attractive is her ankles. She is anarchy on stilts.

More respectable femininities are defined against this kind of imagery. A respectable working-class background can be embraced as a source of positive identification, but as the structural bases of collective working-class identity are now less strong (see Introduction to Part III), some may seek to dissociate themselves from it. In her ethnographic study of working-class young women enrolled in vocational training as carers, Beverly Skeggs (1997) found that they typically dis-identified with the working class, investing instead in femininity as cultural capital, as a possible avenue to social mobility and a means of constructing a positive sense of self. Interestingly here the disavowal of class affiliation was accompanied by greater investment in gendered identification.

An example of racialized misidentification can be seen in the case of young Muslim women in western cultures who wear the *hijab*, which we discussed in Chapter 8.3. From a dominant western perspective this covering is often seen as signalling oppression. For young Muslim women themselves, however, adopting the *hijab* in the contemporary western context represents a positive choice – and a very public statement of identity, as Myfanwy Franks (2000) points out. Although it can mean that they become easier targets of racism, it also has positive consequences. As well as being a statement of religious identity and commitment, veiling may represent a deliberate rejection of the sexualized style of femininity prevalent among non-Muslim women and the risk of sexual objectification that goes with it. Franks' British respondents saw this avoidance of the objectifying male gaze as one of the benefits of veiling. From this perspective the supposed freedoms of western femininity might represent no more than the freedom to become a sexual object, and wearing the *hijab* becomes a means of asserting oneself as an autonomous gendered and sexual subject.

Misidentification can also occur across the heterosexual/homosexual binary, as in the case of the Korean woman discussed in the Introduction to Part IV, but in either direction. A young heterosexual man who appears effeminate might be misidentified as gay, just as a gay man may pass (intentionally or not) as straight. Dis-identification can also occur: lesbians and gay men often report going through a period, especially in their teenage years, of heterosexual dating in order to 'fit in' and appear normal (Savin-Williams, 2004). It is much easier to maintain a positive sense of oneself as lesbian or gay in the context of a supportive community. Young people often find it easier to come out once they have left home, and many gravitate towards large cities where there is an established lesbian or gay community. Such opportunities, however, are not evenly distributed. Leaving home is easier for the more privileged – whether by going to university or finding a well-paid job. Those less fortunate can be forced to leave home because of their sexuality (Dunne et al., 2002). Moreover, queer spaces in cities may be more accessible and welcoming to those with the economic and cultural resources necessary to adopt the appropriate style (see, for example, Taylor, 2004).

In these examples gender and sexuality clearly intersect with other identities (ascribed or adopted), most notably those based on class, ethnicity and religion. We all, however, potentially occupy multiple intersecting identity categories. These exist simultaneously as part of who we are and how we are located in the social world, though particular identities may come to the fore in specific contexts. Not all of the social categories attributable to us give rise to consciously adopted identities; in particular there is an asymmetry between normative and non-normative categories. We have already noted that heterosexuals rarely name themselves as such, though they may distance themselves from the homosexual other as 'not gay'. Similarly in white-dominated societies whiteness is rarely adopted as an identity or even recognized as an ethnicity, except by white supremacists. Those who belong to oppressed, subordinate and marginalized social groups are labelled as 'other' to the norm, but those labels may become sites of resistance; an identity label that was once derogatory or exclusionary such as 'black' or 'queer' can then be reclaimed collectively as a locus of positive identification and/or political action and thus provide a basis for individual identity and a positive sense of self.

Not only do we each embody multiple intersecting identities, but subjective aspects of the self, which are not necessarily associated with definable identities, are also multiple. Different facets of the self come into play in the varied social settings in which we interact with diverse others. Becoming a competent gendered and sexual adult in a complex society involves being able to negotiate transitions between settings and to manage presentations of self (Goffman, 1969). Thus the self is never a fixed structure even in adulthood, though we are usually able to construct for ourselves an ongoing and reasonably coherent sense of who we are through our reflexive capacities. Moreover, the self continues to evolve and change over time. Although it is likely that the self becomes more settled as we adapt to the predictable routines of adult life, there is always the possibility of it becoming unsettled by unforeseen events: for example a new love affair or the end of a long-term relationship. Thus gendered and sexual self-hood is always subject to revision through ongoing interaction with others and retrospective reinterpretation from the standpoint of new situations in which we can find ourselves.

11

Sexual Selves in Global Late Modernity

11.1 Normative Heterosexuality and Alternative Sexualities

Patterns of sexual life are clearly undergoing change. In many parts of the world the weakening link between sexuality and reproduction, more liberal attitudes to sexuality and a greater diversity of sexual lifestyles are changing the conditions that shape sexual selves and identities. Nonetheless, heterosexuality retains its normative status, and within heterosexual relations gender and sexuality remain closely intertwined, often in rather predictable ways. Heterosexuality is, by definition, a gendered institution based on gendered relationships: social and personal relations between women and men. As we pointed out in Chapter 5, heterosexual relationships involve far more than sexual relationships: for example how heterosexual couples organize household finances and domestic chores is as much a part of the everyday doing of heterosexuality as their sex life. The mundane day-to-day patterns of heterosexual life have implications for self and identity that are often taken for granted but bear closer examination.

While heterosexuality is rarely consciously adopted as an identity, many of the identities that are likely to be important to heterosexual adults derive from their location within heterosexually ordered family or kin relations – such as husband or wife, mother or father – and these identities may in turn be important to their sense of self as competently masculine or feminine. For example, a man's idea of himself as a good husband and father, able to provide a decent standard of living for his wife and children, is often important to his masculine identity, which comes under threat if he is made redundant. In the days when women with small children were usually full-time 'housewives' they often complained that they lost their sense of an independent identity, becoming defined only in relation to others: as 'John's wife' or 'Sarah's mother'. Now, when a mother more frequently juggles the 'double shift' of waged work and domestic work, she may worry about the impact of her competing responsibilities on her ability to be a 'good mother'. Parental identities are also related to expectations about children's properly heterosexual futures. This is most evident when these expectations are disrupted. For example, a mother's response to discovering that a son is gay, particularly if he is an only child, might be to express regret that he will not 'make her a grandmother', thus depriving her of an identity proper to the later stages of the normative heterosexual life-cycle.

The differing locations of women and men within heterosexual relations also impact upon the self in more subtle ways. If we remember that the self, as conceptualized by George Herbert Mead, is constructed in relation to others, then *how* we relate to others has consequences for the self. As we have seen in Chapter 4, women still do most of the care work within heterosexual families, which means that men have that work done for them. The care work that women do is not merely 'caring for' others; it is enmeshed with caring *about* them. This 'labour of love' is not merely a matter of physical chores but involves anticipating others' wants and needs, which engenders a heightened relational self-reflexivity in which the self is constantly located in relation to the requirements of others. Men's freedom from having to be concerned with the maintenance of their own bodies and the fact that the space in which they are serviced is the domestic, or private, realm (Smith, 1988) facilitates a more individualized, autonomous form of self-hood, which is especially important in orienting themselves in the public sphere of work. Thus the relational reflexivity that women practise in the day-to-day running of heterosexual family life may actually *enable* men's sense of individuality.

Caring for others extends to the sexual aspects of heterosexual relations. One obvious example of this is the practice of faking orgasm. It is no longer enough to 'have sex' with a woman to confirm competent masculinity; it is increasingly seen to be a man's responsibility to 'give' his partner an orgasm. Women will therefore fake orgasm in order not to cast doubt on the virility of their partner. And, it seems, most are very skilled at this. In an Australian study (Roberts et al., 1995), most of the women interviewed admitted to 'faking it' on occasion, while very few of the men were willing to believe they had ever been with a partner who had faked. Similar performances accompany both 'faked' and 'authentic' orgasms, since the need to reassure men about their sexual proficiency exists whether or not orgasm 'really' happened (Jackson and Scott, 2007). Thus certain kinds of gendered, sexual selves are reconfirmed in sexual interaction, involving interplay between care for the other and adequate performance: he affirms himself as a caring lover and virile man through her orgasm; her feminine sensitivity is underlined by appropriate appreciation of his sexual skills and her care for his ego through her performance of orgasm.

In a British study of long-term heterosexual relationships, Jean Duncombe and Dennis Marsden (1996) found that women carried out a great deal of emotional work in keeping the relationship working, including pretending desire and agreeing to unwanted sex. Again these women were extending the work of care to sexual relations. Both men and women, however, expressed dissatisfaction with sex, but for different reasons. Women complained about the *quality* of the sex. One, for example, said: 'It was like he knew there had to be foreplay so – a couple of squeezes up here and a quick rummage about down there and straight in.' Men, on the other hand, complain about the *quantity* (lack of) sex. As one, rather bluntly, put it: 'It would be no skin off her nose. . . . Sometimes I just want her to let me put it in and do it' (Duncombe and Marsden, 1996: 230). It is not difficult to imagine why this man's partner may have been less than enthusiastic about sex! These tensions reveal the continuing gendered construction of sexual desires, including essentialist assumptions about men's sexual 'needs'.

This has become more evident with the medicalization of sexual problems. It is no coincidence that traditionally male failure to perform vaginal penetration was termed 'impotence' (literally powerlessness), while women's lack of interest in sex was (and sometimes still is) seen as 'frigidity' (coldness). These are, of course, highly gendered terms, reflecting men's and women's positioning within heterosexuality. For many men, being able to perform sexually remains central to their self-conception as properly masculine, even though impotence has now been re-branded in medical parlance as 'erectile dysfunction'. And, where once men may have accepted declining 'potency' as an inevitable consequence of ageing, now Viagra and similar pharmaceuticals promise to keep them 'forever functional' and also reinforce the coital imperative (Marshall and Katz, 2002). These pharmaceutical developments may also undermine women's attempts to develop more equitable and enjoyable heterosexual relations. Annie Potts and her colleagues (2003) found that women complained that when men took Viagra, foreplay was abandoned;

moreover, men often took the pill without consulting their wives and then pressured them to agree to sex.

All this may seem to paint a very pessimistic picture of adult heterosexuality. Yet for much of the population, heterosexual relationships provide them with their most meaningful sources of identity construction as well as valued personal relationships. It should also be clear that even where heterosexual relations clearly disadvantage women, this disadvantage is not merely imposed upon them from above. In some instances what might objectively be seen as inequality, such as women's caring responsibilities, may be actively and reflexively reconstructed as providing a sense of self-worth, while in other cases women are clearly contesting the inequities they encounter. There is a little evidence that some heterosexuals are consciously pursuing alternative lifestyles and modes of being heterosexual: seeking more egalitarian domestic arrangements (VanEvery, 1995), finding alternatives to couple relationships (Roseneil and Budgeon, 2004) or maintaining couple relationships while living apart (Holmes, 2004). These might be a small minority, but they do demonstrate the possibility of doing heterosexuality differently.

Most heterosexuals, however, view their own sexuality as given and natural even when they express tolerance towards other sexualities. For example, the men and women interviewed by Paul Johnson for his study of heterosexual love saw 'love' as an emotion that could be experienced irrespective of gender and sexual orientation. When asked whether they could love someone of the same gender, however, they found that they could not imagine themselves engaging in a same-gender sexual relationship – and in some cases expressions of disgust, previously concealed beneath a veneer of tolerance, came to the surface. As Johnson argues, 'through a rejection of homosexuality as "outside" of themselves, heterosexuals establish an ontological validity for their own identities and . . . as a consequence, their own intimate practices are naturalized' (Johnson, 2005: 119).

What of those who are not heterosexual? Since the last few decades of the twentieth century, movements for gay and women's liberation and the advance of lesbian and gay rights in many western countries have made sexually dissident identities and lifestyles more liveable and alternative identities more available to those who feel they do not fit into the heterosexual mainstream. There are a range of possible identities on offer – for example lesbian, gay, queer, bisexual, transgendered – or even, as in academic queer theory, the refusal of all identities (see Ch. 7.4), though in activist circles queer is more often adopted as a radically oppositional identity. It is now possible for lesbians and gay men to forge 'families of choice' and create new understandings of kinship and friendship (Weston, 1991; Weeks et al., 2001). There have been a number of empirical studies showing that these domestic arrangements are considerably more egalitarian than those in heterosexual households, though this does not necessarily mean that they are free of conflict (for example, Dunne, 1991; Weeks et al., 2001). Without the conventional scripts and expectations that inform heterosexual relationships, those forming same-gender relationships must construct their own, and many consciously pursue a more equal form of partnership. For some a lesbian, gay or queer identity is consciously framed in opposition to heteronormativity – whether or not they live in couple relationships – while others downplay their difference. For example, in her study of lesbian parents in the UK, Jacqui Gabb (2004) found that most stressed the ordinariness of their families.

Transgendered identities are also becoming more visible, particularly when public figures change gender. In the summer of 2009, Chastity Bono, the daughter, now son, of sixties singing duo Sonny and Cher, came out as 'Chas', announcing his FTM (female to male) transition – having previously identified as a lesbian. This was certainly enough of an event to be discussed in the media, but was largely treated in tones of taken-for-granted acceptance. We seem, then, to have come a long way from the situation of Agnes described in Chapter 9. Where Agnes sought to conceal her male past and 'pass' as a 'normal' woman, it is now possible openly to claim a transgendered identity. There are a number of examples from history of cross-gendered individuals (often women passing as men), but the possibility of physically changing sex depended on advances in medicine, which made a 'transsexual' identity possible (Hausman, 1995). At first most of those who changed sex, usually from male to female (MTF), tended to adopt conventional styles of femininity, much like Agnes. Indeed medical protocols demanded, and sometimes still demand, this conformity. Often such individuals represented themselves as women trapped in a male body (for example, Morris, 1978), and some still take this view. Others, however, publicly proclaim a transgendered identity and refuse to accept the trappings of conventional femininity or masculinity or subvert them in some way (for example, by refusing to be identified as heterosexual), taking up identities as 'gender outlaws' (Bornstein, 1994).

In a social world divided into two genders it is easy to see why those uncomfortable with the gender they were originally assigned seek to cross the gender divide, changing a fundamental aspect of their identity. This does disrupt one of the everyday assumptions about gender that Garfinkel identified: that people stay one gender for life (see Ch. 9.2). Analytically we can also see that changing gender can also reconfirm it: an individual switches gender but the gender categories remain intact and so does the assumption that we have to embody certain characteristics in order to be properly gendered. Gender reassignment surgery also perpetuates the assumption that gender depends on having the appropriate genitals. It can also reinforce normative heterosexuality. For example, a man who is sexually attracted to other men may refuse an identity as homosexual, insisting that he is 'really' a heterosexual woman and seek medical treatment to transform his body to that of a woman. This has been a controversial issue, particularly among feminists, some of whom see transitioning from one gender to the other as maintaining gender division and compulsory heterosexuality while others see it as disrupting gender and heteronormativity.

> **TASK: Is it possible to be a straight man trapped in a lesbian's body?**
>
> Imagine an individual who follows the same route as Chastity/Chas Bono, from a lesbian woman to a straight man. In small groups list the ways in which this subverts gender and sexual binaries and the ways in which it might confirm them. Discuss how this transition might impact on the individual themselves, their relationships with others and the wider society.

11.2 Modern Western Transformations of Self and Identity

The idea that we can choose to develop new sexual identities has been attributed to the development of modernity, characterized by increasing opportunities for self-reflexivity, as in Anthony Giddens' (1991) reflexive project of the self, which we discussed in Chapter 8. Theorists such as Ulrich Beck and Elisabeth Beck-Gernsheim have associated increasing life choices in modernity with de-traditionalization and individualization, where the 'de-routinization of the mundane' breaks down the habitual 'into a cloud of possibilities to be thought about and negotiated' (Beck and Beck-Gernsheim, 2002: 6). Life, they tell us, is no longer predictable in this age of the 'do-it-yourself biography' where old certainties have broken down (2002: 7).

Choice can, from these perspectives, be associated with the possibility of envisaging different selves one might be. There is, however, a possible disjuncture between the self as posited by Giddens and Beck and that of George Herbert Mead, which we discussed in Chapter 9. Mead emphasized that self-reflexivity is always a social product (see Ch. 9.3), but more recent theorizations of the self in late modernity posit a self that is cast adrift from traditional cultural expectations, from taken-for-granted ways of living. This can, as some critics have noted, underestimate the degree to which our sense of self is dependent on the cultural resources available to us. Even the very idea of individuality derives from our wider culture We may have more responsibility for making sense of our own experience, and more freedom to do so in new ways, but in so doing we 'still rely on common cultural forms' (Adams, 2003: 229).

An alternative approach to the self in late modernity, which gives more weight to the influences of the wider culture, derives from theorists influenced by Foucault. Over the last few centuries, there has been an increasing concern with exploring the self's interiority and with self-surveillance – and sexuality came to be seen as something intrinsic to the self (Foucault, 1981). The late modern preoccupation with self-fashioning has, from this perspective, been associated with the rise of a confessional culture, the emergence and institutionalization of the 'psy' professions (Rose, 1989) and the popularization of 'psy' discourse (from psychology, psychoanalysis and psychotherapy). For example, in any bookstore now you will find a multitude of self-help texts instructing on how to improve your personal relationships and your sex life and much else. These ideas are also spread through television documentaries, talk shows and magazines. We are thereby provided with numerous resources enabling (and encouraging) us to analyse our inner selves, to know ourselves better and to pursue self-improvement projects. At the same time sexuality has come to be seen as increasingly important to individual self-fulfilment and mental health (see Heath, 1982; Jackson and Scott, 1997).

One way in which these ideas are circulated is through stories of sexual lives and we are also prompted to tell stories about ourselves, which are one way in which we reflexively make sense of ourselves and our lives. We construct such stories not solely on the basis of individual experience but by drawing on our wider cultural knowledge, including the copious resources for self-fashioning provided by our confessional culture. The stories we can tell are always historically and culturally situated (Plummer, 1995). Not only do socially located individual biographies and particular cultural understandings of the sexual provide materials for self-composition, but the social and cultural worlds each of us inhabits may affect what stories can be told, how they are told – and whether they are heard. For example, in *Telling Sexual Stories* (1995), Ken Plummer talks about the ways in which specific stories emerge at particular historical moments. For example, prior to the rise of second wave feminism it was rarely possible for women to talk about being raped. Although this is still not easy, the existence of counsellors in rape crisis centres who listen to women's stories and help them to see themselves as survivors rather than as defiled victims has enabled a reframing of rape narratives. Similarly gay liberation made possible 'coming out' stories and created an audience that encouraged the telling of such stories and was eager to hear them.

We are often prompted to tell stories by others or by our assumptions about others' expectations of us. Stories are called for when we do something unexpected or when something out of the ordinary happens to us. Stories are therefore often constructed around turning points in our lives, and even those whose lives are normatively heterosexual will generally have some stories to tell and retell about why their lives have followed a particular path – though they are unlikely to construct a narrative about becoming heterosexual. The ordinary, routine and expected does not usually produce a story. For example, a woman who was labelled a girl at birth and has always been female would not be expected to tell a story about why she became a woman – and if she did her audience would be likely to be either bemused or bored. Those who change gender, by contrast, usually do have a story to tell and many have told them in print [4].

Of course we all tell little stories about ourselves as a routine part of everyday interaction, but only when a story of self is re-told over time, to oneself and others, does it become part of a conscious fashioning of the self or the construction and adoption of an identity. Such self-stories depend on identities and forms of self-knowledge available to us. Take, for example, a gay man who tells a story of having been born gay, of having 'always been' gay. First that story depends on the existence of the identity 'gay' in his culture, enabling him to apply it to himself. Secondly, his account depends on retrospectively reinterpreting his childhood to fit that identity – perhaps that he always enjoyed certain 'feminine' activities such as dressing up. For this interpretation to be made, there has to be a cultural association between dressing up and not being properly masculine and a further association between not being masculine and being gay. Moreover, an account of being 'born that way' relies on essentialist ideas of gay identity circulating in the wider culture (see Ch. 7.1). In other cultures or other historical epochs, this story could be neither told nor heard.

11.3   Globalized Identities, Global Social Change

One aspect of modernization is held to be the increasing globalization of society and culture. The extent to which globalization is new can be overestimated (see Ch.5.5), but the degree of global connectedness through movements of people (as travellers, migrants, refugees) and ideas (through mass media and the internet as well as interpersonal contact) can be seen as intensifying. Given the global reach of western culture industries and the legacy of colonialism, these flows are asymmetrical: western (especially US) ideas and identity categories have far more influence in other regions of the world than, say, Asian culture has on the West, though there are flows in both directions. Globalized culture and interaction has potential consequences for sexual selves and identities and for the negotiation of transnational sexual relationships.

One aspect of this that has received some scholarly attention is the spread of lesbian and gay identities to countries where they had previously not existed or where there were alternative ways of constructing same-gender desire (Altman, 2001; Binnie, 2004). Now the global availability of gay, lesbian and queer identities makes possible new modes of self-making and identity formation. There are, however, local variations arising from particular cultures and social circumstances, as the story with which we began Part IV demonstrates. Identities as lesbian and gay have become available in Korea and elsewhere in Asia but are locally mediated. Diana Khor and Saori Kamono (2006), writing of 'lesbians' in Asia, caution against assuming that the term has the same meaning in all cultures. Often local identities coexist with translations of western ones. For example, the term *tongzhi* (comrade) is widely used in Hong Kong and Taiwan to identify individuals or communities we would define as gay or queer – an ironic twist on communist and nationalist discourse that shares a first syllable/character (*tong*, meaning same) with the word for homosexuality, *tongxinglian* (Martin, 2003).

In many parts of the world there are local transgendered phenomena: men who take on, in some sense, a feminine identity and have sex with men – such as Indian *hijra*, Filipino *batut* and Samoan *fa'afafine* (see, for example, Herdt, 1999). Although in some cases such groups are beginning to define themselves as 'gay' (see, for example, Johnson, 1997), care should be taken in interpreting locally based identities: we should not assume that they simply constitute a local variation of some universal gay or transgendered identity, or even that they fit easily into our accepted definitions of these categories. Let us look at one example: Don Kulick's ethnographic study of Brazilian *travesti* (1998), transgendered prostitutes. *Travesti* adopt a feminine persona, are known by women's names and alter their bodies to appear feminine. Since they are largely poor, they use do-it-yourself methods: black market hormones and industrial-grade silicon injected to enhance breasts and buttocks. They thus take considerable pains – and risks – to reconstruct themselves as women. At the same time they consider any man who alters his genitals to a feminine form to be insane and cannot imagine doing so. They see themselves as 'better' at being women than 'real' women – particularly in servicing their male clients and their boyfriends – and having a heterosexual, macho boyfriend confirms their femininity. Yet they also define themselves as homosexuals, *viados*, and as embodying 'homosexual desire in its truest and most perfect form' (Kulick, 1998: 225) – and this, for them, means that they would not contemplate having a relationship with another *travesti* or anyone else definable as gay. They do not, therefore, fit easily within dualistic notions of gender: for example, they see their gender as defined not by their genitals but rather by their ability to perform femininity and relate as women to straight men; at the same time their 'authentic' homosexuality is also defined by their performance of femininity and their relationships with 'real' men.

Conventional heterosexual prostitution can also take different forms in local cultural contexts, as in the example of Thai sex tourism that we discussed in the Introduction to Part II, and this has implications for the identities of those involved. The men who use Thai prostitutes are able to construct these women as more like girlfriends (and therefore distance themselves from the identity of client or 'john') because there is no fixed fee for the services offered and they can hire women for long periods (O'Connell Davidson, 1995). The identities of women working in the sex trade are also variable. In many western countries and sometimes elsewhere, the term 'sex worker' is preferred to 'prostitute' both as an occupational identity and as a basis for claims to rights; it is also a way of negating stigma, affirming agency and highlighting the fact that sex work is work. Seeing sex as work also means that sex workers must somehow demarcate the boundaries of sex for work (with clients) and sex for pleasure in intimate relationships and do 'boundary work' to maintain the distinction between themselves as workers and as lovers (Brewis and Linstead, 2000; Chen, 2008). The idea of sex work, along with the identity 'sex worker' is not, however, universally embraced. In her study of women working in the sex trade in the Pearl River Delta region of Southern China, Ding Yu (2009) found that these women preferred another identity, that of *xiaojie*, a term traditionally used as a term of address for young women but now associated with prostitution. *Xiaojie* reject the identity of sex worker on two grounds: first, they think it overemphasizes the sexual aspect of their contact with clients at the expense of other services they offer, such as emotional labour; and, secondly, they do not define what they do as work – precisely because it was not a regular job, but more of a lifestyle. Instead they construct a positive self-identity as modern and cosmopolitan in contrast to the poor, 'backward' villages in inland China from which most of them had migrated (Ding and Ho, 2008).

In this example being 'modern' becomes a component of identity, and this has been observed in studies of other groups of migrants in Asia (for example, Lan, 2008a). This is also part of the motivation of the foreign brides marrying into richer countries, which we discussed in Chapter 5.5. In the metropolitan centres of countries such as India and China where national identities are being reconstructed around modernization projects, we also find modernity being incorporated into self-identity (Farrer, 2002; Tokita-Tanabe, 2003). The modernity of the eastern imaginary is not, however, identical to western conceptions. The Japanese sociologists Akio Tanabe and Yumiko Tokita-Tanabe argue that, precisely because of the dominance of western modernity, maintaining a self-identity as distinct from the West entails 'a complex self-reflexive endeavour to position oneself for *and* against "European modernity" and "indigenous tradition"' (2003: 4, emphasis in original). In these post-colonial contexts it is often women who become bearers of tradition while simultaneously seeking to reconcile it with a sense of self as modern.

Gender and sexuality often figure in the maintenance of national self-identity: women reproduce nations both biologically and culturally so that their bodies figure literally and metaphorically in marking national boundaries (Yuval-Davis, 1997). In western countries, for example, immigrant groups are often stigmatized because they do not adopt the host country's patterns of gender and sexual relations: hence the negative attitudes to arranged marriages or the wearing of the *hijab*. Immigration policies often subtly or more overtly encode assumptions about the gendered sexual conduct of the foreign 'other'

(Fekete, 2006). Pei-Chia Lan (2008b) illustrates the way women's bodies become sites of national boundary marking in her study of Taiwanese attitudes towards foreign brides and migrant domestic workers. Here South East Asian immigrant women are marked as 'other' to the 'civilized' Chinese culture of Taiwan, with domestic workers positioned as potential seducers of Taiwanese husbands and foreign wives stigmatized as potentially unfit mothers.

National identities are a very obvious example of collective identities, but many identities are collective in that they identify us as part of a social group or category – though of course every group is fluid and internally differentiated. Thus, as we have seen, 'women' are constituted as a category but that category comprises women of different nationalities, ethnicities, classes, sexualities, religion, and so on – and all these categories can become the basis of individual and collective identities and components of the complex, multiple intersecting identities we each inhabit.

Learning Outcomes

After reading the chapters in Part IV you should:

- understand that self and identity are always socially constructed, but that we are active agents in that construction – we neither passively accept given 'roles' and identities nor freely create any self or identity we choose;
- be able to demonstrate knowledge of the ways in which interpretive sociologies conceptualize self and identities as socially, reflexively constructed in interaction with others in specific social contexts;
- understand how gender and sexuality are intertwined in the process of self and identity construction, whether we become gay/lesbian or straight;
- be aware that gender and heterosexuality reinforce each other in the construction of both gay and straight sexualities and that the normative status of heterosexuality has consequences for those who do not conform;
- understand that sexuality is scripted at the level of culture, interpersonal relationships and intrapsychic conversations with ourselves, but that scripts are constantly renegotiated by us throughout our lives as we construct and reconstruct self and identity;
- be aware that there are various ways of becoming and being a man or a woman (whether heterosexual or lesbian/gay), resulting from individual biographies, our social location and our reflexive processing of our experience;
- understand that we all simultaneously embody multiple selves/identities, and that gender and sexuality exist in intersection with other identities, such as those based on class, nationality or 'race';
- demonstrate knowledge of the consequences of modernity and globalization for the construction of gendered and sexual identities.

Notes and Resources for Further Study

1 For an introduction to sociological approaches to self and identity, see Richard Jenkins' *Social Identity* (1996). An accessible introduction to the poststructuralist conceptualization of subjectivity, focusing specifically on gender, is to be found in Chris Weedon's *Feminist Practice and Postructuralist Theory* (1987). An interesting account combining elements of interactionist, ethnomethodological and poststructuralist perspectives is James A. Holstein and Jaber F. Gubrium's *The Self We Live By* (2000).

2 See the websites of the Intersex Society of North America (ISNA) – *http://www.isna.org* – and the UK Intersex Association (UKIA) – *http://www.ukia.co.uk* – for more details. The ISNA dissolved in 2008 to join the more mainstream Accord Alliance (*www.accordalliance.org*), but the website will continue to be available as an historical resource. There are a number of books on intersex other than those cited in this chapter. Alice Dreger's *Hermaphrodites: The Medical Invention of Sex* (1998) provides a fascinating historical account of intersex. For further discussions of

contemporary issues see Myra Hird's *Sex, Gender and Science* (2004), Ch. 7, and Catherine Harper's *Intersex* (2007).

3 A more detailed conceptual discussion of the process of becoming sexual can be found in Stevi Jackson and Sue Scott's *Theorizing Sexuality* (2010). There are numerous studies of young people and sexuality, many of which we have cited in the text. A selection of extracts from such studies can be found in Michael Kimmel and Rebecca Plante (eds) *Sexualities: Identities, Behaviors and Society* (2004).

4 For some examples of personal accounts of sex change from various eras and perspectives, see Jan Morris's *Conundrum* (1978), Kate Bornstein's *Gender Outlaw* (1994) and Claudine Griggs' *Journal of a Sex Change* (2004).

Part V

Conclusion

Introduction

In 2007–8, we witnessed the presidential primary campaign of Hillary Clinton, former First Lady and Senator from the state of New York. Although Clinton eventually lost the Democratic nomination to Senator Barack Obama, she was regarded as the frontrunner for most of the campaign, thus marking the first time in American history that a woman had run successfully for a Presidential nomination. Moreover, the Republican Party nominated a woman, Governor Sarah Palin, to be the vice-presidential running mate of their nominee, Senator John McCain. No doubt 2008 will go down in history as the year of diversity. We shall consider what social changes have occurred that made Clinton's campaign possible. In doing so, we aim to illustrate the complexities and ambiguities of contemporary issues around gender and sexuality, both demonstrating the changes in structures, identities and culture that made Clinton's candidacy possible, and exploring the limits of such change.

In the Introduction to this book we identified how issues of sexuality were manifestations of some key sociological concerns:

- social change;
- social conflict, social cohesion and social order;
- social hierarchies, divisions and inequalities;
- social identities;
- dimensions of the social – structures/cultures/identity and agency.

Throughout we have used these key dimensions of the social to discuss and explain other issues, from how social change comes about and the impact of structural and cultural changes, to why certain sexual identities are such a source of social conflict. Instead of repeating our key points from the individual chapters, we want to consider these issues in relation to another key sociological concept: that of power. The assertions around Clinton's candidacy speak to social power: they direct us to consider the sociological changes in power divisions between the genders at home, work and public life; the power of feminist ideas in changing core democratic values; the power available to individuals to conduct their lives as they choose; and the power to which stigmatized sexual identities have been subjected and also the empowerment they have achieved. Power is a resource that is a complex outcome of the interactions of structures, cultures, identities and action in society and it remains a pertinent issue today for feminist and sexual politics. This concluding discussion therefore aims to show you how to relate the issues we have been discussing to questions of power, taking us through discussions of power and politics, identities and the fragmentation of power.

12

Power, Politics, Identities and Social Change

12.1   '18 Million Cracks': The Triumph of Liberal Feminism?

Given her success at university and in her legal career, Hillary Clinton illustrates that professional working women can now rise to the top of their occupations. More specifically, it illustrates that the professional political realm is equally open to the participation and success of women (as long as, in the US context, they are rich or can raise enough money), and, perhaps most significantly, that the public audience/voters can now respond to a woman in political life not simply as a 'female', but as a generic politician. In a very broad sense, one might see a parallel with Obama's candidacy and what it symbolizes about 'race', and one could infer that together these campaigns suggest a new era of 'equality' in gender and racial divisions. The questions for us, as sociologists, are: how has this change been made possible, and what implications does it have for contemporary gender and sexual formations?

The first wave feminist movement saw inequalities of gender as open to remedy by equalizing opportunity and treatment under the law. For example, Mary Wollstonecraft's argument for the rights of women emphasized such issues. These arguments were focused on the developing democratic values and practices of their time. Ultimately, the main aim of both legal and symbolic reform became the right to vote, since this would bring women into the citizenship of liberal democracies. As we explained in Chapter 2, the strand of feminism pursuing equal rights, equal access and equal opportunities has come to be termed liberal feminism. One of the reasons why many women responded to Hillary Clinton's campaign is precisely because it embodied the promise of equal citizenship: she has been able to participate and succeed in education, her professional career and now the most powerful profession in democracy – that of politician. Does Clinton's existence suggest that the inequalities of gender have been largely remedied by liberal feminist strategies and successes?

Clinton herself thinks so to some extent: she argued in her concession speech that the votes for her candidacy represented '18 million cracks' in the 'highest, hardest, glass ceiling' [1] – using the popular phrase that signifies invisible barriers to the advancement and promotion of women which persist despite equal opportunity laws and policies. Her speech thus not only acknowledges the advances that women have made through hard-fought political campaigns and how individual women have benefited from these (Clinton reminds her supporters of suffragette campaigns from first wave feminism), it also reminds us that there are still unspoken, cultural or social biases against women that mean that they are treated differently (and create 'glass ceilings'). In many ways, these acknowledgements illustrate the ambiguities of contemporary gender politics and the social constructions of gender.

First, on the positive side, it is clear that there have been both structural and ideological changes, resulting in cultural and political values shifting towards public gender equality. Political movements, from first wave feminist campaigns to the second wave movements, have impacted most recently on western democracies but are also influential in international organizations such as the United Nations, and within individual countries in the developed and developing worlds [2]. Indeed, the United Nations has many agreements or conventions on the rights of women, recognizing these as part of fundamental human rights and focusing on achieving gender equality in important areas such as work and education. At the national level, in Canada, a recent survey on the importance of the country's constitutional Charter of Rights found that 76 per cent of respondents thought that gender equality was very important to Canadian 'values' (Jedwab, 2007). Canada is also one of the few countries to have full equal rights for lesbians and gays, including the right to marriage.

Your World: Look at gender equality policies in your own country or region, and establish to what extent they are present and an accepted part of national culture.

There are indeed some problems with such assertions of progress, but for now we invite you simply to reflect upon the fact that gender equality has become a mainstream democratic ideal in a relatively short space of time – such values were not mainstream ideas at the beginning of the second wave feminist movement. Of course, the acceptance of sexual diversity is much less secure and widespread, but at the very least one can say that social change has occurred over the last forty years in the liberal feminist sense that equal opportunity and equality under the law are widely accepted in many cultures. These changes have brought social conflict, particularly in political arenas (think of the controversies surrounding abortion rights, for example), and often the progress of women's rights and those of non-heterosexuals has been seen as a threat to social cohesion and order. On the positive side, however, such progress illustrates the social power that political movements can have in influencing and sometimes fundamentally reshaping cultural values.

Moreover, as Hillary Clinton's support demonstrates, public identities made possible by such change provide resources and resonances for individuals living out their lives. Despite the fact that Clinton is most definitely not a typical American working mother, many of her supporters cited her candidacy as a symbol of their own lives as women in the contemporary USA, both drawing a sense of personal empowerment from her campaign and finding in its very existence a representation of the social power of women. Thus, we can see in this micro-example how both personal and political identities have changed over the last thirty to forty years, demonstrating the link between structural and cultural change and their impact as resources for identities and action.

However, even in first wave feminism and most liberal feminisms, there was an awareness that while cultural values would need to be changed to allow for greater gender equality, material circumstances, or structural conditions, were also important. This basis of power and inequality received far more attention in the second wave feminist movement and through gay liberation, thus bringing an emphasis on radical social change and a questioning of the very basis of citizenship, as well as the functioning of democracies. Feminism and sexual liberation movements have brought into question the claim that the liberal democratic state does not regulate the 'private' domestic realm or the 'natural' one beyond protecting people from harm, immorality and obscenity. Sociological analyses of gender and sexuality have clearly demonstrated that the realm of the sexual is regulated not just through prohibition, but more commonly through prescription, constructing social norms through structures, cultures and identities.

12.2   Sometimes, It's (Still) Hard to be a Woman (and Really Hard to be Non-Heterosexual and/or Non-White): Structural Inequalities, Intersecting Oppressions and Hetero-Orthodoxy

Clinton did not run as a 'female' candidate: she was not advocating a specific feminist platform or emphasizing the novelty of her candidacy; rather, she emphasized her experience of public service and political life, especially in the area of national security and foreign policy, with constant references to the experience she gained over her eight years in the White House as First Lady and subsequent time as a Senator. In short, she appealed to the traditional national roles of an American President – her establishment credentials – and argued that she could fulfil these better than any other candidate, rendering her gender as a *neutral* category.

For much of the campaign, Clinton pursued this strategy successfully, winning the argument that she was more experienced and established, particularly through the comparison this invited with the relatively inexperienced Obama. Of course, this position then became a negative factor, given that Obama's campaign and public polling began to emphasize 'change': change from traditional American partisan politics; change from the usual moneyed candidates running for office; change from having a 'dynastic' Bush–Clinton tradition – above all, change from the 'Establishment'. This charge of Clinton being part of the political establishment became a potentially fatal one, identifying her with traditional politics when all the polls suggested the voters wanted anything but. However, her strategy was an attempt to manage what feminists have characterized as the 'dilemma of difference' (Young, 1989). This dilemma turns on the positive and negative power of identity: on the one hand, running as a woman who can bring women's experiences to the fore and represent them has been an important part of feminist activism and attempts to change policy agendas, and yet, on the other, there remains the danger of being seen as only able to represent the interests of those who share one's identity, rather than a wider constituency. Clinton had to appeal to a wider vote than just women, but in doing so she de-emphasized the novelty and radical change that her candidacy represented – themes that could have helped her fend off the strategy of her opponent.

The problem with being a 'woman' (Clinton) or an 'African-American' (Obama) remains that these categories are not socially neutral, but outwith the traditional expectations of 'President' (male, white, socially privileged) and still signify subordinate groups in American society. Inequalities of gender remain not only in the USA, but in many other democracies that espouse equal rights, particularly those in the West that are identified with gender equality. Moreover, as theorists of intersectionality have pointed out, inequalities of gender and sexuality are absolutely constituted through vectors of racialization, challenging the conceptual and theoretical basis of much of the second wave sociology of gender and sexuality. Clinton is not just a woman; she is a white, educated, privileged woman with obvious political connections. Indeed, as one key theorist of intersectionality pointed out, feminists who supported Clinton did not apply a critical analysis to her candidacy that acknowledged her multiple intersecting privileges (Crenshaw, 2008).

Aside from structural inequalities of power, there remains a widespread cultural acceptance of essentialism, particularly in everyday understandings of gender and sexuality. The structural inequalities discussed above demonstrate that gender inequalities remain throughout most of the world, and this is even more stark when thinking about diverse sexualities. There remains a hetero-orthodoxy in most societies and thus it has taken longer to argue for homosexual rights. You could also argue that feminist insights into the power dimensions of sexuality have had only a partial and uneven effect upon the wider culture of western societies. While manifestations of sexual exploitation such as sex work, sexual violence and trafficking have become mainstream issues in gender policies, there has been a less successful connection made to the everyday manifestations of gender, particularly in intimate interactions and how institutionalized heterosexuality has created non-heterosexualities as stigmatized identities.

One consequence is a continued ambivalence around non-heterosexualities because they so clearly represent a social and symbolic challenge to the 'norm' of the hetero-gendered order. In the Introduction to this book, we discussed this challenge in relation to the controversy that gay marriage provokes. While the recent 'War on Terror' has seen participant governments routinely cite women's subordination as a rationale for imposing democracy on countries such as Iraq and Afghanistan, the sociologically related oppression of homosexuals is routinely absent from such legitimizations (Waites, 2008). Many feminists are highly sceptical of the motives behind the apparent concern about women's status within the 'War on Terror' discourse because it is perceived as politically opportunist and fuelled by Islamophobia (Phillips, 2007; Razack, 2008). Yet it is precisely the now taken-for-granted identification of women's rights as part of the 'democratic West' that begets such usage. By contrast, gay rights are not yet a settled part of western democracy. Where they have succeeded, what we have seen has been a framing of lesbian, gay, bisexual and transgender politics in the powerful discourse of human rights. However, here we find another dilemma of difference, one that routinely sees diverse sexualities characterized and represented in essentialist ways in order to argue for rights, rather than a wider critique of the hetero-orthodoxy that still dominates our culture (Kollman and Waites, 2009).

12.3   The Persistence of (Reflexive) Essentialism

Structural inequalities of gender, race and class remain, as do those resulting from the continued institutionalization of heterosexuality, but political movements for women and for sexual diversity have had significant impacts on law and politics, particularly in challenging the dominant explanations of sexual inequalities as 'natural'. However, in this historical period we have also seen the decline of traditional social structures, resulting in a range of post-class identities and an increasing emphasis on individual rather than collective identities.

Thus during the period of feminist advances in the West, we have also seen an increasing emphasis on the commercialized and commodified reflexive project of the self which has intensified the pressures on and expectations of women's presentation, body management and sexuality. This has also been true of lesbian and gay identity and more recently, of heterosexual male identity. This emphasis on the body, pleasures and lifestyles has necessarily manifested itself through gendered identities and their related sexualities, and while it may no longer be overtly homophobic or sexist in many forms, the emphasis on sexual identity remains trapped within an overwhelmingly essentialist framework. In Foucauldian terms, technologies of the self have almost totally focused on the development of a gendered-sexual self, wherein resides the power of wider social discourses around gender, sexuality and morality. Perhaps the new moral frameworks that permit the existence of women's rights and some gay rights indicate the shift towards new self identities, but, as discussed in the section above, it is far from certain that such individual 'projects' of the self are occurring in the context of wider, structural gender and sexual equality. There is a complex visibility of both lesbian and gay sexualities (Streitmatter, 2009) and of empowered women (Gill, 2008), but it is not necessarily progressive, often reasserting a hetero-orthodox culture (Rahman, 2004; Gill, 2008). Moreover, this is happening in the context of the wider circulation of essentialist ideas, also propagated by the media, through which we continue to be encouraged to think of gender differences and sexual desires as governed by our evolutionary and genetic inheritance (Jackson and Rees, 2007).

These concluding examples are woven together by the theme of how power operates in society and how often it is contradictory: there is both progress and remaining inequality in the structural organization of gender and sexuality; cultural discourses are now more plural, but again, they are complex, and alongside challenges to traditional essentialism and the advance of equal rights, we have seen the consolidation of new forms of essentialism focused on the self as a consumer project and a locus of individual rights. Nonetheless, these examples reiterate our overall argument that gender and sexuality are fundamental aspects of the social organization of human societies rather than merely natural 'facts'.

Notes and Resources for Further Study

1 You can view this speech, together with many others from the campaign, at *http://www.youtube.com/watch?v=DHxPHKM6sPE&feature=related*. In this final speech of her campaign, delivered on 7 June 2008, Clinton begins by saying that although she was proud to be running as a woman, she ran because she thought she would be the best president, thereby invoking a gender neutrality to her candidacy. However, she then goes on to discuss more openly than ever her feelings about how her campaign was symbolically important for women, and how both her and Obama's campaigns have answered the question of whether a woman or black man can run successfully for the American Presidency.

2 See the United Nations Commission on the Status of Women and related links found at *http://www.un.org/womenwatch/daw/csw/*.

Bibliography

Abercrombie, N., Hill, S. and Turner, B.S. (2006). *Dictionary of Sociology*. London: Penguin Books.

Abraham, I. (2009). ' "Out to Get Us": Queer Muslims and the Clash of Sexual Civilization in Australia', *Contemporary Islam* 3 (1): 79–97.

Adam, B. (1985). 'Structural Foundations of the Gay World', *Comparative Studies in Society and History* 27: 658–71.

Adams, M. (2003). 'The Reflexive Self and Culture: A Critique.' *British Journal of Sociology* 54 (2): 221–38.

Adams, P., Brown, B. and Cowie, E. (1978). 'Editorial', *m/f* 2: 3–5.

Adkins, L. (1995). *Gendered Work: Sexuality, Family and the Labour Market*. Milton Keynes: Open University Press.

Agustín, L.M. (2007). *Sex at the Margins: Migration, Labour Markets and the Rescue Industry*. London : Zed Books.

Alexander, M.J. (1997). 'Erotic Autonomy as a Politics of Decolonialization: An Anatomy of Feminist and State Practice in the Bahamas Tourist Industry', in M.J. Alexander and C.T. Mohanty (eds) *Feminist Genealogies, Colonial Legacies and Democratic Futures*. New York: Routledge.

Alexander, M.J. and Mohanty, C.T. (1997a). 'Introduction: Genealogies, Legacies, Movements', in M.J. Alexander and C.T. Mohanty (eds) *Feminist Genealogies, Colonial Legacies and Democratic Futures*. New York: Routledge.

Alexander, M.J. and Mohanty, C.T. (eds) (1997b) *Feminist Genealogies, Colonial Legacies and Democratic Futures*. New York: Routledge.

Allen, L. (2005). *Sexual Subjects: Young People, Sexuality and Education*. Basingstoke: Palgrave.

Allen, S. and Leonard, D. (1996). 'From Sexual Divisions to Sexualities: Changing Sociological Agendas', in J. Weeks and J. Holland (eds) *Sexual Cultures: Community, Values and Intimacy*. Basingtoke: Palgrave Macmillan.

Alsop, R., Fitzsimons, A. and Lennon, K. (2002). *Theorizing Gender*. Cambridge: Polity Press.

Althusser, L. (1971). 'Ideology and the Ideological State Apparatuses', in *Lenin and Philosophy*. London: New Left Books.

Altman, D. (2001). *Global Sex*. Chicago: University of Chicago Press.

Amos, V. and Parmar, P. (1984). 'Challenging Imperial Feminism', *Feminist Review* 17: 3–19.

Anderson, E. (2002). 'Openly Gay Athletes: Contesting Hegemonic Masculinity in a Homophobic Environment', *Gender and Society* 16 (6): 860–77.

Anthias, F. (2001). 'The Material and the Symbolic in Theorizing Social Stratification: Issues and Gender, Ethnicity and Class', *British Journal of Sociology* 43 (3): 367–90.

Anthias, F. and Yuval-Davis, N. (1992). *Racialized Boundaries: Race, Nation, Gender, Colour and Class and the Anti-Racist Struggle*. Oxford: Blackwell.

Banks, O. (1990). *Faces of Feminism*. Oxford: Blackwell.

Barker, D.L. and Allen, S. (eds) (1976). *Sexual Divisions in Society: Process and Change*. London: Tavistock Publications.

Barrett, M. (1990 [1980]). *Women's Oppression Today*. London: Verso.

Barrett, M. (1992). 'Words and Things: Materialism and Method in Contemporary Feminist Analysis', in M. Barrett and A. Phillips (eds) *Destabilizing Theory*. Cambridge: Polity Press.

Barrett, M. and McIntosh, M. (1979). 'Towards a Materialist Feminism?', *Feminist Review* 1: 95–106.

Bauman, Z. (2001). 'Consuming Life', *Journal of Consumer Culture* 1 (1): 9–30.

Beal, F.M. (1970). 'Double Jeopardy: To be Black and Female', in R. Morgan (ed.) *Sisterhood is Powerful: An Anthology of Writings from the Women's Liberation Movement*. New York: Vintage Books.

Beauvoir, S. de (1972 [1949]) *The Second Sex*. Harmondsworth: Penguin.

Beck, U. and Beck-Gernsheim, E. (1995). *The Normal Chaos of Love*. Cambridge: Polity.

Beck, U. and Beck-Gernsheim, E. (2002). *Individualization: Institutionalized Individualism and Its Social and Political Consequences*. London: Sage Publications.

Beechey, V. (1979). 'On Patriarchy', *Feminist Review* 3: 66–83.

Bell, C. and Newby, H. (1976). 'Husbands and Wives: The Dynamics of the Deferential Dialectic', in D. Leonard Barker and S. Allen (eds) *Dependence and Exploitation in Work and Marriage*. London: Longman.

Benston, M. (1969). 'The Political Economy of Women's Liberation', *Monthly Review* 21 (4): 13–27.

Berger, J. (1972). *Ways of Seeing*. London: BBC Books.

Bhambra, G.K. (2007). *Rethinking Modernity: Postcolonialism and the Sociological Imagination*. Basingstoke: Palgrave.

Bhavnani, K.-K. and Coulson, M. (1986). 'Transforming Socialist Feminism: The Challenge of Racism', *Feminist Review* 23: 81–92.

Binnie, J. (2004). *The Globalization of Sexuality*. London: Sage Publications.

Birch, K. (1988). 'A Community of Interests', in B. Cant and S. Hemmings (eds) *Radical Records*. London: Routledge.

Blackwood, E. (2000). 'Sexuality and Gender in Certain Native American Tribes: The Case of Cross-Gender Females', in C.L. Williams and A. Stein (eds) *Sexuality and Gender*. Malden, MA: Blackwell.

Blumer, H. (1969). *Symbolic Interactionism: Perspective and Methods*. Englewood Cliffs, NJ: Prentice Hall.

Bordo, S. (1993). *Unbearable Weight: Feminism, Western Culture and the Body*. Berkeley: University of California Press.

Bordo, S. (1998). 'Bringing Body to Theory', in D. Welton (ed.) *Body and Flesh: A Philosophical Reader*. Oxford: Blackwell.

Bordo, S. (1999). *The Male Body: A New Look at Men in Public and in Private*. New York: Farrar, Straus and Giroux.

Bornstein, K. (1994). *Gender Outlaw: On Men, Women and the Rest of Us*. New York: Routledge.

Boswell, J. (1980). *Christianity, Social Tolerance and Homosexuality*. Chicago: University of Chicago Press.

Boswell, J. (1992). 'Concepts, Experience and Sexuality', in E. Stein (ed.) *Forms of Desire*. New York: Routledge.

Brah, A. (1991). 'Questions of Difference and International Feminism', in J. Aaron and S. Walby (eds) *Out of the Margins: Women's Studies in the Nineties*. London: Falmer.

Brah, A. and Phoenix, A. (2004) 'Ain't I a Woman; Revisiting Intersectionality', *Journal of International Women's Studies* 5 (3): 75–86.

Brake, M. (1976). 'I May be Queer but At Least I'm a Man: Male Hegemony and Ascribed versus Achieved Gender', in D.L. Barker and S. Allen (eds) *Sexual Divisions in Society: Process and Change*. London: Tavistock Publications.

Breugel, I. (1979). 'Women as a Reserve Army of Labour', *Feminist Review* 3: 12–23.

Brewis, J. and Linstead, S. (2000). 'The Worst Thing is the Screwing: Consumption and the Management of Identity in Sex Work', *Gender, Work and Organization* 7 (2): 84–97.

Bristow, J. (1997). *Sexuality*. London: Routledge.

Browne, K. (forthcoming). '"By Partner We Mean. . .": Alternative Geographies of "Gay Marriage"', *Sexualities*.

Brownmiller, S. (1975). *Against Our Will: Men, Women and Rape*. London: Secker and Warburg.

Buckingham, D. and Bragg, S. (2004). *Young People, Sex and the Media: The Facts of Life?* Basingstoke: Palgrave.

Butler, J. (1990a). *Gender Trouble: Feminism and the Subversion of Identity*. New York: Routledge.

Butler, J. (1990b). 'Gender Trouble, Feminist Theory and Psychoanalytic Discourse', in L. Nicholson (ed.) *Feminism/Postmodernism*. New York: Routledge.

Butler, J. (1993a). 'Imitation and Gender Insubordination', in H. Abelove, M.A. Barale and D. Halperin (eds) *The Lesbian and Gay Studies Reader.* New York: Routledge.

Butler, J. (1993b). *Bodies that Matter.* New York: Routledge.

Butler, J. (1997). 'Merely Cultural', *Social Text* 15: 265–78.

Byron, S. (1972). 'The Closet Syndrome', in K. Jay and A. Young (eds) *Out of the Closets: Voices of Gay Liberation.* New York: Quick Fox Publications.

Califia, P. (1981). 'Feminism and Sadomasochism', *Heresies* 12: 30–4.

Callinicos, A. (1999). *Social Theory: A Historical Introduction.* New York: New York University Press.

Cameron, D. (ed.) (1998). *The Feminist Critique of Language: A Reader.* London: Routledge.

Cameron, D. and Frazer, E. (1987). *The Lust to Kill: A Feminist Investigation of Sexual Murder.* Cambridge: Polity; New York: New York University Press.

Carby, H. (1982). 'White Woman Listen! Black Feminism and the Boundaries of Sisterhood', in the Centre for Contemporary Cultural Studies (eds) *The Empire Strikes Back: Race and Racism in 70s Britain.* London: Hutchinson.

Cashmore, E. and Parker, A. (2003). '"One David Beckham?": Celebrity, Masculinity and the Soccerati', *Sociology of Sport Journal* 20 (3): 214–31.

Castells, M. (2004) *The Power of Identity* (2nd edn). Oxford: Blackwell.

Chambers, D. Tinknell, E and Van Loon, J. (2004). 'Peer Regulation of Teenage Sexual Identities', *Gender and Education* 16 (3): 397–415.

Charles, N. and Kerr. M. (1988). *Women, Food and Families.* Manchester: Manchester University Press.

Chauncey, G. (1994). *Gay New York: Gender, Urban Culture, and the Making of the Gay Male World, 1890–1940.* New York: Basic Books.

Chen Mei-Hua (2008). 'Sex and Work in Sex Work: Negotiating Sex and Work among Taiwanese Sex Workers', in S. Jackson, Liu Jieyu and Woo Juhyun (eds) *East Asian Sexualities: Modernity, Gender and New Sexual Cultures.* London: Zed.

Cheng, Shu-ju Ada (2003). 'Rethinking the Globalization of Domestic Service: Foreign Domestics, State Control and the Politics of Identity in Taiwan', *Gender and Society* 17 (2): 166–86.

Clarke, C. (1981). 'Lesbianism: An Act of Resistance', in C. Moraga and G. Anzaldua (eds) *This Bridge Called My Back.* New York: Kitchen Table, Women of Color Press.

Collins, P.H. (2000). *Black Feminist Thought: Knowledge, Consciousness and the Politics of Empowerment* (2nd edn). New York: Routledge.

Combahee River Collective (1983 [1977]). 'The Combahee River Collective Statement', in B. Smith (ed.) *Home Girls: A Black Feminist Anthology.* New York: Kitchen Table, Women of Color Press.

Connell, R. (1987). *Gender and Power.* Cambridge: Polity Press.

Connell, R. (1995). *Masculinities.* Cambridge: Polity Press.

Connell, R. (2000). *The Men and the Boys*. Cambridge: Polity Press.

Connell, R. (2002). *Gender*. Cambridge: Polity Press. (Now in 2nd edn, 2009.)

Connell, R. and Dowsett, G.W. (1992). 'The Unclean Motion of the Generative Parts: Frameworks in Western Thought on Sexuality', in R.W. Connell and G.W. Dowsett (eds) *Rethinking Sex: Social Theory and Sexuality Research*. Melbourne: Melbourne University Press.

Constable, N. (2003). *Romance on a Global Stage: Pen Pals, Virtual Ethnography and 'Mail Order' Marriages*. Berkeley: University of California Press.

Constable, N. (2005). 'Cross-Border Marriages, Gendered Mobility and Global Hypergamy', in N. Constable (ed.) *Cross-Border Marriages, Gender and Mobility in Transnational Asia*. Philadelphia: University of Pennsylvania Press.

Coward, R. and Ellis, J. (1977). *Language and Materialism*. London: Routledge and Kegan Paul.

Crenshaw, K. (1989). 'Demarginalizing the Intersection between Race and Sex: A Black Feminist Critique of Anti-Discrimination Doctrine, Feminist Theory and Anti-Racist Politics', *University of Chicago Legal Forum*: 139–67.

Crenshaw, K. (1991). 'Mapping the Margins: Identity Politics, Intersectionality and Violence against Women', *Stanford Law Review* 43: 1241–79.

Crenshaw, K. (2008). 'The Curious Resurrection of First Wave Feminism in the US Elections: An Intersectional Critique of the Rhetoric of Solidarity and Betrayal', in L. Gunnarsson (ed.) *GEXcel Work in Progress, Report Volume III*. Linköping: University of Linköping; Örebro: University of Örebro. Available online at *http://www.genderexcel. org/?q=node/90*

Crossley, N. (2001) *The Social Body: Habit, Identity and Desire*. London: Sage Publications.

Dahlerup, D. (ed.) (1990). *The New Women's Movement: Feminism and Political Power in Europe and the USA*. London: Sage Publications.

Daly, M. (1970). 'Women in the Catholic Church', in R. Morgan (ed.) *Sisterhood is Powerful: An Anthology of Writings from the Women's Liberation Movement*. New York: Vintage Books.

Darwin, C. (1859). *The Origin of Species*. London: John Murray.

Darwin. C. (1871). *The Descent of Man: Selections in Relation to Sex*. London: John Murray.

Davidoff, L. and Hall, C. (1987). *Family Fortunes: Men and Women of the English Middle Class 1780–1850*. Hutchinson: London.

Davidoff, L., McClelland, K. and Varikas, E. (1999). *Gender and History: Retrospect and Prospect*. Oxford: Blackwell.

Davies, B. (1989). *Frogs and Snails and Feminist Tales*. Sydney: Allen & Unwin.

Davis, Kathy (2008). 'Intersectionality as Buzzword: A Sociology of Science Perspective on What Makes a Feminist Theory Successful', *Feminist Theory* 9 (1): 67–84.

Davis, Kingsley (1937). 'The Sociology of Prostitution', *American Sociological Review* 2: 744–55.

Dawkins, R. (1996 [1976]). *The Selfish Gene*. Oxford: Oxford University Press.

Delphy, C. (1976). 'Continuities and Discontinuities in Marriage and Divorce', in D. Leonard Barker and S. Allen (eds) *Sexual Divisions and Society*. London: Tavistock Publications.

Delphy, C. (1977). *The Main Enemy: A Materialist Analysis of Women's Oppression*. London: Women's Research and Resources Centre.

Delphy, C. (1984). *Close to Home: A Materialist Analysis of Women's Oppression*. London: Hutchinson.

Delphy, C. (1993). 'Rethinking Sex and Gender', *Women's Studies International Forum* 16 (1): 1–9.

Delphy, C. and Leonard, D. (1992). *Familiar Exploitation*. Cambridge: Polity Press.

D'Emilio, J. (1993). 'Capitalism and Gay Identity', in H. Abelove, M.A. Barale and D. Halperin (eds) *The Lesbian and Gay Studies Reader*. New York: Routledge.

Dex, S. (1999). *Families and the Labour Market: Trends, Pressures and Policies*. London: Family Policy Studies Centre/Joseph Rowntree Foundation.

Diamond, J. (1997). *Why is Sex Fun? The Evolution of Human Sexuality*. London: Weidenfeld and Nicolson.

Ding Yu (2009). 'Transitions and Possibilities: A Study of *Xiaojies* in the Pearl River Delta'. Unpublished Ph.D. thesis, University of Hong Kong.

Ding Yu and Ho Sik-Ying (2008). 'Beyond Sex Work: An Analysis of *Xiaojies'* Understandings of Work in the Pearl River Delta, China', in S. Jackson, Liu Jieyu and Woo Juhyun (eds) *East Asian Sexualities: Modernity, Gender and New Sexual Cultures*. London: Zed.

Dreger, A. (1998). *Hermaphrodites: The Medical Invention of Sex*. Cambridge, MA: Harvard University Press.

Duncombe, J. and Marsden, D. (1996). 'Whose Orgasm is This Anyway? "Sex Work" in Long-Term Relationships', in J. Weeks and J. Holland (eds) *Sexual Cultures: Communities and Intimacy*. London: Macmillan

Dunne, G. (1991). 'A Passion for Sameness? Sexuality and Gender Accountability', in E. Silva (ed.) *The New Family*. London: Sage.

Dunne, G., Prendergast, S. and Telford, D. (2002). 'Young, Gay, Homeless and Invisible: A Growing Population?' *Culture, Health & Sexuality: An International Journal for Research, Intervention and Care* 4 (1): 103–15.

Durkheim, É. (1964 [1893]). *The Division of Labour in Society*. New York: Free Press.

Dworkin, A. (1981). *Pornography: Men Possessing Women*. London: Women's Press.

Ellis, H. (1936 [1897]). *Sexual Inversion: Studies in the Psychology of Sex*. New York: Random House.

Engels, F. (1942 [1884]). *The Origin of the Family, Private Property and the State*. New York: International Press.

Epstein, D, O'Flynn, S. and Telford, D. (2003). *Silenced Sexualities in Schools and Universities*. London: Tretham Books.

Evans, D. (1993). *Sexual Citizenship: The Material Construction of Sexualities*. London: Routledge.

Farrer, J. (2002). *Opening Up: Youth Sex Culture and Market Reform in Shanghai*. Chicago: University of Chicago Press.

Fausto-Sterling, A. (1992). *Myths of Gender: Biological Theories about Men and Women*. New York: Basic Books.

Fausto-Sterling, A. (2000). *Sexing the Body: Gender Politics and the Construction of Sexuality* (2nd edn). New York: Basic Books.

Fekete, L. (2006). 'Enlightened Fundamentalism? Immigration, Feminism and the Right', *Race and Class* 48 (2): 1–22.

Finch, J. (1983) *Married to the Job: Wives' Incorporation Into Men's Work*. London: Allen and Unwin.

Fine, M. (1988). 'Sexuality, Schooling and Adolescent Females: The Missing Discourse of Desire', *Harvard Educational Review* 58 (1): 29–51.

Fine, M. and McClelland, S. (2006). 'Sexuality, Education and Desire: Still Missing after All These Years', *Harvard Educational Review* 76 (3): 297–338.

Firestone, S. (1972). *The Dialectic of Sex*. London: Paladin.

Flax, J. (1990). 'Postmodernism and Gender Relations in Feminist Theory', in L. Nicholson (ed.) *Feminism/Postmodernism*. London: Routledge.

Ford, C.S. and Beach, F.A. (1951). *Patterns of Sexual Behavior*. New York: Harper and Brothers.

Foucault, M. (1980). 'Truth and Power' (an interview with A. Fontana and P. Pasquino), in C. Gordon (ed.) *Michel Foucault: Power/Knowledge*. Brighton: Harvester/Wheatsheaf.

Foucault, M. (1981). *The History of Sexuality, Volume One*. London: Pelican.

Ford, C.S. and Beach, F.A. (1951). *Patterns of Sexual Behaviour*. New York: Harper and Row.

Frankham, J. (2006). 'Sexual Antinomies and Parent/Child Sex Education: Learning from Foreclosure', *Sexualities* 9 (2): 236–54.

Franks, M. (2000). 'Crossing the Borders of Whiteness? White Muslim Women Who Wear the Hijab in Britain Today', *Ethnic and Racial Studies* 23 (5): 917–29.

Fraser, N. (1997). 'Heterosexism, Misrecognition and Capitalism: A Response to Judith Butler', *Social Text* 15: 279–89.

Freud, S. (1995a [1905]). 'Three Essays on the Theory of Sexuality', in P. Gay (ed.) *The Freud Reader*. London: Vintage Books.

Freud, S. (1995b [1925]). 'Some Physical Consequences of the Anatomical Differences between the Sexes', in P. Gay (ed.) *The Freud Reader*. London: Vintage Books.

Friedan, B. (1963). *The Feminine Mystique*. New York: Norton.

Fuss, D. (1991). 'Introduction', in D. Fuss (ed.) *Inside/Out: Lesbian Theories, Gay Theories*. New York: Routledge.

Gabb, J. (2004). 'Critical Differentials: Querying the Incongruities within Research on Lesbian Parent Families', *Sexualities* 7 (2): 167–82.

Gagnon, J.H. (2004). *An Interpretation of Desire*. Chicago: University of Chicago Press.

Gagnon, J.H. and Simon, W. (1974). *Sexual Conduct*. London: Hutchinson.

Gagnon, J.H. and Simon, W. (2005). *Sexual Conduct* (2nd edn). New Brusnwick, NJ: Aldine Transaction.

Garfinkel, H. (1967). *Studies in Ethnomethodology*. Englewood Cliffs, NJ: Prentice Hall.

Gay, P. (ed.) (1995). *The Freud Reader*. London: Vintage Books.

Gay Left Collective (eds) (1980). *Homosexuality, Power and Politics*. London and New York: Allison and Busby.

Giddens, A. (1990). *The Consequence of Modernity*. Cambridge: Polity Press.

Giddens, A. (1991). *Modernity and Self Identity*. Cambridge: Polity Press.

Giddens, A. (1992). *The Transformation of Intimacy*. Cambridge: Polity Press.

Gill, R. (2007). *Gender and the Media*. Cambridge: Polity Press.

Gill, R. (2008). 'Empowerment/Sexism: Figuring Female Sexual Agency in Contemporary Advertising', *Feminism and Psychology* 18 (1): 35–60.

Gill, R. (2009). 'Beyond the "Sexualization of Culture" Thesis: An Intersectional Analysis of "Sixpacks", "Midriffs" and "Hot Lesbians" in Advertising', *Sexualities* 12 (2): 137–60.

Gilman, C.P. (2008 [1898]). 'Women and Economics', in S. Applerouth and L. Desfor Edles (eds) *Classical and Contemporary Sociological Theory: Text and Readings*. Los Angeles: Pine Forge Press.

Goffman, E. (1969). *The Presentation of Self in Everyday Life*. London: Allen Lane.

Goffman, E. (1977). 'The Arrangement between the Sexes', *Theory and Society* 4 (3): 301–31.

Goffman, E. (1979). *Gender Advertisements*. London: Macmillan.

Greer, G. (2001). 'Long Live the Essex Girl', *The Guardian*, 5 March 2001. Available online at *http://www.guardian.co.uk/world/2001/mar/05/gender*

Griggs, C. (2004). *Journal of a Sex Change*. Oxford: Berg.

Grosz, E. (1994). *Volatile Bodies: Towards a Corporeal Feminism*. Bloomington: Indiana University Press.

Grosz, E. (1995). 'Experimental Desire: Re-Thinking Queer Subjectivity', in E. Grosz (ed.) *Space, Time and Perversion*. New York: Routledge.

Guillaumin, C. (1995 [1978]). 'The Practice of Power and the Belief in Nature. Part I: The Appropriation of Women', in C. Guillaumin, *Racism, Sexism, Power and Ideology*. London: Routledge.

Gupta, R. (ed.) (2003). *From Homebreakers to Jailbreakers: Southall Black Sisters*. London: Zed.

Hall, C. (1979). 'The Early Formation of Victorian Domestic Ideology', in S. Burman (ed.) *Fit Work for Women*. London: Croom Helm.

Hall, C. (1992). *White, Male and Middle Class: Explorations in Feminism and History*. London: Routledge.

Halperin, D.M. (1995). *Saint Foucault: Towards a Gay Hagiography*. Oxford: Oxford University Press.

Harper, C. (2007). *Intersex*. Oxford: Berg.

Hartmann, H. (1976). 'Capitalism, Patriarchy and Job Segregation by Sex', *Signs* 1: 137–68.

Hartmann, H. (1979). 'Capitalism, Patriarchy and Job Segregation by Sex', in Z.R. Eisenstein (ed.) *Capitalist Patriarchy and the Case for Socialist Feminism*. New York: Monthly Review Press.

Hartmann, H. (1981). 'The Unhappy Marriage of Marxism and Feminism: Towards a More Progressive Union', in L Sargent (ed.) *Women and Revolution: The Unhappy Marriage of Marxism and Feminism*. London: Pluto Press.

Hausman, B. (1995). *Changing Sex: Transsexualism, Technology and the Idea of Gender*. Durham, NC: Duke University Press.

Heaphy, B. (2007). *Late Modernity and Social Change: Reconstructing Social and Personal Life*. London: Routledge.

Heath, S. (1982). *The Sexual Fix*. London: Macmillan.

Hemmings, C. (2005). 'Telling Feminist Stories', *Feminist Theory* 6 (2): 115–39.

Hennessy, R. (1993). *Materialist Feminism and the Politics of Discourse*. London: Routledge.

Hennessy, R. (1995). 'Queer Visibility in Commodity Culture', in L. Nicholson and S. Seidman (eds) *Social Postmodernism*. Cambridge: Cambridge University Press.

Hennessy, R. (2000). *Profit and Pleasure*. New York: Routledge.

Hennessy, R. and Ingraham, C. (1997). *Materialist Feminism: A Reader in Class, Difference and Women's Lives*. New York: Routledge.

Herdt, G. (ed.) (1999). *Third Sex, Third Gender*. New York: Zone Books.

Hersberger, R. (1948). *Adam's Rib*. New York: Pellegrini and Cudahy.

Hird, M. (2004). *Sex, Gender and Science*. Basingstoke: Palgrave Macmillan.

Holland, J, Ramazanoğlu, C., Sharpe, S. and Thomson, R. (1996). 'In the Same Boat? The Gendered (In)experience of First Heterosex', in D. Richardson (ed.) *Theorizing Heterosexuality: Telling it Straight*. Buckingham: Open University Press.

Holmes, M. (2004). 'An Equal Distance? Individualisation, Gender and Intimacy in Distance Relationships', *Sociological Review* 52 (2): 180–2000.

Holstein, J.A. and Gubrium, J.F. (2000). *The Self We Live By*. New York: Oxford University Press.

Hood, J. (1999). *The Silverback Gorilla Syndrome: Transforming Primitive Man*. Santa Fe: Adventures in Spirit.

hooks, b. (1982). *Ain't I a Woman? Black Women and Feminism*. London: Pluto Press.

Ingraham, C. (1996). 'The Heterosexual Imaginary', in S. Seidman (ed.) *Queer Theory/Sociology*. Oxford: Blackwell.

Ingraham, C. (1999). *White Weddings: Romancing Heterosexuality in Popular Culture*. New York: Routledge.

Irigaray, L. (1985). *This Sex Which is Not One*. Ithaca, NY: Cornell University Press.

Irving, Z. (2008). 'Gender and Work', in D. Richardson and V. Robinson (eds) *Introducing Gender and Women's Studies*. Basingstoke: Palgrave.

Irwin, S. (1999). 'Resourcing the Family: Gendered Claims and Obligations', in E. Silva (ed.) *The New Family?* London: Sage Publications.

Irwin, S. (2005). *Reshaping Social Life*. London: Routledge.

Jackson, M. (1989). '"Facts of Life" or the Eroticization of Women's Oppression? Sexology and the Social Construction of Heterosexuality', in P. Caplan (ed.) *The Cultural Construction of Sexuality*. New York: Routledge.

Jackson, S. (1982). *Childhood and Sexuality*. Oxford: Blackwell.

Jackson, S. (1996). *Christine Delphy*. London: Sage Publications.

Jackson, S. (1998). 'Feminist Social Theory', in S. Jackson and J. Jones (eds) *Contemporary Feminist Theories*. Edinburgh: Edinburgh University Press.

Jackson, S. (1999). *Heterosexuality in Question*. London: Sage Publications.

Jackson, S. (2001). 'Why a Materialist Feminism is *Still* Possible (and Necessary)', *Women's Studies International Forum* 24 (2–3): 283–93.

Jackson, S. (2005). 'Sexuality, Heterosexuality and Gender Hierarchy: Getting Our Priorities Straight', in C. Ingraham (ed.) *Thinking Straight: The Power, the Promise and the Paradox of Heterosexuality*. New York: Routledge.

Jackson, S. (2006a). 'Gender, Sexuality and Heterosexuality: The Complexity (and Limits) of Heteronormativity', *Feminist Theory* 7(1): 105–21.

Jackson, S. (2006b). 'Heterosexuality, Sexuality and Gender: Re-Thinking the Intersections', in D. Richardson, M. Casey and J. McLaughlin (eds) *Intersections between Feminist and Queer Theory*. London: Palgrave.

Jackson, S. (2010a [1997]). 'The Amazing Deconstructing Women', in D. Cameron and J. Scanlon (eds) *The Trouble and Strife Reader*. London: Bloomsbury Academic. Available online at *http://www.bloomsburyacademic.com/index.html*

Jackson, S. (2010b). 'Self, Time and Narrative: Re-Thinking the Contribution of G.H. Mead', *Life Writing* 7 (2).

Jackson, S. (forthcoming). 'Materialist Feminism, Pragmatism and the Sexual Self in Global Late Modernity', in A.G. Jónasdóttir, V. Bryson and K.B. Jones (eds) *Sexuality, Gender and Power: Intersectional and Transnational Perspectives*. New York: Routledge.

Jackson, S. and Rees, A. (2007). 'The Appalling Appeal of Nature: The Popular Influence of Evolutionary Psychology as a Problem for Sociology', *Sociology* 41 (5): 917–30.

Jackson, S. and Scott, S. (1996a). 'Sexual Skirmishes and Feminist Factions: Twenty-Five Years of Debate on Women and Sexuality', in S. Jackson and S. Scott (eds) *Feminism and Sexuality*. Edinburgh: Edinburgh University Press.

Jackson, S. and Scott, S. (eds) (1996b). *Feminism and Sexuality*. Edinburgh: Edinburgh University Press.

Jackson, S. and Scott, S. (1997). 'Gut Reactions to Matters of the Heart: Reflections on Rationality, Irrationality and Sexuality', *Sociological Review* 45 (4): 551–75.

Jackson, S. and Scott, S. (1999). 'Risk Anxiety and the Social Construction of Childhood', in D. Lupton (ed.) *Risk and Sociocultural Theory: New Directions and Perspectives*. Cambridge: Cambridge University Press.

Jackson, S. and Scott, S. (2007). 'Faking Like a Woman? Towards an Interpretive Theorization of Sexual Pleasure', *Body & Society* 13 (2): 95–116.

Jackson, S. and Scott, S. (2010). *Theorizing Sexuality*. Maidenhead: Open University Press.

Jackson, S., Liu Jieyu and Woo Juhyun (eds) (2008). *East Asian Sexualities: Modernity, Gender and New Sexual Cultures*. London: Zed Books.

Jackson, Sue (2005a). 'I'm 15 and Desperate for Sex: "Doing" and "Undoing" Desire in Letters to a Teenage Magazine', *Feminism and Psychology* 15 (3): 295–313.

Jackson, Sue (2005b). '"Dear Girlfriend. . .": Constructions of Sexual Health Problems and Sexual Identities in Letters to a Teenage Magazine', *Sexualities* 8 (3): 282–305.

Jamieson, L. (1999). 'Intimacy Transformed?', *Sociology* 33 (3): 477–94.

Jedwab, J. (2007). 'Shared Canadian Values, Social Cohesion and the Charter of Rights: Is it Time to Re-think the Terms of the Debate?', *Canadian Issues* Fall: 20–6.

Jeffreys, S. (1990). *Anticlimax: A Feminist Perspective on the Sexual Revolution*. London: The Women's Press.

Jeffreys, S. (1993). *The Lesbian Heresy: A Feminist Perspective on the Lesbian Sexual Revolution*. Melbourne: Spinifex Press.

Jeffreys, S. (1997). *The Idea of Prostitution*. Melbourne: Spinifex Press.

Jenkins, R. (1996). *Social Identity*. London: Routledge.

Johnson, M. (1997). *Beauty and Power: Transgendering and Cultural Transformation in the Southern Philippines*. Oxford: Berg.

Johnson, P. (2005). *Love, Heterosexuality and Society*. London: Routledge.

Kaluzynska, E. (1980). 'Wiping the Floor with Theory: A Survey of writings on Housework', *Feminist Review* 6: 27–54.

Karras, R.M. (1996). *Common Women: Prostitution and Sexuality in Medieval England*. Oxford: Oxford University Press.

Kelly, L., Lovett, J. and Reagan, L. (2005). *A Gap or a Chasm? Attrition in Reported Rape Cases*. London: Home Office.

Kent, S.K. (1990). *Sex and Suffrage in Britain, 1860–1914*. London: Routledge.

Kessler, S.J. (1998). *Lessons from the Intersexed*. New Brunswick, NJ: Rutgers University Press.

Kessler, S.J. and McKenna, W. (1978). *Gender: An Ethnomethodological Approach*. New York: Wiley.

Khor, D. and Kamano, S. (2006). 'Introduction', in D. Khor and S. Kamano (eds) *'Lesbians' in East Asia: Diversity, Identities and Resistance*. Binghampton, NY: Harrington Park Press.

Kimmel, M. (2004). *The Gendered Society*. New York: Oxford University Press.

Kimmel, M. (2005). *The Gender of Desire*. Albany: State University of New York Press.

Kimmel, M. (2008). 'Hooking Up, Party Rape and Predatory Sex: The Sexual Culture of the American College Campus', in L. Gunnarsson, A. Jónasdóttir and G. Karlsson (eds) *GEXcel Work in Progress Report, Volume II*. Linköping: University of Linköping; Örebro: University of Örebro.

Kimmel, M. and Plante, R. (eds) (2004). *Sexualities: Identities, Behaviors and Society*. New York: Oxford University Press.

Kirkman, M., Rosenthal, D.A. and Feldman, S.S. (2005). 'Being Open with Your Mouth Shut: The Meaning of "Openness" in Family Communication about Sexuality', *Sex Education* 5 (1): 49–66.

Kitzinger, C. (2005). '"Speaking as a Heterosexual": (How) Does Sexuality Matter for Talk-in-Interaction?', *Research on Language and Social Interaction* 38 (3): 221–65.

Kitzinger, C. and Wilkinson, S. (1993). 'Theorizing Heterosexuality', in S. Wilkinson and C. Kitzinger (eds) *Heterosexuality: A Feminism and Psychology Reader*. London: Sage Publications.

Klein, V. (1946). *The Feminine Character: History of an Ideology*. London: Kegan Paul.

Koedt, A (1996 [1972]). 'The Myth of the Vaginal Orgasm', in S. Jackson and S. Scott (eds) *Feminism and Sexuality*. Edinburgh: Edinburgh University Press

Kollman, K. and Waites, M. (2009). 'The Global Politics of Lesbian, Gay, Bisexual and Transgender Human Rights: An Introduction', *Contemporary Politics* 15 (1): 1–17.

Komarovsky, M. (1946). 'Cultural Contradictions and Sex Roles', *American Journal of Sociology* 52 (3): 184–9.

Komarovsky, M. (1962). *Blue-Collar Marriage*. New York: Random House.

Krafft-Ebing, R. von (1965 [1886]). *Psychopathia Sexualis: With Especial Reference to the Antipathic Sexual Instinct*. New York: Stein and Day.

Kuhn, A. (1978). 'Structures of Patriarchy and Capital in the Family', in A. Kuhn and A. Wolpe (eds) *Feminism and Materialism: Women and Modes of Production.* London: Routledge and Kegan Paul.

Kulick, D. (1998). *Travesti: Sex, Gender and Culture among Brazilian Transgendered Prostitutes.* Chicago: University of Chicago Press.

Lan, Pei-Chia (2003). 'Maid or Madam? Filipina Migrant Workers and the Continuity of Domestic Labour', *Gender and Society* 17 (2): 187–208.

Lan, Pei-Chia (2006). *Global Cinderellas.* Durham, NC: Duke University Press.

Lan Pei-Chia (2008a). 'Global Cinderellas: Sexuality, Power and Situational Practices across Borders', in S. Jackson, Liu Jieyu and Woo Juhyun (eds) *East Asian Sexualities: Gender, Modernity and New Sexual Cultures.* London: Zed Books.

Lan, Pei-Chia (2008b). 'Migrant Women's Bodies as Boundary Markers: Reproductive Crisis and Sexual Control in the Ethnic Frontier of Taiwan', *Signs: Journal of Women in Culture and Society* 33 (4): 833–62.

Laqueur, T. (1990). *Making Sex: Body and Gender from the Greeks to Freud.* Cambridge, MA: Harvard University Press.

Laumann, E. and Gagnon, J. (1995). 'A Sociological Perspective on Sexual Action', in R. Parker and J. Gagnon (eds) *Conceiving Sexuality: Approaches to Sex Research in a Postmodern World.* New York: Routledge.

Laumann, E., Gagnon, J., Michael, R.T. and Michaels, S. (1994). *The Social Organization of Sexuality: Sexual Practices in the United States.* Chicago: University of Chicago Press.

Leeds Revolutionary Feminist Group (1981). 'Political Lesbianism: The Case against Heterosexuality', in Onlywomen Press (eds) *Love your Enemy? The Debate between Heterosexual Feminism and Political Lesbianism.* London: Onlywomen Press.

Leonard, D. and Adkins, L. (1996). *Sex in Question.* London: Taylor and Francis.

LeVay, S. (1993). *The Sexual Brain.* Cambridge, MA: MIT Press.

Levine, J. (2002). *Harmful to Minors: The Perils of Protecting Children from Sex.* Minneapolis: University of Minnesota Press.

Lewis, B. (2002). *What Went Wrong? The Clash between Islam and Modernity in the Middle East.* New York: Harper Perennial.

Lewis, J. (2001). *The End of Marriage? Individualism and Intimate Relations.* London: Edward Elgar.

Liu Jieyu (2008). 'Sexualized Labour?: "White-Collar Beauties" in Provincial China', in S. Jackson, Liu Jieyu and Woo Juhyun (eds) *East Asian Sexualities: Modernity, Gender and New Sexual Cultures.* London: Zed.

Lorber, J. (2008). 'Believing is Seeing: Biology as Ideology', in M. Kimmel, A. Aronson and A. Kaler (eds) *The Gendered Society Reader: Canadian Edition.* Don Mills, ON: Oxford University Press.

Lyotard, F. (1984). *The Postmodern Condition.* Manchester: Manchester University Press.

McBride-Stetson, D. (2004). *Women's Rights in the USA: Policy Debates and Gender Roles.* New York: Routledge.

McCaughey, M. (2008). *The Caveman Mystique: Pop-Darwinism and the Debates over Sex, Violence, and Science.* London: Routledge.

McClintock, A. (1995). *Imperial Leather: Race, Gender and Sexuality in the Colonial Context.* London: Routledge.

McDonough, R. and Harrison, R. (1978). 'Patriarchy and Relations of Production', in A. Kuhn and A. Wolpe (eds) *Feminism and Materialism.* London: Routledge and Kegan Paul.

McIntosh, M. (1978). 'Who Needs Prostitutes? The Ideology of Male Sexual Needs', in C. Smart and B. Smart (eds) *Women, Sexuality and Social Control.* London: Routledge and Kegan Paul.

McIntosh, M. (1996 [1968]). 'The Homosexual Role', in S. Seidman (ed.) *Queer Theory/Sociology.* Cambridge, MA: Blackwell.

MacKinnon, C.A. (1982). 'Feminism, Marxism, Method and the State: An Agenda for Theory', *Signs* 7 (3): 515–44.

MacKinnon, C.A. (1996). 'Feminism, Marxism, Method and the State: An Agenda for Theory', in S. Jackson and S. Scott (eds), *Feminism and Sexuality.* Edinburgh: Edinburgh University Press.

MacKinnon, C.A. (2002). 'Pleasure under Patriarchy', in C.L. Williams and A. Stein (eds) *Sexuality and Gender.* Malden, MA: Blackwell.

McNay, L. (2000). *Gender and Agency.* Cambridge: Polity Press.

Marshall, B. (1994). *Engendering Modernity: Feminism, Social Theory and Social Change.* Boston: Northeastern University Press.

Marshall, B. and Katz, S. (2002). '"Forever Functional": Sexual Fitness and the Ageing Male Body', *Body and Society* 8 (4): 43–70.

Marshall, B. and Witz, A. (eds) (2004). *Engendering the Social: Feminist Encounters with Sociological Theory.* Maidenhead: Open University Press.

Martin, F. (2003). *Situating Sexualities: Queer Representations in Taiwanese Fiction, Film and Popular Culture.* Hong Kong: Hong Kong University Press.

Martin, K. (1996). *Puberty, Sexuality and the Self: Girls and Boys at Adolescence.* New York: Routledge.

Mason, M. (1994). *The Making of Victorian Sexuality.* New York: Oxford University Press.

Maynard, M. (1995). 'Beyond the "Big Three": The Development of Feminist Theory in the 1990s', *Women's History Review* 4: 259–81.

Mead, G.H. (1964 [1929]). 'The Nature of the Past', in A.J. Reck (ed.) *Mead: Selected Writings.* Indianapolis/New York: Bobbs-Merrill.

Mead, G.H. (1934). *Mind, Self and Society.* Chicago: University of Chicago Press.

Mead, G.H. (2002 [1932]). *The Philosophy of the Present.* New York: Prometheus Books.

Mead, M. (1962 [1950]). *Male and Female.* Harmondsworth: Penguin.

Mead, M. (1965 [1935]). *Sex and Temperament in Three Primitive Societies.* New York: William Morrow.

Millett, K. (1971). *Sexual Politics.* London: Rupert Hart-Davis Ltd.

Mills, C.W. (1959). *The Sociological Imagination.* Harmondsworth: Penguin.

Mirza, H.S. (ed.) (1997). *Black British Feminism: A Reader.* London: Routledge.

Mitchell, J. (1975). *Psychoanalysis and Feminism.* Harmondsworth: Penguin.

Modleski, T. (1991). *Feminism without Women.* New York: Routledge.

Mohanty, C.T. (1991a). 'Introduction: Cartographies of Struggle: Third World Women and the Politics of Feminism', in C. Mohanty, A. Russo and L. Torres (eds) *Third World Women and the Politics of Feminism.* Bloomington: Indiana University Press.

Mohanty, C.T. (1991b). 'Under Western Eyes', in C. Mohanty, A. Russo and L. Torres (eds) *Third World Women and the Politics of Feminism.* Bloomington: Indiana University Press.

Mohanty, C.T. (1997). 'Women Workers and Capitalist Scripts: Ideologies of Domination, Common Interests and the Politics of Solidarity', in M.J. Alexander and C.T. Mohanty (eds) *Feminist Genealogies, Colonial Legacies, Democratic Futures.* New York: Routledge.

Moi, T. (1985). *Sexual/Textual Politics.* London: Methuen and Co.

Molyneux, M. (1979). 'Beyond the Domestic Labour Debate', *New Left Review* 116: 3–27.

Monzini, P. (2005). *Sex Traffic: Prostitution, Crime and Exploitation.* London: Zed.

Moraga, C. and Anzaldua, G. (eds) (1991). *This Bridge Called My Back.* New York: Kitchen Table, Women of Color Press.

Morgan, R. (ed.) (1970). *Sisterhood is Powerful: An Anthology of Writings from the Women's Liberation Movement.* New York: Vintage Books.

Morgan, R. (1977). *Going Too Far: The Personal Chronicle of a Feminist.* New York: Random House.

Morris, J. (1978). *Conundrum.* London: Coronet Books.

Mort, F. (1980). 'Sexuality: Regulation and contestation', in Gay Left Collective (ed.) *Homosexuality: Power and Politics.* London: Allison and Busby.

Mort, F. (1987). *Dangerous Sexualities: Medico-Moral Politics in England since 1830.* London: Routledge and Kegan Paul.

Motha, S. (2007). 'Veiled Women and the Affect of Religion in Democracy', *Journal of Law and Society* 34 (1): 139–62.

Mozini, P. (2005). *Sex Traffic: Prostitution, Crime, and Exploitation.* London: Zed Books.

Myrdal, A. and Klein, V. (1956). *Women's Two Roles.* London: Routledge and Kegan Paul.

Nanda, M. (1997). '"History is what Hurts": A Materialist Feminist Perspective on the Green Revolution and Its Ecofeminist Critics', in R.

Hennessy and C. Ingraham (eds) *Materialist Feminism: A Reader in Class, Difference and Women's Lives*. New York: Routledge.

Nelson, A. (2010). *Gender in Canada* (4th edn). Pearson: Toronto.

Nixon, S. (1996). *Hard Looks: Masculinities, Spectatorship and Contemporary Consumption*. London: UCL Press.

Nye, R. (ed.) (1999). *Sexuality*. Oxford: Oxford University Press.

Oakley, A. (1972). *Sex, Gender and Society*. London: Temple Smith.

O'Brien, M. (1981). *The Politics of Reproduction*. Boston, MA: Routledge and Kegan Paul.

O'Connell Davdison, J. (1995). 'British Sex Tourists in Thailand', in M. Maynard and J. Purvis (eds) *(Hetero Sexual Politics*. London: Taylor and Francis.

O'Faolain, J. and Martines, L. (1974). *Not in God's Image*. Glasgow: Collins/ Fontana.

Pampel, F.C. (2000). *Sociological Lives and Ideas: An Introduction to the Classical Theorists*. New York: Worth Publishers.

Oosterhuis, H. (1997). 'Richard von Krafft-Ebing's "Step-Children of Nature": Psychiatry and the Making of Homosexual Identity', in V.A. Rosario (ed.) *Science and Homosexualities*. New York: Routledge.

Parkin, F. (1972). *Class Inequality and Political Order*. London: Paladin.

Parsons, T. (1951) *The Social System*. London: Routledge and Kegan Paul.

Parsons, T. and Bales, R. (1956). *Family, Socialization and Interaction Process*. London: Routledge and Kegan Paul.

Petty, C., Roberts, D. and Smith, S. (1987). *Women, Liberation and Socialism*. London: Bookmarks.

Phillips, A. (2007) *Multiculturalism without Culture*. Princeton: Princeton University Press.

Phillips, L.M. (2000). *Flirting with Danger: Young Women's Reflections on Sexuality and Domination*. New York: New York University Press.

Phoenix, A., Frosh, S. and Pattman, R. (2003). 'Producing Contradictory Masculine Subject Positions: Narratives of Threat, Homophobia and Bullying in 11–14 Year Old Boys', *Journal of Social Issues* 59 (1): 179–95.

Pilcher, J. (2005). 'School Sex Education: Policy and Practice in England 1970 to 2000', *Sex Education* 5 (2): 153–70.

Plummer, K. (1975). *Sexual Stigma*. London: Routledge and Kegan Paul.

Plummer, K. (1995). *Telling Sexual Stories: Power, Change and Social Worlds*. London: Routledge.

Plummer, K. (2005). 'Intimate Citizenship in an Unjust World', in M. Romero and E. Margolis (eds) *The Blackwell Companion to Social Inequalities*. Oxford: Blackwell.

Potts, A., Gavey, N., Grace, V.M. and Vares, T. (2003). 'The Downside of Viagra: Women's Experiences and Concerns', *Sociology of Health and Illness* 25 (7): 697–719.

Questions Féministes Collective (1997 [1981]). 'Variations on a Common Theme', in E. Marks and I. de Courtivron (eds) *New French Feminisms: An Anthology.* Brighton: Harvester/Wheatsheaf.

Rahman, M. (2004). 'Beckham as an Historical Moment in the Representation of Masculinity', *Labour History Review* 69 (2): 219–34.

Rayside. D. and Wilcox, C. (eds) (2010). *Religion, Sexuality, and Politics in Canada and the United States.* Vancouver, UBC Press.

Razack, S.H. (2008). *Casting Out: The Eviction of Muslims from Western Law and Politics.* Toronto: University of Toronto Press.

Reddy, V., Sandfort, T. and Rispel, L. (eds) (2009). *From Social Silence to Social Science: Same-Sex Sexuality, HIV & AIDS and Gender in South Africa.* Cape Town: HSRC Press.

Reed, K. (1998). 'Racing the Feminist Agenda: Exploring the Intersections between Race, Ethnicity and Gender', in D. Richardson and V. Robinson (eds) *Introducing Gender and Women's Studies.* Basingstoke: Macmillan.

Renold, E. (2005). *Girls, Boys and Junior Sexualities.* London: Routledge Falmer.

Renold, E. (2006). 'They Won't Let us Play. . .Unless You're Going Out With One of Them': Girls, Boys and Butler's "Heterosexual Matrix" in the Primary Years', *British Journal of the Sociology of Education* 27 (4): 489–509.

Rich, A. (1980). 'Compulsory Heterosexuality and Lesbian Existence', *Signs* 5 (4): 631–60.

Richardson, D. (ed.) (1996). *Theorizing Heterosexuality: Telling It Straight.* Buckingham: Open University Press.

Riley, D. (1988). *Am I That Name? Feminism and the Category of 'Women' in History.* New York: Macmillan.

Roberts, C., Kippax, S., Waldby, C. and Crawford, J. (1995). 'Faking It: The Story of "Ohh!"', *Women's Studies International Forum* 18 (5–6): 523–32.

Romero, M. (1992). *Maid in the USA.* New York: Routledge.

Romero, M. (1999) 'Who Takes Care of the Maid's Children? Exploring the Costs of Domestic Service', in H.L. Nelson (ed.) *Feminism and Families.* New York: Routledge.

Rosario, V. (1997). 'Homosexual Bio-Histories: Genetic Nostalgias and the Quest for Paternity', in V.A. Rosario (ed.) *Science and Homosexualities.* New York: Routledge.

Rose, N. (1989). *Governing the Soul.* London: Routledge.

Roseneil, S. and Budgeon, S. (2004). 'Cultures of Intimacy and Care Beyond "The Family": Personal Life and Social Change in the Early 21st Century', *Current Sociology* 52 (2): 135–59.

Rothfield, P. (1996). 'Menopausal Embodiment', in P. Komesaroff, P. Rothfield and J. Daly (eds) *Reinterpreting Menopause: Cultural and Philosophical Issues.* London: Routledge.

Rowbotham, S. (1981). 'The Trouble with Patriarchy', in R. Samuel (ed.) *People's History and Socialist Theory*. London: Routledge and Kegan Paul.

Rubin, G. (1975). 'The Traffic in Women: Notes on the "Political Economy" of Sex', in R. Reiter (ed.) *Toward an Anthropology of Women*. New York: Monthly Review Press.

Rubin, G. (1984). 'Thinking Sex: Notes for a Radical Theory of the Politics of Sexuality', in C. Vance (ed.) *Pleasure and Danger*. London: Routledge and Kegan Paul.

Ruby, T.F. (2008). 'Listening to the Voices of Hijab', in M. Kimmel, A. Aronson and A. Kaler (eds) *The Gendered Society Reader: Canadian Edition*. Don Mills, ON: Oxford University Press.

Savin-Williams, R.C. (2004). 'Dating and Romantic Relationships among Gay, Lesbian and Bisexual Youth', in M.S. Kimmel and R.F. Plante (eds) *Sexualities: Identities, Behaviors and Society*. New York: Oxford University Press.

Schofield, M. (1965). *The Sexual Behaviour of Young People*. London: Longman.

Seidler, V. (1989). 'Reason, Desire and Male Sexuality', in P. Caplan (ed.) *The Cultural Construction of Sexuality*. New York: Routledge.

Seidman, S. (1996). 'Introduction', in S. Seidman (ed.) *Queer Theory/ Sociology*. Cambridge, MA: Blackwell.

Seidman, S. (1997). *Difference Troubles: Queering Social Theory and Sexual Politics*. Cambridge: Cambridge University Press.

Seidman, S. (2002). *Beyond the Closet: The Transformation of Gay and Lesbian Life*

Simon, W. (1996). *Postmodern Sexualities*. New York: Routledge.

Simon, W. and Gagnon, J. (1986). 'Sexual Scripts: Permanence and Change', *Archives of Sexual Behaviour* 15 (2): 97–120.

Skeggs, B. (1997). *Formations of Class and Gender: Becoming Respectable*. London: Sage Publications.

Smart, C. and Shipman, B. (2004). 'Visions in Monochrome: Families, Marriage and the Individualization Thesis', *British Journal of Sociology* 55 (4): 491–509.

Smith, D.E. (1988). *The Everyday World as Problematic*. Milton Keynes: Open University Press.

Solomon, Y., Warin, J., Lewis, C. and Langford, W. (2002). 'Intimate Talk between Parents and Their Teenage Children: Democratic Openness or Covert Control?', *Sociology* 36 (4): 965–83.

Spender, D. (1985). *For the Record: The Making and Meaning of Feminist Knowledge*. London: The Women's Press.

Spivak, G.C. (1988). 'Can the Subaltern Speak?' in C. Nelson and L. Grossberg (eds) *Marxism and the Interpretation of Culture*. London: Macmillan.

Stanley, L. and Wise, S. (1983). *Breaking Out: Feminist Consciousness and Feminist Research*. London: Routledge.

Stanley, L. and Wise, S. (1993). *Breaking Out Again*. London: Routledge.

Streitmatter, R. (2009). *From 'Perverts' to 'Fab Five': The Media's Changing Depiction of Gay Men and Lesbians*. New York: Routledge.

Sullivan, A. (2004). *Same-Sex Marriage, Pro and Con: A Reader*. New York: Vintage Books.

Suzuki, N. (2005) 'Filipina–Japanese Marriages and Fantasies of Transnational Traversal', in N. Constable (ed.) *Cross-Border Marriages, Gender and Mobility in Transnational Asia*. Philadelphia: University of Pennsylvania Press.

Swingewood, A. (2000). *A Short History of Sociological Thought*. Basingstoke: Macmillan.

Sydie, R.A. (1994[1987]). *Natural Women, Cultured Men: A Feminist Perspective on Sociological Theory*. Vancouver: University of British Columbia Press.

Tanabe, A. and Tokita-Tanabe, Y. (2003). 'Introduction: Gender and Modernity in Asia and the Pacific', in Y. Hayami, A. Tanabe and T. Tokita (eds) *Gender and Modernity: Perspectives from Asia and the Pacific*. Kyoto: Kyoto University Press.

Taylor, Y. (2004). 'Negotiation and Navigation: An Exploration of the Spaces/Places of Working-Class Lesbians', *Sociological Research Online* 9 (1). Available online at *http://www.socresonline.org.uk/9/1/taylor.html*

Taylor, Y. (2007). *Classed Outsiders: Working-Class Lesbians' Life Experiences*. Basingstoke: Palgrave.

Thomson, R. and Scott, S. (1991). *Learning about Sex*. London: Tufnell Press.

Thorne, B. (1993). *Gender Play: Boys and Girls in School*. Buckingham: Open University Press.

Thornhill, R. and Palmer, C. (2000). *A Natural History of Rape: Biological Bases of Sexual Coercion*. Cambridge, MA: MIT Press.

Tokita-Tanabe, Y. (2003). 'Aesthetics of the Female Self: Modernity and Cultural Agency of Urban Middle-Class Women in Orissa', in Y. Hayami, A. Tanabe and Y. Tokita-Tanabe (eds) *Gender and Modernity: Perspectives from Asia and the Pacific:* Kyoto: Kyoto University Press.

Tolman, D. (2002). *Dilemmas of Desire*. Cambridge, MA: Harvard University Press.

Torr, R. (2007). 'What's Wrong with Aspiring to Find Out What Has Really Happened in Academic Feminism's Recent Past?: Response to Clare Hemmings' "Telling Feminist Stories"', *Feminist Theory* 8 (1): 59–67.

Trinh T. Minh-ha (1989). *Woman, Native, Other: Writing Postcoloniality and Feminism*. Bloomington: Indiana University Press.

Tseëlon, E. (1995). *The Masque of Femininity: The Presentation of Woman in Everyday Life*. London: Sage.

Turner, B.S. (1993). 'Baudrillard for Sociologists', in C. Rojek and B.S. Turner (eds) *Forget Baudrillard?* London: Routledge.

Turner, G. (2004). *Understanding Celebrity*. London: Sage Publications.

Vance, C. (ed.) (1984). *Pleasure and Danger: Exploring Female Sexuality.* New York: HarperCollins.

VanEvery, J. (1995). *Heterosexual Women Changing the Family: Refusing to be a 'Wife'!* London: Taylor and Francis.

Vines, G. (1993). *Raging Hormones.* London: Virago.

Waites, M. (2008). 'Analysing Sexualities in the Shadow of War: Islam in Iran, the West and the Work of Reimagining Human Rights', *Sexualities* 11 (1–2): 64–73.

Walby, S. (1986). *Patriarchy at Work.* Cambridge: Polity Press.

Walkowitz, J. (1980). *Prostitution and Victorian Society: Women, Class and the State.* Cambridge: Cambridge University Press.

Watney, S. (1980). 'The Ideology of the GLF', in Gay Left Collective (eds) *Homosexuality: Power and Politics.* London: Allison and Busby.

Weedon, C. (1987). *Feminist Practice and Poststructuralist Theory.* Oxford: Blackwell.

Weeks, J. (1980). 'Capitalism and the Organization of sex', in Gay Left Collective (eds) *Homosexuality: Power and Politics.* London: Allison and Busby.

Weeks, J. (1989). *Sex, Politics and Society* (2nd edition). London: Longman.

Weeks, J. (2007). *The World We Have Won: The Remaking of Erotic and Intimate Life.* London: Routledge.

Weeks, J., Donovan, C. and Heaphy, B. (2001). *Same-Sex Intimacies: Families of Choice and Other Life Experiments.* London: Routledge.

West, C. and Zimmerman, D. (1987). 'Doing Gender', *Gender and Society* 1 (2): 125–51.

Weston, K. (1991). *Families We Choose: Lesbians, Gays, Kinship.* New York: Columbia University Press.

Whannel, G. (2002). *Media Sports Stars: Masculinities and Moralities.* London and New York: Routledge.

Whelehan, I. (1995). *Modern Feminist Thought: From the Second Wave to 'Post-Feminism'.* New York: New York University Press.

Whisman, V. (1996). *Queer by Choice.* New York: Routledge.

Whitehead, H. (1981). 'The Bow and the Burden Strap: A New Look at Institutionalized Homosexuality in Native North America', in S.B. Ortner and H. Whitehead (eds) *Sexual Meanings: The Cultural Construction of Gender and Sexuality.* Cambridge: Cambridge University Press.

Wight, D. (1996). 'Beyond the Predatory Male: The Diversity of Young Glaswegian Men's Discourses to Describe Heterosexuality', in L. Adkins and V. Merchant (eds) *Sexualizing the Social.* London: Macmillan.

Wight, D., Raab. G.M., Henderson, M., Abraham, C., Buston, K., Hart, G. and Scott, S. (2002). 'Limits of Teacher Delivered Sex Education: Interim Behavioural Outcomes from Randomized Trial', *British Medical Journal* 324: 1430.

Wittig, M. (1992). *The Straight Mind and Other Essays.* Hemel Hempstead: Harvester Wheatsheaf.

Witz, A. (2000). 'Whose Body Matters? Feminist Sociology and the
    Corporeal Turn in Sociology and Feminism', *Body and Society* 6 (3): 1–24.
Witz, A. and Marshall, B.L. (2004). 'The Masculinity of the Social: Towards
    a Politics of Interrogation', in B.L. Marshall and A. Witz (eds) *Engendering
    the Social: Feminist Encounters with Sociological Theory*. Maidenhead: Open
    University Press.
Wollstonecraft, M. (1972 [1792]). 'A Vindication of the Rights of Woman',
    in M. Schneir (ed.) *Feminism: The Essential Historical Writings*. New York:
    Vintage Books.
Woo, J. (2007). 'Sexual Stories Go to Westminster: Narratives of Sexual
    Citizens/Outsiders in Britain'. Unpublished Ph.D. thesis, University of
    York.
Young, I.M. (1994). 'Gender as Seriality: Thinking about Women as a
    Social Collective', *Signs* 19 (3): 713–38.
Young, I.M. (1989). 'Polity and Group Difference', *Ethics* 99 (2): 250–74.
Yuval-Davis, N. (1997). *Gender and Nation*. London: Sage Publications.
Yuval-Davis, N. (2006). 'Intersectionality and Feminist Politics', *European
    Journal of Women's Studies* 13 (3): 193–209.

Index